# Salesforce Architect's Handbook

## A Comprehensive End-to-End Solutions Guide

Dipanker Jyoti
James A. Hutcherson

Apress®

*Salesforce Architect's Handbook: A Comprehensive End-to-End Solutions Guide*

Dipanker Jyoti
Rockville, MD, USA

James A. Hutcherson
Orlando, FL, USA

ISBN-13 (pbk): 978-1-4842-6630-4
https://doi.org/10.1007/978-1-4842-6631-1

ISBN-13 (electronic): 978-1-4842-6631-1

Managing Director, Apress Media LLC: Welmoed Spahr
Acquisitions Editor: Susan McDermott
Development Editor: Laura Berendson
Coordinating Editor: Rita Fernando

Cover designed by eStudioCalamar

Cover image designed by Pixabay

Distributed to the book trade worldwide by Springer Science+Business Media New York, 1 New York Plaza, New York, NY 10004. Phone 1-800-SPRINGER, fax (201) 348-4505, e-mail orders-ny@springer-sbm.com, or visit www.springeronline.com. Apress Media, LLC is a California LLC and the sole member (owner) is Springer Science + Business Media Finance Inc (SSBM Finance Inc). SSBM Finance Inc is a **Delaware** corporation.

For information on translations, please e-mail booktranslations@springernature.com; for reprint, paperback, or audio rights, please e-mail bookpermissions@springernature.com.

Apress titles may be purchased in bulk for academic, corporate, or promotional use. eBook versions and licenses are also available for most titles. For more information, reference our Print and eBook Bulk Sales web page at http://www.apress.com/bulk-sales.

Any source code or other supplementary material referenced by the author in this book is available to readers on GitHub via the book's product page, located at www.apress.com/9781484266304. For more detailed information, please visit http://www.apress.com/source-code.

Printed on acid-free paper

*This book is dedicated to the Ohana of the Salesforce ecosystem. Each person who contributes to its Trust, Customer Success, Innovation, and Equality makes it possible to extend the ecosystem to amazing heights.*

# Table of Contents

# About the Authors

**Dipanker "DJ" Jyoti** is an industry veteran with over two decades of experience in managing digital transformation engagements with Fortune 500 companies. Dipanker holds a total of 23 industry certifications, among which 13 certifications are in Salesforce, including the Salesforce Certified System Architect and Salesforce Certified Architect certifications. Some of his other architect-level certifications include AWS Certified Solutions Architect - Professional, Google Cloud Certified Professional Architect, Microsoft Certified Azure Solutions Architect, and Certified Blockchain Expert.

Dipanker currently works for IBM as an associate partner, managing IBM's Global Salesforce Assets. Previous to IBM, he held executive positions at Capgemini, Accenture, and Citibank. Dipanker's involvement with Salesforce began a decade ago, as part of a strategic business transformation engagement, where he got intimately involved in building a Salesforce proof of concept to demonstrate the capabilities of using a low code/no code CRM solution. He instantly fell in love with Salesforce and has since continued his journey to grow and share his knowledge of Salesforce among his peers and the cloud community. He currently manages an online blog on cloud architecture concepts, accessible at `www.cloudmixdj.com`. Dipanker lives with his wife, Junko, and two sons, Kazuya and Ouji, in Rockville, MD. In his free time, he enjoys cooking for his family and watching premier league soccer. For more details about Dipanker, you can follow him on LinkedIn at `www.linkedin.com/in/dipanker-dj-jyoti-3104974`.

**James A. Hutcherson** is a seasoned business leader with more than 40 years of technology experience. His first Salesforce project was implemented in 2004 where he started his Salesforce journey. During this time, James had taken every opportunity to grow his Salesforce knowledge. He holds 17 Salesforce certifications including Certified Salesforce Application Architect and Certified Salesforce System Architect. James is an avid educator and has hosted several *no-cost* Salesforce training sessions over the last few years to give back and grow the Salesforce ecosystem.

James is currently a principal and the chief technical architect at Capgemini Government Solutions where he leads the Salesforce Practice delivering enterprise-class solutions to US federal government customers. He earned an MBA from Baldwin Wallace College, an MSCIS from the University of Phoenix, and a BA from Southern Illinois University - Carbondale. James and his wife, Sherry, live in Orlando, FL, where they enjoy spending time with their family and four wonderful grandchildren. Follow him on LinkedIn at `www.linkedin.com/in/jim-hutcherson-2018/` and Twitter at `https://twitter.com/hutchersonj`.

# About the Technical Reviewer

**Kal Chintala** is one of about 300 Salesforce Certified Technical Architects (CTAs) worldwide with over 15 years of experience in delivering Salesforce and other CRM systems architectures, software design, and data modeling. Most of these projects are executed in Agile fashion while managing technical risk and change and software quality assurance for enterprise-wide transformation of many federal and Fortune 500 companies. Kal has managed Salesforce architectures for up to 65,000 users globally, including achieving more than $1.2 million in operational efficiencies by consolidating services onto Salesforce. His demonstrated industry experience achieves operational efficiencies through innovative applications of technology and business process enhancements. Kal currently serves as a Salesforce Practice strategy advisor, a technology lead, and an SME on road map and delivery of complex enterprise-wide Salesforce implementations across federal civilian and defense clients. Kal earned his bachelor's from Madras University, India, and has a master's from La Trobe University, Australia. He has earned more than 25 certifications including multiple certifications in Salesforce. Kal lives with his wife and two beautiful kids in Ashburn, Virginia. You can follow him on LinkedIn: `www.linkedin.com/in/kalch/`.

# Acknowledgments

A book like this cannot be accomplished without the support and compromise made by my family. My beautiful and amazing wife, **Junko Maki**, who has spent the last 9 years of her life unconditionally loving me and selflessly supporting my ambitions. She is my best friend, philosopher, coach, and therapist. The last part is probably something I need a lot of. Her understanding and compromise to allow me to spend several nights and weekends in my office room by myself is an equal contribution made by her in completing this book, as it has been for me. Thank you for all you do for me and the kids every single day, in addition to your real estate career. I could not have been where I am without you in my life.

I am also the proud father of two teenage sons, **Kazuya Jyoti** and **Ouji Jyoti**, who were the first reviewers of the initial chapters of this book. My efforts were already paid in full the day they both read the first chapter of this book and said they really want to become cloud architects. Their persistent request to write more chapters so they could learn more about Salesforce kept me going with a relentless motivation to research and write each chapter with love and dedication.

Giving back to the community is something I learned at a young age by simply observing my mother, **Arati Jyoti**, who is a Reiki Grandmaster and a volunteer at Mother Teresa's order of missionaries and St. Jude Children's Hospital in Mumbai, India. She dedicated the last 30 years of her life to offering Reiki treatments to people with various physical, emotional, and mental illnesses. In addition to this, she volunteers her remaining time to St. Jude Children's Hospital. My father, **Haran Jyoti**, who has selflessly dedicated his life to meeting his family's every need and raising his only son with the belief that everything is achievable as long as you don't give up. He was the person to tell me "you can do it" when I said I wanted to write a book on Salesforce architecture.

I am truly blessed to have my friend and co-author, **James Hutcherson**, partnering with me on this book, without whom this book could not have been completed. Thanks for trusting me and diving in with all your dedication. Your collaboration and contribution has been truly invaluable.

ACKNOWLEDGMENTS

I want to thank **Matt Francis** for his constant support and feedback on this book. Matt is a Salesforce veteran and a Salesforce Certified Technical Architect (CTA), who has not only been a Salesforce mentor to me but has been an unstoppable force in my success with my Salesforce career. His nonstop encouragement and endless motivation each day at work has led my Salesforce journey to be where it is today.

A book is only as good as its reviewer, for which I want to thank **Kal Chintala**. His invaluable knowledge in Salesforce in general and as a Salesforce Certified Technical Architect (CTA) has helped us tremendously in correcting many parts of this book and getting new perspectives on our content.

Similarly, a great contribution was made by the Salesforce Generations CTA group that reviewed our book and provided their unbiased review for our material. The Salesforce Generations CTA group is a weekly CTA study group that includes **Sudhir Durvasula**, **Waruna Buwaneka**, **Chetan Devraj**, **Brock Elgart**, **Jim Hutcherson**, and **Julia Kantarovsky**, in addition to James and me. We dedicated several of our study group sessions to reviewing each chapter line by line and getting collective feedback from the group.

Last but not the least, I would like to thank **Rita Fernando** and **Susan McDermott** from Apress for believing in me and giving me an opportunity to write this book for Apress. I still remember the day I contacted both of you, and never in a thousand years could I have imagined what this journey was going to be. Thanks for your patience and continuous support throughout the entire process.

—**Dipanker "DJ" Jyoti**


I would like to thank my adorable wife, **Sherry Hutcherson**, for her loving support along this journey. She is my best friend and has been my champion for more than 40 years. She allowed me to accomplish more than I ever could have done without her giving me advice and inspiration. Her encouragement made my contribution to this book a reality. Thank you, Sherry, for everything you do and for allowing me to have and obtain the "big dreams."

I am honored that **Dipanker "DJ" Jyoti** invited me to join in this endeavor. Without all the hard work you invested from start to finish, it would still just be a thought in my head. Your hard work getting this book approved and supported by **Apress** made it a reality. Thank you for letting me join your effort to write this book.

I would like to thank the members of the Salesforce Generations weekly CTA study group including **DJ**, **Sudhir Durvasula**, **Waruna Buwaneka**, **Chetan Devraj**, **Brock Elgart**, **Jim Hutcherson** (my son), and **Julia Kantarovsky**. They have provided thought leadership and assistance for both studying for the CTA exam and allowing DJ and me to ask hard questions and test topics with seasoned professionals in the field.

I am grateful to my family for the words of encouragement and the support over the years. My son, **Jim Hutcherson**, has shown me that even an *old dog* like me can still learn new tricks. You are an amazing Salesforce architect. But more importantly, you are the best son I could have ever asked for. You are an exemplary father, husband, and role model for everyone you meet. **Maureen Hutcherson**, thank you for the love, support, and fun you bring to the family. **Dave** and **Vickie Magill**, **Kathy Bevec**, and **Patty** and **Ronnie Eamich**, thank you for accepting me even when I'm "preoccupied" and still providing assistance and encouragement at just the right times. Thank you to **Renee and Richard Abell** and **Chis and Jim Sabo** for cheering me on over the years. You helped more than you will ever know.

I would not have co-written this book without the opportunities, challenges, and successes I gained from the amazing organizations I have worked with over the years, including **Capgemini**, **Adnubis**, **Apollo Education**, **Net Direct**, **Advizex**, **Agilysys/Pioneer-Standard**, **NCR**, **Anderson Jacobson**, and the **US Navy**. My architectural knowledge evolved and matured from each of you allowing me to try, succeed, and sometimes fail. I would like to make a shout-out to **Capgemini Government Solutions** for investing actively in my career and the larger Salesforce ecosystem. Thank you.

I would like to offer a special thank you to **Kal Chintala** for his tireless support and guidance as the technical reviewer for this book. Your comments and ideas truly helped make it more valuable to our readers. Thank you for the effort and your friendship. It is greatly appreciated.

Finally, I would like to offer my sincere gratitude to **Rita Fernando**, **Susan McDermott**, and the staff at **Apress** who saw the value of this material and partnered with **DJ** and me in its publication. You have consistently provided the highest level of support, directions, and patience throughout the entire writing process, and for that you have my greatest appreciation.

—James A. Hutcherson

# Introduction

This book is intended for several different audiences including (1) Salesforce implementation partners who are building their practice and want to define the overall strategy and architecture approach, (2) Salesforce industry professionals who need a one-stop educational resource to Salesforce architecture and for the Salesforce architecture domain certification exams, and (3) enterprise cloud champions who are involved in implementing, optimizing, and architecting Salesforce-based solutions within their organization.

## What This Book Is About

This book takes an in-depth look into the seven key architecture domains that form the pillars of any Salesforce-based solution.

## Platform as a Service Architecture

- Provides an overview of the Force.com platform as a service (PaaS) architecture and the key components that empower the Salesforce SaaS model.

- Understand the microservices-based architecture of Salesforce Lightning consisting of highly scalable and reusable Salesforce Lightning components, Salesforce Lightning pages, and Salesforce Lightning apps.

- Understand "When to Use What" standard features of Salesforce and the considerations, limitations, and trade-offs of declarative vs. programmatic configurations.

- Understand the AppExchange marketplace and the significance of considering third-party AppExchange microservices components and AppExchange apps.

- Understand the considerations, limitations, and trade-offs between declarative and programmatic design on the Salesforce platform.

# Salesforce Data Architecture

- Provides an overview of the Salesforce platform architecture considerations when working with large data volumes (LDVs).

- Understand the object-oriented data modeling concepts within Salesforce and key considerations in designing the right Salesforce object model.

- Understand the data migration strategy, considerations, and appropriate tools to use.

# Salesforce Security Model Architecture

- Understand the "Who Sees What and How" within Salesforce.

- Architect a solution that utilizes the appropriate platform security mechanisms.

- Design a secure Salesforce community portal architecture including access by both internal and external users.

- Identify declarative platform security features that can be used to meet record-level security requirements.

- Identify the programmatic platform security features that can be used to meet security requirements.

- Describe how to incorporate the platform security features into a solution.

# Salesforce Integration Architecture

- Understand and evaluate the integration strategy for cloud-to-cloud, cloud-to-on-premise, and multi–Salesforce org integration scenarios.

- Understand when to use Canvas apps vs. integrating with Heroku apps vs. integrating using Salesforce Connect vs. integrating using a middleware such as MuleSoft.

- Understand the various integration patterns and justify their use as part of the overall integration architecture.

- Recommend and justify the appropriate integration strategy and integration patterns.

- Recommend the appropriate platform-specific integration technology.

## Salesforce Identity and Access Management Architecture

- Understand the concepts of identity provider (IDP)–initiated and service provider (SP)–initiated protocols.

- Understand the out-of-the-box declarative capabilities to configure single sign-on (SSO).

- Understand the capabilities of integrated apps and ODATA integrations.

- Understand the benefits, considerations, and trade-offs of incorporating external applications.

- Understand the considerations, trade-offs, and benefits of using middleware solutions vs. Salesforce Identity.

## Mobile Architecture

- Understand the concepts of Mobile Device Management (MDM) and Mobile Device Federation (MDF).

- Understand the considerations for a mobile platform strategy.

- Understand the Salesforce mobile architecture options, design trade-offs, and benefits.

- Understand the design approaches of architecting a Salesforce mobile solution using Mobile SDK or Salesforce1 Mobile App or the Field Service Lightning app.

- Understand the capabilities of the Salesforce Mobile SDK.

- Understand the strategies and use cases for wearables and connected devices and the appropriate architecture patterns.

# Development and Deployment Lifecycle

In addition to the six architecture concepts outlined previously, this book also offers the industry best practices and the recommended framework for approaching, managing, delivering, and continuously improving a Salesforce solution using the Salesforce Development and Deployment Lifecycle:

- Understand the Salesforce Development Lifecycle Methodology (SDLM).

- Learn to evaluate and mitigate Salesforce implementation risks, dependencies, and constraints.

- Understand the key stakeholders needed for any Salesforce projects and understand their roles and responsibilities.

- Understand the best practices for setting up a Center of Excellence and a Salesforce Governance Model.

- Identify the appropriate test strategy and user acceptance strategy for Salesforce implementations.

- Learn to evaluate and use the appropriate tools for Salesforce project management, business requirements management, testing, and release management.

- Understand benefits and best practices for using source control and continuous integration for Salesforce release management.

# What This Book Is *Not*

This book is not a screen-by-screen configuration guide for Salesforce, nor does it have any code snippets to learn programming. Although configuration, Apex, and Visualforce capabilities are discussed in this book, they are explained at the level that is necessary for an architect to architect an ideal Salesforce solution.

This book is not an encyclopedia covering every feature of Salesforce as we did not intend to replace the user manuals and Salesforce Trailhead[1] published by Salesforce. We have made the best attempt to add as many references as possible to Salesforce content, Salesforce trailheads, and other Salesforce contents throughout the book. Even if we could have covered every feature of Salesforce, it would be outdated by the time you read this book, given the pace at which Salesforce changes every day.

Instead, this book covers the consistent context needed by a Salesforce architect to group old and new features for their architectural use. It also connects the dots between any two features by categorizing their relevance within the seven architectural domains.

# How Best to Read This Book

We have arranged each chapter in this book in the most logical order possible to match the sequence of architecting an ideal Salesforce solution. We have decoupled each chapter from other chapters such that they can be read independently on their own. For the readers who are just beginning their architect journey, we would definitely recommend completing Chapters 1 and 2 before jumping into any domain-specific chapters located within Chapters 3–9.

For some of our advanced architects, we would highly recommend starting with Chapter 2 before jumping into any domain-specific chapters located within Chapters 3–9.

This book is meant to be an architecture handbook that should be referenced and revisited by Salesforce architects throughout their architectural practice. For instance, if you are working on an assignment which requires heavy integrations, you can jump directly to Chapter 6 or Appendix B to get everything needed to design your integrations.

The content in this book is a culmination of our combined industry experiences and consultations with Multiple Salesforce Certified Technical Architects (CTAs) and aspiring CTAs in their approach to architecting a Salesforce solution. The content in this book comprises the learning materials we used to achieve our Salesforce Certified Application Architect and Salesforce Certified System Architect certifications. This book is also a reference guide to studying for the Salesforce CTA board exam.

---

[1]https://help.salesforce.com/articleView?id=mth_what_is_trailhead.htm&type=5.

# CHAPTER 1

# Salesforce Architecture

You have been assigned to build something in Salesforce. You may have been an admin or developer or merely heard about Salesforce. Where do you begin?

You probably started by searching on YouTube, Google, or even Trailhead, Salesforce's free learning management tool, to learn everything about Salesforce, but all you found was piecemeal information about Salesforce and its architecture. There are several books on administration and development with Salesforce, but what about architecting with Salesforce? Here we will start with the fundamentals of Salesforce architecture and what makes it unique compared to other technologies.

This chapter covers some key points, including

- Why companies choose Salesforce over other cloud solution alternatives

- Distinctions between on-premise, infrastructure as a service (IaaS), platform as a service (PaaS), and software as a service (SaaS) options to build solutions

- How Salesforce can be used as a PaaS as well as a SaaS solution

- The mechanics of a multi-tenant architecture and the metadata-driven framework that drives Salesforce

- The seven architectural domains of Salesforce that need to be considered when architecting with Salesforce

© Dipanker Jyoti and James A. Hutcherson 2021
D. Jyoti and J. A. Hutcherson, *Salesforce Architect's Handbook*, https://doi.org/10.1007/978-1-4842-6631-1_1

# Why Do Companies Choose Salesforce?

Salesforce was started in 1999 by Marc Benioff, Parker Harris, Dave Moellenhoff, and Frank Dominguez.[1] In its 20 years of exponential growth, Salesforce has surpassed a market cap of more than $180 billion[2] with a total annual revenue of $13.3 billion in the year 2019 and employing over 36,000 global employees.[3] The annual revenue for the year 2020 is estimated to surpass $16.5 billion, which is over $3 billion in revenue growth within a single year (see Figure 1-1).[4]

## Salesforce's Exponential Growth (as of 2020)

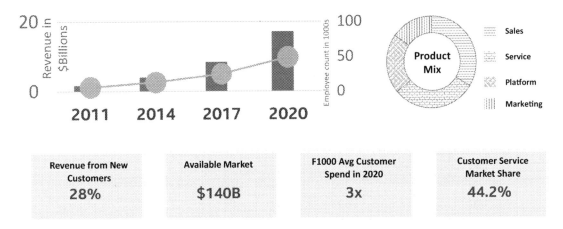

**Figure 1-1.** *Salesforce Growth Over the Years*

[1]"The History of Salesforce." Salesforce News, September 18, 2020, www.salesforce.com/news/stories/the-history-of-salesforce/.

[2]Jordannovet. "Marc Benioff's Salesforce Has Eclipsed Larry Ellison's Oracle in Market Cap." CNBC, July 10, 2020, www.cnbc.com/2020/07/10/salesforce-eclipses-oracle-in-market-cap.html.

[3]"2019 Annual Report: Celebrating 20 Years of Salesforce." www.annualreports.com/HostedData/AnnualReportArchive/s/NYSE_CRM_2019.pdf.

[4]"The History of Salesforce." Salesforce News, September 18, 2020, www.salesforce.com/news/stories/the-history-of-salesforce/.

Salesforce provides several benefits over other cloud solutions, including

1. **No Code/Low Code Platform:** Most things in Salesforce can be configured by a business user with no programming skills. Almost everything in Salesforce is configured using and by just using a GUI interface with drag and drop capabilities that support reusable components.

2. **Time to Market:** Building production-ready business applications in Salesforce can be achieved within days, not months.

3. **No Additional Costs for All Upgrades Made to the Platform Each Year:** Salesforce constantly improves its SaaS and PaaS offerings by releasing new features three times a year that are automatically released to all Salesforce customers at no additional cost. The three major upgrades each year keep the platform in sync with the latest technology features in the industry, such as upgrades related to artificial intelligence, block chain, and machine learning.

# Modern-Day Options to Build Technology Solutions

Before we begin architecting in Salesforce, it is important to understand all the options out there to build a solution and when building something in Salesforce makes sense.

Every solution requires a technology stack to operate in. A typical technology stack consists of eight tiers:

1. Application code

2. Runtime engine

3. Integration server

4. Operating system (OS)

5. Virtualization engine

6. Network device

7. Computation server

8. Data storage server

In this book, we will not get into the details of each tier, as each tier merits its own book. But for our context, it's important to realize that an organization needs to invest in all eight tiers to build even the simplest of solution. Whether they build one or multiple solutions, the eight tiers are the required building blocks. For any organization, investing in these eight tiers can range from a few thousand dollars to millions of dollars.

Given the investments needed, every organization has four options to build solutions. They are as follows:

1.  Invest in an on-premise solution.

2.  Leverage an infrastructure as a service (IaaS) cloud solution.

3.  Leverage a platform as a service (PaaS) cloud solution.

4.  Leverage a software as a service (SaaS) cloud solution.

The four approaches listed here differ from each other based on which tiers a company manages on their own vs. which tiers the company outsources to an external cloud service provider (CSP) such as Salesforce, ServiceNow, Appian, AWS, Microsoft Azure, Google, and so on.

In Figure 1-2, I have outlined the four options in a side-by-side comparison based on who manages which tier.

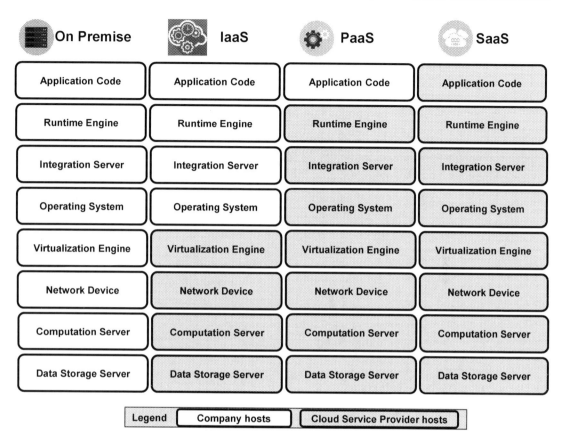

*Figure 1-2.* *Comparison of On-Premise, IaaS, PaaS, and SaaS[5]*

The various technology options can also be viewed in terms of a nested diagram with each option being an improvement over the other.

In Figure 1-3, I have illustrated such a nested diagram with a few examples of the popular CSPs that provide each type of service.

---

[5]https://www.redhat.com/en/topics/cloud-computing/iaas-vs-paas-vs-saas

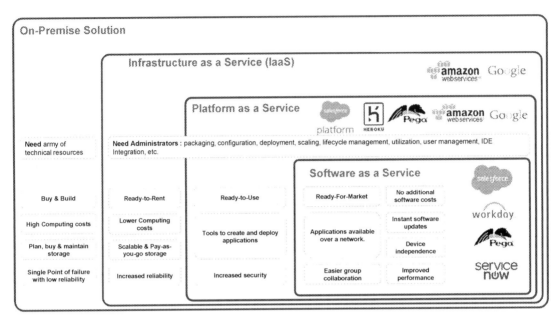

***Figure 1-3.*** *Nested Diagram of Solution Development Options*

# On-Premise Solution

Traditionally, any company interested in building a business application had to size up, buy, and set up all the tiers of the technology stack in-house from scratch. They would also need to manage and maintain each tier set up within the organization's premises, *hence the industry term "on-premise."* With this approach, the organization requires dedicated staff to manage the technology infrastructure, often at a stack-by-stack *(i.e., each infrastructure component)* level.

Some key advantages and disadvantages of the on-premise option are provided in Table 1-1.

***Table 1-1.*** *Advantages and Disadvantages of On-Premise Solution Development*

| Advantages | Disadvantages |
|---|---|
| Full ownership and control of the technology stack used to support the business operations. Every tier of the stack can be custom designed and managed to meet the unique needs of the organization. | Higher initial capital outlay and cost for specialty resources. On-premise solutions are expensive to build, and a single company cannot have economies of scale to support resources and component cost compared to other CSP solutions. |
| Internally administered security for the organization's data, application code, and user base is proprietary to – and managed entirely within – the organization. Access to the entire technology stack resides within the organization's premises. Each technology component can be custom tailored or entirely replaced to meet the organization's needs for adherence to security standards. | Time intensive to build with slower time to market. It is time consuming to plan, size up, and procure the hardware and software needed. The initial planning also does not consider seasonal spikes and load demands. Additionally, resources at each tier need to coordinate and self-organize their divisions to support the solution, which could take months or even years to launch a single solution in production environment. |
| Controlled solution deployment can be entirely self-managed and timed as per the availability of in-house technical staff and without any reliance on third-party cloud providers because each component of the technology stack can be designed, tested, approved, and launched for live production use through internal coordination and readiness. | Difficult to keep up with industry standards in security and best practices. The technology industry is changing at a rapid pace with new standards emerging on a daily basis. Some standards may be nice-to-haves for a company, but some may be critical to compliance and market adherence. Failure to comply with these standards could even mean closing down business completely. |

# Infrastructure as a Service (IaaS)

In an infrastructure as a service (IaaS) model, cloud service providers such as Amazon Web Services, Microsoft Azure, or Google Cloud Platform provide outsourced raw computing infrastructure, data storage, and virtualization that are provisioned on demand within minutes and can be available instantly.

Some advantages and disadvantages of the IaaS approach are provided in Table 1-2.

***Table 1-2.*** *Advantages and Disadvantages of IaaS-Based Solution Development*

| Advantages | Disadvantages |
| --- | --- |
| Flexibility and scalability. Infrastructure components can be upscaled or downscaled on demand. Most CSPs offer a pay-as-you-go licensing model so companies can start small and grow their infrastructure, as needed, to meet a gradual growth or seasonal demands of the solution. | Time intensive to build with slower time to market compared to PaaS or SaaS. It is needless to say that in order for the CSP-provided infrastructure to work with the other components of the technology stack managed by the company, a technical coordination effort is required from the company's technical resources, along with additional setup needed to both the IaaS settings and the settings of the on-premise systems. |
| No initial investments needed. The CSP manages the supporting infrastructure components, so no up-front investments are needed for the company to get started. The costs of the infrastructure setup are absorbed entirely by the CSP, with only a pay-as-you-go subscription fee charged to the company based on the company's actual usage. | Larger investments needed than PaaS or SaaS. Although there are some major cost savings in this approach compared to the on-premise approach, the company still has to employ technical resources to manage the common operating system, any integration servers, runtime engines, and the actual code to run the business application.  Any future changes to the CSP's infrastructure components could result in a refactoring required toward all other components managed by the company. This could be both time intensive and expensive for the company. |
| Disaster recovery and infrastructure support provided by the CSP. Most CSPs have an extensive disaster recovery and failover process built into their IaaS offering. Companies can benefit from the disaster recovery and other infrastructure support offered by the CSP at no additional costs. | No control over infrastructure decisions. Companies can choose various types of infrastructure qualities; however, the companies do not have any control over the management or security of the infrastructure. Although CSPs adhere to most industry standard compliance requirements, these cannot address requirements specific to a single company. |

# Platform as a Service (PaaS)

Platform as a service (PaaS) uses the provided technology stack components to build applications without the overhead of procuring and managing the individual components. This allows the architect and company to focus on the software solution. Companies such as Salesforce, Appian, and ServiceNow have included options to provide PaaS access to their respective platforms. Often, like Salesforce, the platform offers the business process tools, a development environment, and a testing and deployment framework. The PaaS options allow for advanced solution development without the need for management and oversight of the underlying infrastructure.[6]

Some advantages and disadvantages of the PaaS approach are provided in Table 1-3.

***Table 1-3.*** *Advantages and Disadvantages of PaaS-Based Solution Development*

| Advantages | Disadvantages |
| --- | --- |
| Development focused. The PaaS approach frees up the company from worrying about the underlying infrastructure and instead allows a company to strictly focus on the code base, proprietary to the company. PaaS is the best approach for developers and development-based companies that build custom software unique to them and their solution needs. | Nonideal for organizations with fewer or no technical staff or with standard business models. Leveraging a PaaS approach means managing the code base for the underlying solution in-house, and hence this approach requires maintaining a staff of technical resources familiar with the code used to build the technology solution. A company with few or no technical resources struggles with this approach, due to its reliance on staffing technical resources, mainly developers, to manage and support the application code component of the technology stack. A PaaS approach would require the development of proprietary code to support business capabilities. Such companies should consider using the SaaS approach instead. |

*(continued)*

---

[6]"What Is PaaS? Platform as a Service: Microsoft Azure." Platform as a Service | Microsoft Azure, azure.microsoft.com/en-us/overview/what-is-paas/.

*Table 1-3.* (*continued*)

| Advantages | Disadvantages |
| --- | --- |
| Built-in auto-scaling and auto-load balancing.<br>Most PaaS providers manage the auto-scaling and auto-load balancing for the platform provisioned by them as an inherent service to their clients. There may still be additional costs associated with such scaling; however, it moves the burden of auto-scaling and performance load balancing to the PaaS provider and occurs with no additional effort or planning. | Maintaining industry standard feature sets.<br>As business applications are built from scratch, it is easy to lose industry-specific context or even to maintain status quo with industry standard feature sets such as responsive design, mobile notifications, etc. This is because every component of the entire application needs to be explicitly designed and coupled with the overall architecture in PaaS. For example, imagine designing the tax software "Intuit TurboTax" on a platform as a service from scratch. The burden of changes to the application code to support every minor design feature application can be overbearing and often missed. |
| Inherits the advantages of an IaaS approach.<br>The PaaS approach has all the advantages available from an IaaS approach and much more, since PaaS is built and managed by the CSP on top of the IaaS-supported components. | Most subscriptions use a pay-per-user model rather than the provisioned infrastructure costs.<br>As a platform, the license cost is accrued based on the number of users rather than the number of applications or processes. This license model may be higher than a traditional infrastructure as a service. The key consideration is whether the organization is using "only" a PaaS environment; some CSPs such as Salesforce offer a hybrid of PaaS and SaaS options. Typically, organizations will purchase the initial Salesforce license as a SaaS expense and then reduce the cost of ownership by using the available PaaS functionality in the environment. |

# Software as a Service (SaaS)

Software as a service (SaaS) uses all of the technology stack components to access commercial off-the-shelf (COTS) applications without the overhead of developing the application and managing the individual components. This allows the company to focus on the business without developing any custom code. Rather, the company can use a solution such as Salesforce Sales Cloud or Microsoft Dynamics 365 to provide an industry-leading solution for typical business issues. Most SaaS products allow the business users to "configure" the details of the solution to match the specific business requirements. The SaaS options allow a company to focus on their core competency without the need for management and oversight of the underlying software or infrastructure.[7]

Some advantages and disadvantages of the SaaS approach are provided in Table 1-4.

***Table 1-4.*** *Advantages and Disadvantages of SaaS-Based Solution Development*

| Advantages | Disadvantages |
|---|---|
| No initial infrastructure investments or development resources needed. | Not ideal for companies with highly customized business processes. |
| Most SaaS providers operate in a pay-as-you-go subscription model for end-to-end business software hosted on-cloud. In a SaaS approach, the CSP manages the infrastructure and the entire solution, eliminating the need for the company to maintain a team of technical resources to support the applications. Most SaaS solutions offer declarative configuration capabilities using drag and drop interface and using clicks instead of writing code. Any nontechnical user with familiarity to the system can configure basic functionalities and personalization and start using the system. | SaaS solutions are built with a one-size-fits-all principle that is designed to serve the majority customer base of an industry, with common and shared business solutions needed. Hence, customizing the SaaS solution beyond a point to meet the unique needs of a single customer is difficult to achieve. For this reason, a SaaS solution may be nonideal for companies with unique business processes requiring highly customized solutions. |

(*continued*)

---

[7]"What Is PaaS? Platform as a Service: Microsoft Azure." Platform as a Service | Microsoft Azure, azure.microsoft.com/en-us/overview/what-is-paas/.

***Table 1-4.*** (*continued*)

| Advantages | Disadvantages |
|---|---|
| Fastest time to market.<br>Compared to the other approaches, with the SaaS approach, companies can launch technology solutions within a few hours from signing up for the SaaS service. | Higher operating expenses.<br>With a SaaS solution, the customer may not have any initial investment to get started, as the SaaS CSP assumes the costs of setting up, maintaining, and monitoring the entire technology stack for this solution. The SaaS CSP typically bakes in the costs for managing the technology stack for its customers in the licenses for the SaaS product, which are typically higher than an IaaS- or PaaS-based subscription model. At the end, the expensiveness of SaaS licenses is subjective, since the premium paid for SaaS licenses offers a worry-free technology environment to its customers, at an all-inclusive monthly license fees, with the flexibility to cancel or change the service as needed. |
| No software installation or infrastructure maintenance required.<br>Users of the system do not need to install any software on their computers or mobile devices to use the SaaS solution. All they need is a web browser and an Internet connection to access the SaaS solution from anywhere. The customers of SaaS products do not need to worry about maintaining the underlying infrastructure, as it is solely the responsibility of the SaaS CSP. | Most subscriptions follow a pay-per-user model rather than provisioned infrastructure costs.<br>As a SaaS platform, the license cost is accrued based on the number of users rather than the number of applications, the number of processes, or the infrastructure required. This license model may be higher than a traditional IaaS and PaaS service. The key consideration is whether the organization is using SaaS "only" as a SaaS environment. Typically, as discussed earlier, organizations will purchase the initial Salesforce license as a SaaS expense and then reduce the cost of ownership by using the available PaaS functionality in the environment. |

# Salesforce as a PaaS- and SaaS-Based Cloud Service Provider (CSP)

Salesforce provides a web-based user interface as part of its SaaS and PaaS offerings. It inherently uses a highly configurable application platform, called the "Salesforce Lightning Platform." The Lightning Platform offers easily configurable features such as data objects and fields, formulas, validation rules, and process management tools such as *Process Builder* and *Lightning Flow* to automate application processes, all without writing a single line of code. Salesforce also provides a standard data model within its products that can be extended and customized further to meet the data storage, data processing, and data retrieval needs of most of its customers. In addition to the data, application, and user interface layers, Salesforce offers a variety of APIs in both SOAP- and REST-based protocols to integrate almost any proprietary or third-party vendor systems used by the customer.

## A Deep Dive into the Technology Stack

It is difficult to find a holistic and detailed architectural view of the Salesforce technology stack, as Salesforce does not publish the "behind-the-scenes" details of the platform architecture in a single definitive source document. However, we participated in countless Salesforce meetings, classroom and Trailhead training, client meetings, and technical sessions at Dreamforce and TrailheaDX conferences to obtain an in-depth understanding of the technology stack used to provide the Salesforce PaaS and SaaS Lightning Platform.

In Figure 1-4, we have summarized the technology stack used by the Salesforce Lightning Platform followed by a more detailed discussion on the individual components.

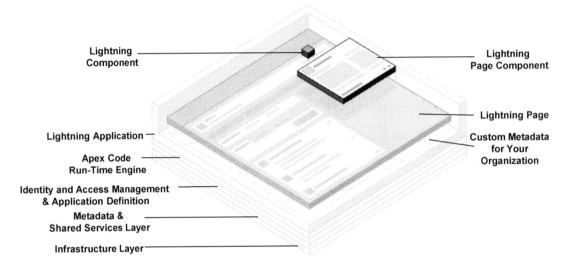

*Figure 1-4.* *Salesforce Lightning Platform Technology Stack*

## Infrastructure Layer

The infrastructure layer is the foundation layer of the Salesforce Lightning Platform. This layer consists of the data centers supporting the primary and replicated disaster recovery instances, plus a separate production-class lab facility. The infrastructure layer utilizes carrier-class components designed to support millions of users. The infrastructure layer also consists of a network topology that regulates Internet traffic into and out of Salesforce in a carrier-neutral network strategy that minimizes the risk of a single point of failure for the platform while still equipped to offer a highly resilient environment with maximum uptime and performance.

Also, at the infrastructure layer, Salesforce stores and protects all customer data by ensuring that only authorized users can access each grain of the data. When Salesforce administrators assign data security rules via the setup mode within Salesforce, the infrastructure layer enforces those security settings directly at this level. Sharing settings that define the organization-wide defaults (OWDs) and role hierarchy–based sharing are also enforced by Salesforce at the infrastructure layer.

All data in transit from client side to server side of Salesforce and data at rest in Salesforce's data center is encrypted. All data access to any data stored within Salesforce data centers is governed by strict password policies that are stored in SHA 256 one-way hash format.[8] At the infrastructure layer, Salesforce has implemented a sophisticated Intrusion Detection System (IDS) to monitor for potential security incidents. The IDS detection rules are automatically updated daily so that custom rules can be updated as needed.[9] Additionally, Salesforce utilizes a system health monitoring component that is configured to generate and distribute alerts as security events occur in the environment.[10]

## Metadata and Shared Services Layer

This is the layer within which Salesforce stores and manages the unique metadata associated with the customer's Salesforce instance. We will talk more about "metadata" a bit later in this chapter. The uniqueness of the metadata for each Salesforce instance at this layer also securely manages the separation of customer data stored in the infrastructure layer.

Each instance of Salesforce is capable of supporting several thousand customers in a secure and efficient manner, and there are appropriate controls in place designed to prevent any given customer's Salesforce instance from being compromised. This layer also maintains a large variety of shared services for the Salesforce Lightning Platform including a messaging bus to support SOAP- and REST-based APIs offered by Salesforce out of the box.

## Identity and Access Management and Application Definition Layer

At this layer of the technology stack, Salesforce manages the provisioning, authentication, authorization, and identity resolution for users and systems permitted to access the customer's Salesforce instance. Given that this layer determines a given user's access rights, it is no surprise that the application that needs to be rendered to the user as per their permitted access is also defined at this layer. Later in this chapter, we will discuss how Salesforce generates and compiles the entire application, dynamically from scratch, on demand based on the metadata defined for the user's org and based on each user's access.

---

[8]Secure Coding Storing Secrets. Developer.force.com, developer.salesforce.com/wiki/ secure_coding_storing_secrets.

[9]"Network Security Planning." Unit | Salesforce Trailhead, trailhead.salesforce.com/en/content/ learn/modules/network-security-planning/detect-network-intrusions.

[10]"Training: Salesforce." Help, help.salesforce.com/articleView?id=security_health_check.htm.

# Apex Code Runtime Engine Layer

Every functionality in Salesforce, whether it is an out-of-the-box functionality or code written by a Salesforce developer, is executed each time on demand by the application layer located in a Salesforce data center. The Apex language is a proprietary language developed by Salesforce to run code exclusively in the Salesforce environment. The syntax of Apex is very similar to that of the Java programming language, and Apex is an object-oriented programming language. Salesforce only supports its proprietary Apex language within the environment. The Apex runtime engine layer consists of two primary components: an Apex compiler and an Apex runtime engine.

In Figure 1-5, we illustrate how the Apex code written by a developer is compiled and executed on demand by Salesforce. When a developer writes a class and saves within Salesforce, the Apex runtime engine layer receives the execution request to store the Apex class in Salesforce for future use. To store the Apex class, the Apex compiler, within the application layer, must first process the class and convert it into an abstract set of machine instructions that can only be interpreted by the Apex runtime engine, also located within the Apex runtime engine layer.

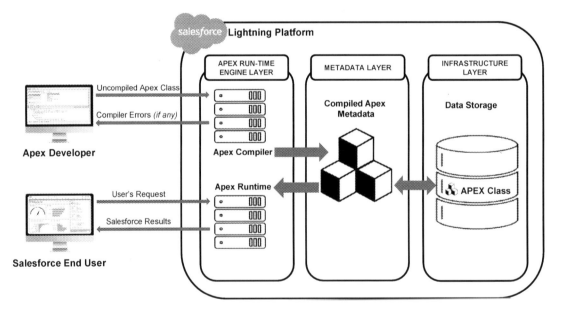

***Figure 1-5.*** *Apex Runtime Engine Processing Apex Code*

The Apex programming language is a tightly written language, and the Apex compiler maintains safeguards and coding standards to ensure that no single code segment or class is written in a way that monopolizes the entire server resources of Salesforce's multi-tenant architecture. When a developer submits an Apex class that is not acceptable by the Apex compiler, the compiler instantly returns the class, along with compile error messages, back to the developer.

The Apex compiler does not process or save the code until the developer fixes the compile errors and resubmits the Apex class. Once the developer resubmits the class, the Apex compiler converts the Apex code into an abstract set of instructions that can only be interpreted by the Apex runtime engine and is stored as metadata within the data storage layer provisioned to your org at an assigned data center of Salesforce.

When a user navigating Salesforce in their web browser or their mobile device uses a functionality that executes Apex code saved by the developer, the request is first received by the Apex runtime engine layer, which retrieves the metadata with the compiled machine instructions from the data storage layer and runs the compiled machine instructions through the Apex runtime engine.

The Apex runtime engine processes the Apex code and delivers the execution results to the Salesforce user via the user's web browser or mobile device to successfully conclude the code execution. All of this happens within milliseconds of the user's clicking the functionality that executes the Apex code. All standard functionalities of Salesforce that are available out of the box also execute in the exact same way as the Apex code custom written and stored by your Salesforce developer.[11]

# The Lightning Application Layer

At this layer, the Salesforce Lightning Platform delivers the capability to customize and personalize the applications within a Salesforce instance through point and click configuration capabilities and manages the business logic of the application, file storage design, analytics, multilanguage support, and social collaboration capabilities. This is also the layer that renders the out-of-the-box Salesforce mobile app and provides access to the Salesforce mobile software development kit (SDK), which a Salesforce developer can use to build a customized mobile experience for your company's users, accessing Salesforce on mobile devices.

---

[11]"How Does Apex Work? Apex Developer Guide: Salesforce Developers." Salesforce Developers
Documentation, developer.salesforce.com/docs/atlas.en-us.apexcode.meta/apexcode/apex_
intro_how_does_apex_work.htm.

# The Lightning Component Layer

The Lightning Component layer provides a user interface framework for rendering the application as a decoupled component of the page rendered to the end user via a Lightning page. Lightning Component uses JavaScript on the client side *(i.e., user's browser)* and Apex on the Salesforce server side. At this layer, Salesforce loads a set of temporary executable files onto the cache memory of the user's browser, which is executed at runtime to provide real-time responsiveness to the end user without making unnecessary server calls to the data center of Salesforce.

# Lightning Page Component

The Lightning page component is a custom layout that lets Salesforce administrators design Lightning pages for use in the Salesforce mobile app or Lightning Experience.

# Lightning Page

Lightning pages occupy a middle ground between page layouts and Visualforce pages. Like a page layout, an administrator is allowed to add standard and custom Lightning components to a specific Lightning page.

# Custom Metadata for Your Organization

Metadata in Salesforce describes the structure of the Salesforce Lightning Platform for your instance of Salesforce along with the structure of standard and custom objects, fields, and the page layouts associated with the respective objects. We will discuss, later in this chapter, the role of metadata within the Salesforce multi-tenant architecture.

Given the preceding discussion of the Salesforce Lightning Platform architecture, here are some key functionalities and features that the platform provides out of the box to all its customers:

- Web-based application that can be customized for most business models, primarily using a graphical point and click user interface, without writing any code and compliant with web standards such as HTML5, AJAX, JavaScript, Flash, and Web 2.0 standards

- A relational database that automatically scales and adheres to the major industry standards and compliances such as HIPAA

- Configurable business automation tools such as workflows, validation rules, process builders, and email service and notifications, using a point and click user interface

- Out-of-the-box reporting and dashboards with drag and drop capabilities to customize and create additional reports as needed

- Out-of-the-box mobile app available via both iOS and Android mobile stores for most mobile devices

- A wide variety of SOAP- and REST-based API capabilities available out of the box to support integrations with other company systems on-cloud or on-premise

- A multilayered security model that is robust yet customizable to meet the security needs of every company

Salesforce also introduces new features and enhancements to its platform through three major releases every year. All customers of Salesforce automatically receive the three upgrades each automatically in their instance of Salesforce. All new upgrades and features delivered as part of the three releases are delivered in a dormant or inactive state to every instance of Salesforce, and a system administrator is required to activate the features in their org, as needed. Salesforce also ensures complete backward compatibility of all code and configurations done by customers on their respective Salesforce instances. The Salesforce API also gets upgraded and gets a new version number with every API-related upgrade.[12]

Salesforce is able to support its SaaS and PaaS offerings by leveraging a multi-tenant architecture that allows for multiple customers to operate off a common platform with shared services accessible to all customers equally. We will talk more about the various SaaS offerings from Salesforce in Chapter 3.

---

[12]"Managing Version Settings for Apex." Help, help.salesforce.com/articleView?id=code_version_settings_apex.htm.

# Multi-tenant Architecture and the Metadata-Driven Framework

To decrease the cost of delivering the same application to all customers, SaaS-based solutions such as Salesforce utilize a multi-tenant architecture rather than a single-tenant architecture. In a single-tenant application architecture such as an on-premise or IaaS strategy, a dedicated set of resources are required to fulfill the needs of just one or a few organizations, whereas in a multi-tenant SaaS architecture model, needs of multiple tenants (companies or departments within a company) are satisfied, using the common hardware resources and staff needed to manage a single software instance.[13]

All customers of Salesforce operate in a complete virtual isolation from one another. Customers can use and customize a Salesforce-based application independently as if they each have a separate cloud technology stack of Salesforce with their own data and their customizations secured and insulated from the activity of all other customers using Salesforce.

For a multi-tenant architecture to work as it does for Salesforce, the technology components powering Salesforce need to be polymorphic *(i.e., the ability to support multiple variations of the business logic and data model, through a single and common interface for all).* For this reason, Salesforce's multi-tenant architecture leverages a metadata-driven framework that makes the underlying platform architecture to be polymorphic and as such allows each customer on its platform to design, build, and deploy their version of the business application through a common interface while still maintaining a complete isolation of individualized business logic and data through dedicated access and security for each customer.

The only thing that separates the experience of one Salesforce customer from another is the unique metadata for each customer's org. A customer can have multiple instances or orgs within their company. The metadata for each instance of Salesforce will be unique to that instance of Salesforce. A Salesforce instance *(also commonly referred to as an "org" in the Salesforce ecosystem)* is nothing more than a container for the unique metadata for your instance of Salesforce. The metadata for your org describes your org, the applications within your org, the user interface appearance, the applicable business logic, and the unique algorithm to access your org's stored data. Everything in your Salesforce org is defined in the metadata for your org, including standard and custom objects, fields, workflows, reports, security permissions, Apex code, Visualforce pages, and so on.

---

[13]`www.developerforce.com/media/ForcedotcomBookLibrary/Force.com_Multitenancy_ WP_101508.pdf.`

In a more traditional architecture without the metadata-driven framework, a developer would write code directly as part of your application's component, which is then interpreted, compiled, and processed by your system each time the code is executed. The system only follows the instructions provided explicitly within your code to determine the exact behavior of your application.

In a metadata-driven framework, the Salesforce Lightning Platform engages a dynamic Apex code runtime engine *(i.e., a computation server in a Salesforce data center that executes Apex code)* to generate and compile the entire application dynamically from scratch on demand by reading the metadata defined for your org each time a system event occurs on your Salesforce org. Following the metadata read, the runtime engine then proceeds to execute any necessary Apex code or standard automation feature that needs to be triggered to render the expected behavior from your Salesforce application.

When a Salesforce administrator configures or customizes your Salesforce org by creating custom objects or writing an Apex code, they are actually creating new metadata in addition to the standard metadata of Salesforce that controls the standard features of Salesforce. The end users of Salesforce, including Salesforce administrators and developers, can never delete or change any of the standard components or standard metadata of Salesforce. All customizations made by Salesforce users are additional to and only extend the standard components of Salesforce to accommodate unique customizations needed for your Salesforce org. When a Salesforce administrator creates a new custom object, for example, the Salesforce Lightning Platform does not create a corresponding data table in the underlying database of Salesforce, nor does it execute any code at this time. Instead, the Salesforce Lightning Platform simply creates a new metadata definition identifying the new custom object and uses this stored metadata later to generate a virtual application, on demand, instantly at runtime.

The point and click declarative configuration made on Salesforce by administrators only changes the metadata for your org, and since all customizations are just metadata stored in the Salesforce database, all configurations are instantly deployed in your org as soon as the metadata records are committed to the Salesforce database. Salesforce sandboxes are nothing more than mirrored metadata records in the Salesforce database. Salesforce's multi-tenant architecture allows Salesforce to resolve any defects for all its customers by making changes to their centralized metadata and code base.

The key point to note here is that, compared to a traditional architecture, all code in Salesforce is considered metadata, but not all metadata in Salesforce is code.

The metadata for each instance is stored within Salesforce in the format of an Extensible Markup Language (XML) file, commonly named within each instance as the "package.xml" file. The package.xml file can be extracted out of Salesforce using a development tool such as VS Code or Workbench,[14] modified independently by a developer, and imported back into Salesforce to reflect new changes and customizations for your Salesforce org based on the modified package.xml file.

Because of this architectural setup of Salesforce, every tenant on the Salesforce Lightning Platform can maintain their own set of customizations and personalization for their Salesforce experience as metadata, without disrupting or compromising the experience, customizations, and personalization of other Salesforce orgs and respective users of other Salesforce orgs.

Because metadata processing is so vital to the Salesforce Lightning Platform, the platform's runtime engine is optimized to access all stored metadata for every Salesforce org on demand. One such optimization technique requires the Salesforce Lightning Platform to cache the metadata for the Salesforce org in the browser memory to improve system performance by avoiding code recompilations at runtime. Salesforce stores the application data for each customer org in large and shared database tables as heap storage (a style of data storage that is not dependent on the execution of any application code). To access a customer's stored data from heap storage, the Salesforce Lightning Platform leverages a set of pivot tables that maintains a denormalized version of the customer's data linked together via data indexes. The Salesforce Lightning Platform references these pivot tables in accordance with the customer's unique metadata information which indicates the format, logic, and access required to present the data to the end user.

For more details on Salesforce's multi-tenant architecture, I would recommend reviewing the multi-tenant architecture section on the official Salesforce website.[15]

To illustrate how Salesforce conducts the multi-tenant magic behind the scenes for a seamless user experience, let me walk you through a user scenario in Figure 1-6, where the user is logging into Salesforce to update the phone number for a customer account.

---

[14]"Package.xml Metadata Management." Unit | Salesforce Trailhead, trailhead.salesforce.com/content/learn/modules/package-xml/package-xml-manifest?trail_id=architect-solutions-with-the-right-api.

[15]"The Force.com Multitenant Architecture." Multi Tenant Architecture – Developer.force.com, developer.salesforce.com/wiki/multi_tenant_architecture.

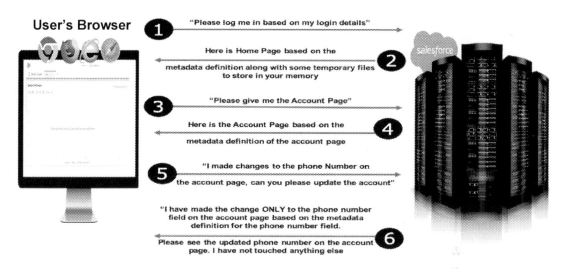

**Figure 1-6.** *Illustration of User Experience in Salesforce with Multi-tenant Architecture Orchestration Executing Behind the Scenes*

In this figure

- **In step 1**, the user logs into Salesforce via a web browser, using their login credentials.

- **In step 2**, Salesforce authenticates and authorizes the user to have access based on the user's access rights defined in the user's profile, which is stored within the metadata of that user's Salesforce org. Upon completing authentication, Salesforce realizes that the user's default page upon login is the Salesforce home page, which is dynamically generated and rendered by Salesforce as per the specifications of the home page defined in the metadata for the user's org. In addition to delivering the home page, Salesforce also returns a set of temporary executable files to be cached in the user's browser memory. The temporary executable files include support for any and all of the functions on the user's current page such as showing more details when the user hovers over the related quick links and so on. The purpose of these executable files is to support all page functions (except for data changes on the page) directly from the browser, without making a number of calls to the Salesforce data servers. For any changes to the underlying data, such as when a user updates a field or adds a new value to a blank field, Salesforce needs to make an API call to the Salesforce server in a Salesforce data center, where the actual data is stored.

- **In step 3**, the user navigates next to a specific customer's account page.

- **In step 4**, Salesforce renders the account page requested by the user, as per the metadata definition of the account page, along with the temporary executable files to support the non-data-related page actions on the account page.

- **In step 5**, the user updates the phone number field on the account and clicks save.

- **In step 6**, Salesforce receives a request to only update one field on the specific account page (i.e., the phone number). Salesforce uses the metadata definition of the account page and the phone number field in the physical database where the user's Salesforce data is stored and updates only that field. Salesforce then responds back to the user's web browser with only the updated field (i.e., the phone number) to display and confirm the data update within Salesforce.

All of these interactions are orchestrated by Salesforce in real time and within a few milliseconds.

The approach where a user's web browser interacts with the Salesforce servers by leveraging the metadata provides an added layer of efficiency for Salesforce to manage the traffic of requests hitting its data servers at any given time. This approach also protects Salesforce from any malicious web browser activities that can be prevented or at worst isolated at the level of the metadata for the org. This level of isolation at a metadata level prevents disruption to other users and services and protects all other orgs when a single org is affected by a security threat or a breach.

# The Seven Architecture Domains to Consider When Architecting with Salesforce

Now that we understand conceptually how Salesforce works, you may have already realized that architecting and implementing a solution on Salesforce, a SaaS-based solution, requires a completely different approach than, let's say, building something on-premise or an IaaS solution.

Every architect, when designing or assessing a Salesforce architecture, needs to align their architecture approach with the following seven architectural domains:

1. Application design architecture

2. Data architecture

3. Security architecture

4. Integration architecture

5. Identity and access management (IAM) architecture

6. Mobile architecture

7. Development lifecycle

# Application Design Architecture

In this domain, you should understand the declarative options available to build a custom application and be able to justify when to use what declarative option and why. Salesforce has more than 20 SaaS- and PaaS-based product offerings, each with its unique license type and features. Salesforce customers can mix and match the product licenses for their users as relevant to each user type. You should be familiar with and able to distinguish between the features of most major Salesforce product types, including, but not limited to, Sales Cloud, Service Cloud, Marketing Cloud, Community Cloud, Salesforce Einstein, and Salesforce Lightning Platform. You should be able to access and utilize the ideal licensing mix for the company users and the capabilities needed by each user group. The ideal licensing mix should accomplish a majority of each user's business requirements via out-of-the-box Salesforce capabilities, supported by the respective license type.

Additionally, you should take into consideration a large variety of prebuilt applications available on Salesforce's ecosystem called Salesforce AppExchange, where third-party vendors provide prebuilt extensible solutions that can be automatically installed in any Salesforce org to extend the out-of-the-box functionalities of the Salesforce platform. Salesforce AppExchange works in a similar way as Apple's App Store works for iPhones and other iOS devices. We will discuss many of the Salesforce license types, the features offered by each license type, and the most popular apps available on AppExchange in Chapter 3.

The programmatic options available within Salesforce support business logic and user interface requirements that cannot be configured using Salesforce out-of-the-box configuration capabilities. The architect should have a working knowledge of Apex (Salesforce's proprietary programming language for coding in Salesforce), Visualforce, Lightning components, and Lightning web components (LWC). In this book, we will address the programmatic options at a high level and as required for design thinking and architectural considerations needed for building a solution.

For a detailed review of the programmatic capabilities available in Salesforce, we would highly recommend starting with the Apex Developer Guide.[16]

# Data Architecture

In this domain, you are required to assess the data management and data stewardship requirements for an organization including data requirements related to large data volumes (LDVs). When designing the data architecture for a Salesforce solution, you need to consider the design approach for data sourcing, data interactions (i.e., internal interactions among data stored within Salesforce and external interactions with data stored in external systems that needs to be accessed via a systems integration approach), data governance, master data management (MDM), and metadata management.

We will cover the Salesforce data architecture in depth a bit later in Chapter 4.

# Security Architecture

In this domain, you are required to design a security model within Salesforce that can support complex requirements, primarily using the out-of-the-box security settings and with consideration of security concepts such as least privilege, defense in depth, and failing securely. The architect, when designing the security settings, needs to consider the appropriate peer-to-peer access provided to users with appropriate usage of sharing rules, both criteria based and ownership based. The architect should design the data object relationships and organization-wide object access in such a way that it can allow for data access through inheritance of data relationships.

---

[16]"Apex Developer Guide – Apex Developer Guide: Salesforce Developers." Salesforce Developers Documentation, developer.salesforce.com/docs/atlas.en-us.apexcode.meta/apexcode/apex_dev_guide.htm.

You also need to consider the appropriate mix of license types for the users to access the appropriate standard objects or features supported by each Salesforce license type such as Sales Cloud licenses vs. Service Cloud licenses. You should be able to design the appropriate hierarchical access required within a company using role hierarchy such that supervisors have access and visibility into their subordinates' work and, in many situations, access and visibility provided to their external partners and customers via Salesforce Community Cloud licenses.

You should be able to recommend the appropriate team-based sharing settings with the appropriate usage of account, opportunity, and case teams, public groups, and queues. When you are designing the security architecture, you must incorporate the security considerations to adhere with the industry standard data security compliances such as PCI, PII, and HIPAA standards. There may be times when the out-of-the-box security settings fall short of accomplishing the required security configuration for your company, during which you will need to recommend and justify the appropriate use of programmatic sharing known as "Apex sharing."

We will cover the Salesforce security architecture in depth in Chapter 5.

## Salesforce Integration Domain

In this domain, you should be able to determine when to use which integration pattern and be familiar with integration patterns such as the Request and Reply pattern, Fire and Forget pattern, Batch Data Synchronization pattern, and Remote Call-In pattern and UI changes based on the Data Update pattern and Data Virtualization pattern. You are required to analyze existing and future state integration architectures and develop an integration architecture blueprint that considers any integration with other company applications and cloud applications.

We will cover the Salesforce integration architecture in depth in Chapter 6.

## Salesforce Identity and Access Management (IAM) Domain

In this domain, you should understand the identity management architecture that spans multiple platforms and includes integration and authentication of non-Salesforce systems with Salesforce. You should describe the configuration requirements of delegated authentication in Salesforce. You should be familiar with SAML (Security

Assertion Markup Language)-based identity configuration including the difference between identity provider–initiated (IDP-initiated) SAML and service provider (SP)–initiated SAML and when to use each.

You should understand the conceptual identity management flow using identity protocols such as OAuth, SAML, OpenID Connect, and social sign-on. You should be able to design the ideal user authentication mechanism when using Salesforce communities. Additionally, you must consider the user management lifecycle, which incorporates the design for automated user provisioning, just-in-time provisioning, and manual account creation.

We will cover the Salesforce identity and access management architecture in depth a bit later in Chapter 7.

## Salesforce Mobile Domain

In this domain, you should be familiar with the four common mobile strategies: 1) leverage the out-of-the-box Salesforce mobile app available on Apple's App Store and Android-based Google Play Store; 2) build a Salesforce-native app using the Salesforce Mobile SDK; 3) build a hybrid app by combining HTML5, JavaScript, and CSS within the Salesforce Mobile SDK framework; and 4) build a web-based app by embedding HTML5 content within custom Visualforce pages.

You should be familiar with the benefits and trade-offs of choosing one mobile strategy over the others. In addition to selecting the ideal mobile strategy, you should also address the requirements related to mobile authentication, mobile security, offline mobile capabilities, and mobile notification capabilities. You should also understand how programmatic developments within Salesforce such as Visualforce pages and Lightning components can be exposed within the mobile app. Additionally, you should be able to optimize the mobile application's performance via design considerations such as lazy loading, JavaScript remoting, and action areas.

We will cover the Salesforce mobile architecture in depth a bit later in Chapter 8.

## Development Lifecycle Management

In this domain, you should be able to analyze the development environment of the company, design an appropriate governance framework, and recommend the best approach in managing the development and deployment lifecycle.

You should be familiar with the capabilities and characteristics of Metadata API and recommend the ideal mix of tools needed to execute deployment strategies and environmental approaches successfully. You should be able to create a development lifecycle blueprint that includes source control management, continuous integration, testing methodologies, system restore, and backup strategies.

We will cover the Salesforce development and deployment lifecycle strategies in depth a bit later in Chapter 9.

# Key Considerations and Limitations When Architecting with Salesforce

To preserve performance consistency for all tenants and to protect all shared resources in their multitenant architecture, Salesforce requires all its customers to adhere to certain governor limits. The limits enforced by Salesforce protect each customer on the Salesforce platform from a single customer misusing or monopolizing the performance of the shared resources powering their Salesforce Lightning Platform.

Salesforce enforces two types of limits:

1. Limit per transaction

2. Limit of transactions within a rolling 24-hour period

A list of all governor limits enforced by Salesforce is available at the Salesforce official developer resource site.[17]

# Summary

In this chapter, we covered

- A brief history of Salesforce and its exponential growth until date in the CRM-related SaaS and PaaS technology market space.

- The distinction between and the advantages and disadvantages of on-premise and IaaS, PaaS, and SaaS solutions.

---

[17]"Execution Governors and Limits – Apex Developer Guide: Salesforce Developers." Salesforce Developers Documentation, developer.salesforce.com/docs/atlas.en-us.apexcode.meta/apexcode/apex_gov_limits.htm.

- The four common approaches to building a technology stack in today's world including building either an on-premise solution, IaaS cloud solution, PaaS cloud solution, or SaaS cloud solution and some key advantages and disadvantages with each approach.

- A deep-dive view into the technology stack utilized by Salesforce which comprises an infrastructure layer, a metadata and shared services layer, an identity and access management and application definition layer, an Apex runtime engine layer, a Lightning application layer, a Lightning Component layer, a Lightning page component, and a Lightning page.

- An overview of Salesforce's multi-tenant architecture and the metadata-driven framework that allows Salesforce to decrease its cost of service delivery to all its customers while maintaining a central repository of its baseline code and offerings.

- The seven architecture domains that need to be considered simultaneously when architecting with Salesforce. These domains are application design architecture, data architecture, security architecture, integration architecture, identity and access management architecture, mobile architecture, and development lifecycle.

# CHAPTER 2

# The Art of Artifacts

The real value of a Salesforce architect comes from the artifacts they produce to keep the solution consistent and aligned with the business objectives. The quality of an artifact differentiates an architect from other Salesforce roles. A Salesforce architect's purview and responsibility is much more comprehensive. It is a common misconception that architects are a luxury item for a Salesforce project, as they are expensive and not needed.

We often tell people, *"If you think Salesforce architects are expensive, try paying for a project without one."*

The key reason for discussing the artifacts so early in this book is to equip you with a Salesforce architect's mindset and allow you to organize the technical details from this book in relevant context. We often see knowledgeable architects struggling to put their thoughts on paper mainly due to a disconnect between their Salesforce knowledge and their approach in developing the artifacts. The intent of this chapter is to bridge that gap.

The architectural artifacts are the first step in your design process. It will equip you to start with a standard approach and strengthen the artifact with granular technical details. The ideal artifacts must include considerations from each of the seven architecture domains outlined in Chapter 1.

We recommend using this chapter as the basis for organizing and absorbing the contents of this book.

This chapter covers some key points, including

- The creation of three key artifacts commonly used in every Salesforce solution design

- Using FUSIAOLA analysis to create artifacts

- An approach to design a system landscape

- Using seven essential data modeling techniques to design a Salesforce solution

© Dipanker Jyoti and James A. Hutcherson 2021
D. Jyoti and J. A. Hutcherson, *Salesforce Architect's Handbook*, https://doi.org/10.1007/978-1-4842-6631-1_2

# Art of Artifacts

The artifacts you create should articulate the design of each component of the solution in the most straightforward format with as few documents as possible. These artifacts become the blueprints of the solution and a reference point for development.

There are three key artifacts that you must produce for every Salesforce solution:

1. FUSIAOLA analysis

2. System landscape

3. Data model

There are, however, a few other artifacts that you may need to produce beyond the preceding three based on an individual project's needs such as

- Role Hierarchy and Sharing Diagram

- Environment and Release Management Diagram

- Source Code Branching Diagram

- System Authorization Flow diagrams

However, in this chapter, we will only focus on the three critical artifacts identified earlier, since they are key to every Salesforce architecture design.

In the next section, we will outline the thought process and an approach to creating each of the three key artifacts. You can create and present these artifacts in any format or style of your choosing, as long as you remain true to the approach outlined in this chapter.

# FUSIAOLA Analysis

The first step in the architectural process is to analyze the business domain and clearly understand all business requirements that need to be accomplished. Each business requirement needs to be assessed against the seven architectural domains introduced previously.

Only a few of us architects are lucky to be engaged in a project from the start. Most of us are brought in only when something is broken or in the middle of the project when the requirements get complex. No matter when you are brought in as an architect, your first question to answer should always be ***"What the FUSIAOLA is going on here?"***

*FUSIAOLA,* pronounced (*fuhs-ee-a-HO-la*), stands for

> **F**: Features
>
> **U**: Users
>
> **S**: Systems
>
> **I**: Integrations
>
> **A**: Authentication
>
> **O**: Objects
>
> **L**: Licenses
>
> **A**: Assumptions

## F: Features

Salesforce solutions need functions to support business requirements. The functional capabilities provided by a system can include any one or all of the following three outcomes:

1. A user interacting with Salesforce

2. A remote system interacting with Salesforce

3. Salesforce interacting with a user or a remote system based on some criteria or an event within Salesforce

To identify the features needed by the users, we need to understand each user's experience with the system in explicit details. Systems do not have commonsense reasoning as humans do, and hence every logic and system expectation must be explicitly expressed within business requirements.

Typically, a business analyst on the project captures these business requirements, so you as architect must start by reviewing the completeness and coverage of the business requirements for the intended solution. Typically, a single business requirement is captured in a single statement such as "The system shall..." or as a user story. A user story is a business requirement written from the point of view of a specific user or a user group, along with the user's achieved objective for the requirement.

Here are two examples of typical user stories and their format:

- **User Story A**: "As a sales user, I would like to create a new opportunity for an existing customer account with the opportunity status of "New" so I can process and track the opportunity throughout the opportunity lifecycle."

- **User Story B**: "As a sales user, I would like to create a new opportunity for a new customer account that does not exist in the system with the opportunity status of "New" so I can process and track the opportunity throughout the opportunity lifecycle."

A user story often considers the business context of the user's needs. However, as an architect, you need to decompose the business requirement a step further to determine the technical context of the user's need.

For instance, in reading these user story examples, you may assume that both user stories are similar, and hence designing for User Story A solves for User Story B. If so, you would be wrong and here is why.

User Story A requires that the sales user can create a new opportunity for an existing account record, and hence the user will be able to associate the new opportunity record with an existing customer account. But what happens when a customer account does not exist? Whom do you associate the new opportunity with? This is where User Story B plays differently. In User Story B, the sales user must create a new opportunity along with a new customer account. In this case, there will always be a new account record which the new opportunity can be associated with.

The difference in the user stories specified in the preceding text is an oversimplification of the nuances that you as an architect will need to spot when reviewing the business requirements or user stories.

As an architect, you must think deeper than the business context and determine the technical context that dominates the business requirement.

The best way of doing this is to look at each business requirement from the lens of three key technical contexts, which are

1. Data context

2. Business logic context

3. Interaction context

Every business requirement exhibits one or all three technical contexts. It is very common for one technical context to be more dominant than the other two for a given business requirement. All Salesforce capabilities, declarative or programmatic, can be mapped to one of these three key technical contexts, and hence categorizing all business requirements into one or more of the three technical contexts will become highly crucial in choosing the right Salesforce feature to meet each business requirement.

## Data Context

A business requirement with a data context typically includes a user creating data, updating data, reviewing data, deleting data, or sometimes associating one data with another.

Both user story examples mentioned earlier are examples of data context–dominant requirements because the underlying objective of both user stories is to create data and associate data with each other. Yes, there is also a user interaction context *(more on interaction context in the next section),* as the user needs to enter data via a screen. And although both contexts are relevant, the data context is the more dominant technical context. If you had to choose one over the other, you would probably choose the data context over the interaction context. Later in this chapter, you will learn why choosing a dominant technical context is important.

## Business Logic Context

A business requirement with a business logic context includes the processing of a user's request or a system transaction with some business logic or calculation. Examples of requirements with dominant *business logic context* are as follows:

1. As a sales user, I want the system to calculate and apply a sales discount in the range of 0–5%, based on the discount thresholds allowed by me so that we can only offer discounts that I am authorized to offer without requiring additional approvals.

2. As a product manager, I want all product inquiries and service requests related to the product we manage to be routed to me based on my geographical territory so that I only address the inquiries and customer support needed for the product we manage in my geographical territory.

# Interaction Context

A business requirement with a dominant interaction context typically refers to a user interaction via a screen or a remote system interacting with Salesforce via a systems integration.

Examples of requirements with a dominant interaction context are as follows:

1. As a sales manager, I want to view my team's opportunity pipeline and forecast details grouped quarterly on a single page so that I can track all opportunities managed by me and my team.

2. As a sales user, I want a new order to be created in the SAP system associated with the customer account when an opportunity is set to closed/won within Salesforce, along with the order number of the newly created order in the SAP system being available within Salesforce, so that a new order is created in SAP automatically when an opportunity is closed/won.

Once you identify the dominant technical context for each business requirement, you will find it easy to map the business requirements with the ideal Salesforce feature. Not only that, you will also be able to justify when you need to use code instead of declarative options. We will cover an approach to choosing the right Salesforce solution based on the three technical contexts in Chapter 3.

Sometimes it is hard to pick a single dominant technical context; this often means that the business requirement is overloaded and needs to be decomposed further and split into multiple requirements. After splitting the requirement, if you are still unable to pick a single technical context, it is okay to pick up to two technical contexts for a single business requirement. But just know that picking more than one or all three technical contexts will blur your choices for the ideal solution.

To capture the technical contexts for each business requirement, we recommend creating a table such as Table 2-1. This table has two additional columns to indicate the declarative and programmatic options available to address the requirement. How to choose the declarative or programmatic option for each requirement is covered in Chapter 3.

***Table 2-1.*** *Illustration of Dominant Characteristics, Identification, and Assignment*

| User Story | Dominant Contexts | | Declarative Option | Programmatic Option |
|---|---|---|---|---|
| | 1 | 2 | | |
| As a sales VP, I want to manage select fields on each account and opportunity than the sales team since I only need to review these particular fields for any account or opportunity. | | | | |
| | Interface | Data | *Page layout or reports and dashboards* | *Visualforce page or Lightning web components* |
| As a sales user, I want a new order to be created in the SAP system associated with the customer account when an opportunity is set to closed/won within Salesforce, along with the order number of the newly created order in the SAP system being available within Salesforce so that a new order is created in SAP automatically when an opportunity is closed/won. | | | | |
| | Business logic | Interface | *Workflow rule and outbound message* | *Lightning web components Or Apex Trigger and Apex class and REST API* |
| As a sales user, I want the system to automatically update the opportunity status as closed/won when the contract status is "Executed" and also send me an email notification after changing the opportunity status so that I can be notified of the closed/won opportunity upon contract execution. | | | | |
| | Data | Business logic | *Process Builder or Lightning Flow* | *Apex Trigger* |
| As a division lead, I only want to see data and functions that are relevant to my sales division so that I only manage functions relevant to my division. | | | | |
| | Interface | Business logic | *Lightning app or record types and page layout* | *Visualforce page or Lightning web components* |
| As a salesperson for division A, I want to manage opportunities only for division A as per division A's opportunity management process which is different for each division so I can adhere to the business process unique to my division. | | | | |
| | Interface | Data | *Record types and page layout* | *Not required* |

# U: User

Refers to the users intending to use the Salesforce solution. In the Salesforce ecosystem, a user or a group of users with common business operations and roles is also referred to as an "actor." Going forward, we will refer to a user or user group unanimously as an "actor."

Each actor can be differentiated from another based on the actor's nature of use of the system.

An actor's nature of use can be evaluated based on four key user attributes:

1. Information role

2. Business function

3. Internal vs. external

4. Role hierarchy index

## Information Role Attribute

An actor can either be an

1. Information provider

2. Information processor

3. Information consumer

An actor can be the creator and provider of the information needed within Salesforce. Actors that are information providers are usually customers, external partners, internal client-facing sales staff, or call center intake staff.

Information processors are typically the back or middle office staff that process the provided information and run it through the workflow of their operations.

The information consumers are typically supervisors, executives, customers, and external partners who monitor and consume the results of the operations executed within the system.

However, there can also be scenarios where a given actor is the provider, processor, and also consumer of the information. This is common in smaller organizations with fewer employees who manage the data intake, process the data internally, and consume the data. In such cases where a user is provider, processor, and consumer, you can safely categorize the user's role as the "information processor." In most cases, the information processor will need to be given the most comprehensive security access and license type within the system anyways. In any case, it is still valuable to assess and differentiate the actors based on their information role attribute in order to assign the appropriate license type, user profiles, permission sets, sharing rules, teams, and public group assignment for the appropriate level of visibility and sharing. More on visibility and sharing will be covered in Chapter 5.

Another value of the information role attribute is to determine the ideal license type for the user. For instance, let's say an actor, identified as primarily an information consumer, may only require read-only access to accounts and contacts within Salesforce; manage CRM content, ideas, and answers within Salesforce; need read-only access to reports and dashboards; view and approve workflows; use the calendar to create and track their activities; and share data only with a group of users. All of these can be accomplished by assigning just a "Chatter Only" license to the actor, instead of a more expensive Sales Cloud or Service Cloud license. The user profile for such a user will also be unique compared to a Sales Cloud– or Service Cloud–licensed user, which will need to be taken into account for visibility and sharing requirements. More on license types will be covered in Chapter 3.

## Business Function Attribute

Another key attribute that distinguishes a type of user from another is the business function(s) of the company that the actor manages. In large organizations, a clear and formal segregation of duties is outlined for each actor. The business division to which an actor belongs could be sales, service, marketing, or IT. Within a service division, the actor may be part of the call center function or the field service function. It is critical to dive deeper into an actor's business functions rather than just classify them to a department or division because Salesforce now offers more than just Sales and Service Cloud licenses. Salesforce licenses vary by industry specialization such as Financial Services Cloud or Health Cloud as well as by functionality such as Field Service Lightning and Einstein Analytics. A single user within Salesforce can only be assigned a single Salesforce license at any given time. Due to this reason, assigning the correct licenses to each actor is highly crucial and the fundamental starting point for what an actor can do within the system. For instance, in a scenario where an actor belongs to the service division and is also part of the field service function of the company, a Salesforce Field Service Lightning license will be more appropriate for the actor than just a Service

Cloud user license because a Field Service Lightning license covers all major functions available via a Service Cloud license, in addition to the field service capabilities that are primarily intended.

In large companies, it is easier to drill down from an actor's business division to the actor's formal business functions. However, in smaller companies and start-ups, there may not be any formal segregation of duties or a clear job function defined for any actor. In this case, an actor within the organization may need the ability to do everything from sales and service to field service functions. In this instance, the "Salesforce Field Service Lightning Plus" license would be more appropriate for most actors, as it provides the capabilities of Sales Cloud, Service Cloud, and Field Service Lightning, all from a single license.

The "Salesforce Field Service Lightning Plus" license is more expensive than an individual Sales Cloud or Service Cloud or Field Service Dispatcher or Field Service Technician license; however, the premium paid for the "Salesforce Field Service Lightning Plus" license is justified by the flexibility and scalability of functions available to a single actor of the system. This is why the Salesforce product mix and license model can be completely different for companies within the same industry with identical business operations. More on license types will be covered in Chapter 3.

## Internal vs. External Attribute

The last but not the least is to identify if the actor is internal to the enterprise (i.e., employed by the enterprise) or external to the enterprise such as a customer or partner with self-service capabilities. Additionally, for external users, it's important to understand the type of relationship they maintain with the enterprise and the functions or features that they are involved in. This is for identifying the appropriate Salesforce community licenses that may be needed for the actor.

---

**Note**    The only licenses that can be applied to external users are either Community Cloud licenses or "Chatter External" licenses.

---

Through Salesforce community licenses, external users are provided access to a subset of the information stored and processed within Salesforce via a personalized portal access. It is however important to note that Salesforce community licenses can also be provisioned to internal users, if needed. We will cover "Salesforce community" and other common Salesforce product types in Chapter 3.

# Role Hierarchy Index Attribute

A key sharing setting offered by Salesforce is the role hierarchy. Access within Salesforce can either be shared laterally with peer associates or vertically with a user's manager and their managers, all the way up to the CEO of the company. The role hierarchy sharing setting within Salesforce addresses the vertical information sharing access between users, the user's manager, and their managers.

A role hierarchy within Salesforce can be assigned to any user at the user's profile level, allowing the user of that profile to view, edit, and report on all data that's owned by the user or shared with the users below them in their role hierarchy. The only exception to access granted via role hierarchy occurs when the specific object (i.e., containing the information being accessed) is a custom object with the object's organization-wide default setting for "Grant Access Using Hierarchies" being "disable." In all other cases, a role hierarchy set for a given user determines the user's access to all data that was either created by them or any user listed in the role hierarchy under them. A role hierarchy allows vertical access for a given user only in the direction of top to bottom and not the other way. By this, we mean a user, let's say user X, who is listed in the role hierarchy above another user, let's say user Y, can view all data that user Y has access to within the system, in addition to their own data within the system. On the other hand, user Y can only access data created by them but has no access to the data created or owned by user X.

Many people assume that the role hierarchy of Salesforce should be set up to replicate the formal organization chart of the company, assuming that the formal organization chart captures the vertical access needed within the system. This is not always the case and not in any way mandatory. The role hierarchy of Salesforce determines who needs to see what from an inherited data ownership perspective, without setting up complicated sharing settings for supervisors and managers to be able to access the data owned by their direct reports.

That being said, in many cases, an administrative assistant user who is shared by multiple executives may need access to the data owned or created by each of the executives whom they support. It would be too complex to create a set of sharing settings to give them access to each executive's data. In such a scenario, it may just be easier to place the administrative assistant user above the executives they support, within the role hierarchy, even though the executives do not report to the administrative assistant. By manipulating the setup of the role hierarchy this way, the administrative assistant automatically gets access to all data managed by the executives they support within the system.

Another reason why a company's formal organization chart may differ from the role hierarchy in Salesforce is that the role hierarchy can also include external users such as partners and customers who access the system for collaboration and self-service. That's right; external users need to be set up in the role hierarchy within Salesforce, if they need to access the system via Salesforce Community Cloud. A role hierarchy index is a number assigned to each user, with respect to their role and position in the company. The role hierarchy index of 1 signifies the highest level in the role hierarchy, which is typically assigned to the CEO of the company. All role hierarchy indexes following the index of 1 (i.e., greater than 1) apply to subordinate users in the role hierarchy. There can be multiple roles with the same role hierarchy index signifying peer roles. For example, it's common to have the role hierarchy index of 2 assigned to VP of sales, as well as VP of service, as well as VP of IT operations.

The best way to capture the user attribute analysis is to create a table such as Table 2-2. We will cover the inputs in the last column named "Ideal License" in Chapter 3, where we will discuss the details of the most commonly used Salesforce license types and how the Salesforce user attribute chart can help us identify the ideal license type to be assigned to each actor.

***Table 2-2.*** *Salesforce User Attribute Chart*

| Actor Name | Actor Description | Information Role | Business Function | Internal vs. External | Role Hierarchy Index | Ideal License |
|---|---|---|---|---|---|---|
| CEO | The chief executive officer (CEO) is the highest-ranking executive of the company, responsible for making major corporate decisions, managing the overall operations and profitability of the company. All vice presidents report to the CEO and share the overall health of the company related to key functions of the company which include sales, service, finance, IT, and human resources. The CEO rarely uses the system, but when they do use the system, it's mainly to view reports and dashboards related to sales and service. | | | | | |
| | | Consumer | Executive oversight | Internal | 1 | Platform Plus license |

(*continued*)

***Table 2-2.***  (*continued*)

| Actor Name | Actor Description | Information Role | Business Function | Internal vs. External | Role Hierarchy Index | Ideal License |
|---|---|---|---|---|---|---|
| Admin assistant of the CEO | The administrative assistant of the CEO keeps track of the CEO's calendar, serving as gatekeeper to all interactions between the CEO and other employees of the company. The administrative assistant of the CEO interacts also with the company's partners and customers on behalf of the CEO relating to logistical correspondence or general follow-ups. The administrative assistant's use of the system includes reviewing the reports and dashboards for format and detail correctness prior to the CEO's review. The administrative assistant of the CEO has almost the same level of access to the system as the CEO and is able to access all the information entered by all users (except for some information entered by the CEO) within the system. | | | | | |
| | | Consumer | Executive oversight | Internal | 2 | Platform Plus license |
| VP of sales | The vice president (VP) of sales is committed to overseeing the achievement of sales targets across all regions for all products sold by the company, which include product A and product B. The VP of sales is also responsible for reviewing and approving all sales contracts over $1 million and any discounts offered to customers that exceed 25% of the original deal value. The RVP of sales only uses the system to generate monthly, quarterly, and annual sales reports and view daily dashboards. The VP of sales is also interested in big deal alerts and deals requiring their review and approval. Occasionally, the VP of sales needs access to account- and deal-level details to review and investigate the account and deal background. | | | | | |
| | | Consumer | Sales | Internal | 3 | Sales Cloud |

(*continued*)

***Table 2-2.*** (*continued*)

| Actor Name | Actor Description | Information Role | Business Function | Internal vs. External | Role Hierarchy Index | Ideal License |
|---|---|---|---|---|---|---|
| RVP of sales of product B | The regional vice president (RVP) of sales is committed to overseeing the achievement of the sales target for their designated geographical region related to product B. The RVP is also responsible for reviewing and approving all sales contracts over $1 million and any discounts offered to customers that exceed 15% and are less than 25% of the original deal value. The RVP only uses the system to generate monthly, quarterly, and annual sales reports and view daily dashboards. The RVP of sales is also interested in big deal alerts and deals requiring their review and approval. Occasionally, the RVP needs access to account- and deal-level details to review and investigate the account and deal background. | | | | | |
| | | Consumer | Sales | Internal | 4 | Sales Cloud |
| VP of service | The vice president (VP) of service is committed to overseeing the achievement of service and support offered across all regions and for all products sold by the company. The VP of service ensures that the service-level agreements offered to the customers are met adequately and the customer satisfaction rating for the company is maintained at the highest level. The VP of service uses the system to monitor a daily dashboard consisting of service KPI metrics and review service quality standards monthly, quarterly, and annually. The VP of service has full access to the system to access all service issues as needed such that they can intervene and address any case that has been escalated multiple times with no resolution. | | | | | |
| | | Processor | Service | Internal | 3 | Service Cloud |

(*continued*)

***Table 2-2.*** (*continued*)

| Actor Name | Actor Description | Information Role | Business Function | Internal vs. External | Role Hierarchy Index | Ideal License |
|---|---|---|---|---|---|---|
| Field sales | The field salesperson is responsible for all direct sales with customers for customer accounts assigned to them within their territory. The field salesperson sets their revenue targets in the beginning of the fiscal year and tracks their sales targets quarterly within the system. The field salesperson often physically visits the customer's location and with their customers on a regular basis and uses the system to enter and track all sales activities using their mobile device. Due to this reason, the field salesperson depends heavily on offline capabilities of their mobile device since many times they are in areas with no Internet or cellular connectivity. The field salesperson needs access to accounts, contacts, opportunities, quotes, cases, and any other data related to their assigned customers that are stored within the system to maintain a complete 360-degree information about the customers. | | | | | |
| | | Processor | Field service | Internal | 5 | Field Service Lightning |
| Product manufacturer for product A | A product manufacturer for product A is an external partner that is responsible for the production and supply of product A, supporting all regions, and collaborates with all field salespeople who sell product A. The product manufacturer for product A has access to all leads and opportunities related to product A across the company. The product manufacturer does not interact directly with the customer but supports any questions or issues related to product A via interactions with the designated field salesperson for product A. | | | | | |
| | | Processor | Sales and service | External | 4 | Partner Community |
| B2B customer | B2B customers are customer organizations that purchase products A and B at large volumes for redistribution at their retail location. A typical B2B customer organization comprises anywhere between 20 and 50 employee firms that primarily interact with the company for placing wholesale orders via a personalized company portal allowing for self-service and allowing member access and member management of the customer organization employees. | | | | | |

(*continued*)

***Table 2-2.*** (*continued*)

| Actor Name | Actor Description | Information Role | Business Function | Internal vs. External | Role Hierarchy Index | Ideal License |
|---|---|---|---|---|---|---|
| | | Provider | Customer | External | 6 | Community Plus |
| B2B customer representative | A B2B customer representative is an employee staff member at the B2B customer organization who is responsible for placing and tracking orders with the company. They conduct all interactions related to order management via the B2B customer portal personalized for that B2B customer organization. The B2B customer representative can manage their own profile within the portal and can see all transactions related to their company, including transactions being managed by the peers in their own organization. | | | | | |
| | | Provider | Customer | External | 7 | Community Plus |
| B2C customer | B2C customers are direct customers who are individuals purchasing the company's products for self-consumption. The B2C customers need the ability to shop for products online, create a personalized account when placing orders, or conduct self-service activities such as tracking orders placed, reviewing previous purchases, and opening support tickets for their transactions. | | | | | |
| | | Provider | Customer | External | 6 | Community |
| IT operations associate | An IT operations associate is a member of the company's IT organization responsible for the administration, management, and maintenance of the CRM system. The responsibilities of the IT operations associate include setting up new users, supporting existing users with access to the CRM system, developing reports and dashboards as per requests from disparate users of the system, and conducting basic enhancements to the system on an ongoing basis and as needed. | | | | | |
| | | Provider | General | Internal | 5 | Service Cloud |

# S: Systems

This refers to all systems in the company's ecosystem that either exist currently or are identified as systems of interest in the future. Note that I am recommending making a list of currently existing systems even if it is planned to be retired or be replaced. We will discuss how we communicate the existing and new systems a bit later in this chapter when we discuss the artifact "system landscape."

For existing systems that are being listed, it's important to address the following questions:

- Is the existing system being listed on-premise, on-cloud, or a hybrid of on-premise and on-cloud?

- Will the existing system remain or be replaced in the desired environment?

- If the existing system remains, will it require a bidirectional or a one-way integration with Salesforce?

- If the existing system remains and requires integration with Salesforce, then does it support the REST API protocol or SOAP API protocol or both?

- If the listed system is to be replaced, will it be replaced partially or fully?

- If the listed system is to be replaced, will there be a need for data migration or data archiving from the existing system?

When identifying new systems, it is important to answer the following questions based on your understanding of the current environment:

- For the systems planned to be retired or replaced, can Salesforce fill all the functional gaps in the desired future state?

- For any functional gaps not fulfilled by any products of Salesforce, are there any third-party apps on Salesforce AppExchange that meet the unfulfilled requirements?

- For any functional gaps still remaining after considering Salesforce products and Salesforce AppExchange, what cloud-based solutions are available that have prebuilt Salesforce adapters or SOAP API protocols compatible with Salesforce? *(More on Salesforce SOAP API protocol compatibility covered in Chapter 6.)*

- Other than the purpose of replacing the existing system(s), what other desired state requirements does the Salesforce-based solution need to address, and which Salesforce product(s) among the large variety of Salesforce products that best meets the requirements? *(More on the most common Salesforce products and their high-level descriptions in Chapter 3.)*

- Are any of the following systems needed in the desired state?

  - Middleware or an Enterprise Service Bus (ESB) tool

  - Extract-Transform-Load (ETL) tool

  - Master data management (MDM) system

  - Identity and access management (IAM) system

  - Data warehouse (DW) system

  - Document management (DMS) system

  - Content Management (CMS) system

Answering these questions should allow you to capture a list of all systems that need to be included and considered for a desired state system landscape, which we will create in the next section of this chapter ("System Landscape Artifact").

# I: Integrations

This refers to the integrations needed between the systems previously identified and Salesforce. Salesforce takes an API-first approach to building all its features on the Salesforce platform. With this approach, every feature and the underlying data within Salesforce can be accessed directly by another system or application without the use of a Graphical User Interface (GUI). This approach allows us to connect all the non-Salesforce systems with Salesforce and vice versa, using one of the many APIs supported by Salesforce. For an in-depth understanding of the integration approaches, pattern choices, and when to use which integration, please refer to Chapter 6.

However, for the purpose of FUSIAOLA analysis, you may add a column or two to Table 2-1, identifying the systems (among the list of all systems identified earlier) to be integrated and, in a separate column, identifying at a high level what each system needs to accomplish with the other. You can repurpose the preceding table to provide justification of each of the integrations that you have identified in your analysis.

# A: Authentication

This refers to the authentication and authorization needed by users and external systems to access Salesforce or access other systems via Salesforce. This specifically considers the identity and access management capabilities needed to secure access to and from the Salesforce solution.

If you are new to the concepts of identity and access management, including authentication vs. authorization, OAUTH, SAML Delegated Authentication, and single sign-on (SSO), then I would recommend reviewing Chapter 7 before conducting the analysis here on authentication methods.

In terms of the FUSIAOLA analysis, it is important to answer the following ten questions to outline the appropriate authentication methods for each actor and systems:

1. **Users and Account Management**: Which users need access to Salesforce, and are they internal or external?

2. **Provisioning:** How will internal and external users be provisioned within Salesforce?

3. **Authentication**: How will users be authenticated, and which system will store the identity of the user?

4. **Authorization**: How will users (when Salesforce is not the identity provider for the user) or external systems using the API get access into Salesforce?

5. **Single Sign-On**: Do users need to access multiple systems using a single authentication and authorization method?

6. **Access Rights**: Once users or systems have access to Salesforce, what can they do in Salesforce?

7. **Session Management**: How long should users be allowed to stay idle within the system before their session is timed out, or in the case of system access, when should the system's access be revoked?

8. **Logout and Redirects**: When a user logs out of Salesforce, where should the user be redirected to?

9. **Deprovisioning**: How will inactive users be deprovisioned access to the system?

10. **Account Recovery**: When user's access is disabled or locked, how can they regain access to Salesforce?

I will cover the lifecycle of identity and access management in detail in Chapter 7.

# O: Objects

This refers to existing and new data tables that need to be created within Salesforce to organize and store the data that is needed to support the functions and features supported by the system. One technique to identify objects easily from your requirements is to look for the "nouns" used in the sentences. Most often, the nouns used in the requirement are something you need to store as data within the system. For instance, in the following user story, I have underlined the nouns that can be considered as objects that need to be created in Salesforce to store data: As a **sales user**, I want a new **order** to be created and associated with the **customer account** when any **opportunity** is set to closed/won, so that I can track all **orders** resulting from closed/won **opportunities**.

In considering the objects, you need to meet this requirement. You can easily identify that you will need to use standard objects or create custom objects to store the following:

1. **User Object**: For sales user

2. **Order Object**: For new order

3. **Account Object**: For customer account

4. **Opportunity Object**: For any opportunity

This is an oversimplified example of how to identify objects from a requirement.

For a deep dive into data modeling and a detailed understanding of the Salesforce object model, along with the data architecture of Salesforce, please refer to Chapter 4.

# L: Licenses

Specifically, this is the optimal mix of Salesforce licenses types that will be needed to support a majority of the solution using out-of-the-box capabilities of Salesforce. The true potential of a SaaS-based solution like Salesforce is best realized only when the majority of capabilities needed are achieved out of the box. Since one size does not fit all in the SaaS world, Salesforce has distinguished its product offerings into several license types based on business functions, such as Sales Cloud or Service Cloud, and industry-specific license types, such as Health Cloud and Financial Services Cloud.

Choosing the right licenses for the solution is the best starting point and a vital step in architecting with Salesforce. As an architect, it is important to optimize the licenses required by each Salesforce actor such that the total licenses required by the organization are optimized for design and cost efficiencies. Salesforce allows its customers to mix and match multiple licenses for its users within a single Salesforce instance. However, each user within Salesforce can only be assigned a single license type at any given time.

For instance, a standard Salesforce Lightning Platform license is significantly cheaper than a Sales or Service Cloud license and may be enough to cover all the functions and features needed by a single actor within the company. On the other hand, an industry-specific license such as a Salesforce Health Cloud license or Field Service Lightning license is more expensive than a standard Sales or Service Cloud license but is completely worth it, given the additional capabilities and specialized features covering a diverse set of functionalities and features required by an actor of this company. In the earlier section where we discussed users and created a user table, I have illustrated the assignment of user licenses within the same table. The exercise of assigning the ideal licenses to each actor requires a strong understanding of the various licenses offered by Salesforce. Although it's hard to cover every Salesforce product license, I have discussed the most commonly used and most popular licenses of Salesforce in Chapter 3.

# A: Assumptions

Assumptions refer to the assumptions that you as an architect have made at the time of designing the desired solution based on the information available to you and your architectural inferences drawn from it. An architect's assumptions form the validity of their understanding of the business needs and an informal permission to fill in the blanks for information that is missing.

Although there can be a variety of topics for an architect to make assumptions, including topics covered in the earlier sections of the FUSIAOLA analysis, here are some recommended topics to consider when looking for assumptions.

## Who Sees What?

During the design stage of the solution, it is often not clear as to which user can see what, why, and how. As an architect, I often make assumptions in this topic by referencing the user attribute table created during the FUSIAOLA analysis related to users. That table allows me to identify internal vs. external users and their information role and business functions. Assumptions in this topic also allow an architect to validate the licenses assigned to each actor. It is also easier to confirm or correct the assumptions related to this topic since it can be effectively done by updating the user attribute table.

## Organization-Wide Defaults and Data Visibility

Another topic area for assumptions is the organization-wide default (OWD) settings for object and data visibility across the organization. The organization-wide default settings are often set up with the principle of "least privilege," which means that the org-wide default settings for each object within Salesforce should be set up keeping in mind the user with the lowest and least access within Salesforce.

Another way of saying that is if any single user within Salesforce cannot access a particular object, let's say "Object A," then the OWD setting for Object A should be set to "Private," which is the most restrictive setting using OWD in Salesforce. As an architect, I often indicate in my assumptions which objects within Salesforce I have considered to be private vs. public due to the principle of least privilege. There are other areas of visibility which are derived from ownership of records, in which case I often indicate how users can access records that they are not owners of (i.e., sharing rules, sharing via teams, sharing via group membership, etc.).

## Scope and Nature of Integrations

Given the out-of-the-box integration capabilities of Salesforce, project stakeholders often assume that there is not much development or setup required in the non-Salesforce system to work with Salesforce. They also assume that since Salesforce offers more than ten different types of APIs readily available for integration, the API will work automatically without a significant amount of configuration within Salesforce. This is a key reason for outlining the different methods being used to integrate the different systems with Salesforce during our FUSIAOLA analysis, the integration part, earlier. The integration options selected will allow an architect to justify the recommended investment in a middleware tool such as MuleSoft or the use of one of the Salesforce APIs over the others.

Assumptions can also be made about the type of protocols supported by the non-Salesforce system, because it is often the case, especially with SOAP API–based integrations, when the WSDL file of the non-Salesforce system is not supported by Salesforce. In such cases, when a WSDL file is not supported by Salesforce and a SOAP API–based integration is warranted, the only option is to use a middleware such as MuleSoft or Informatica, which orchestrates a protocol conversion to map the SOAP API schema of the non-Salesforce system with Salesforce SOAP API.

# Identity Provider–Initiated vs. Service Provider–Initiated Authentication

When designing a solution with seamless experience for users, it is critical for an architect to clarify which system acts as the identity provider for which users and which system(s) acts as the service provider. It is often the case that users within a company need access to many systems within the company other than Salesforce, and hence most companies implement single sign-on strategies that assign one system such as Microsoft Active Directory (AD) or PingFederate or Okta as the central repository and true source of all user details. In such cases, it's important to indicate the identity management system as the identity provider for Salesforce and Salesforce as the service provider to the identity management system. In other cases where a user accesses other systems from within Salesforce by using the Salesforce Canvas app, Salesforce becomes the identity provider for the external system being accessed, and the external system becomes a service provider for Salesforce. It is important to lay out which system acts as the identity provider vs. which system acts as the service provider, because, more often than not, project stakeholders assume all systems can act as identity providers simultaneously.

# Format of the FUSIAOLA Analysis

Earlier in this chapter, we talked about how the format of the FUSIAOLA analysis really does not matter, and oftentimes an architect may need to quickly draw a back-of-the-napkin sketch in front of the client. In Figure 2-1, we have illustrated what a quick back-of-the-napkin FUSIAOLA analysis would look like.

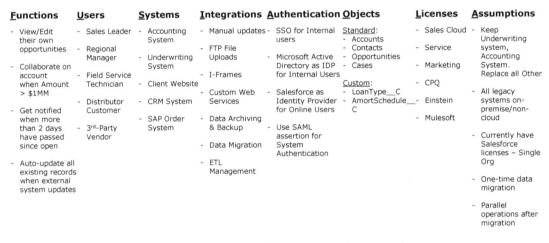

*Figure 2-1.* *High-Level FUSIAOLA Analysis Example*

For a detailed FUSIAOLA analysis in the right format, we recommend creating this artifact in Microsoft Excel with multiple worksheet tabs for each analysis, respectively.

Now that we have conducted the FUSIAOLA analysis, the artifacts from here on can be created based on the information gathered during the FUSIAOLA analysis. The FUSIAOLA analysis will be the basis for the next two artifacts that we will be discussing. We will start next with the system landscape artifact.

# System Landscape Artifact

A Salesforce system landscape is a blueprint of the interoperability between Salesforce and all other systems existing within the company's technical environment.

In Figure 2-2, you will see an illustrative example of what a typical Salesforce system landscape artifact would look like.

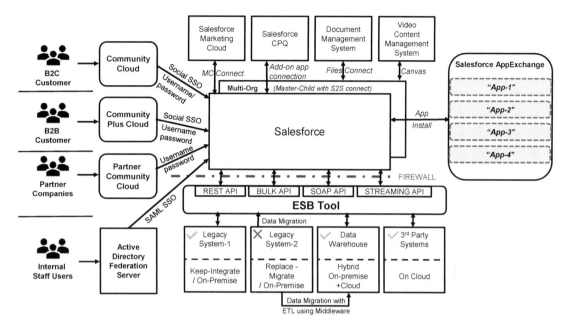

***Figure 2-2.*** *Illustrative System Landscape*

You would replace the generic names in the preceding diagram with the relevant external system names, such as "Microsoft ADFS" instead of the Active Directory Federation server or "SAP ERP" instead of third-party systems or "MuleSoft" instead of middleware/ESB tool.

At first look, the Salesforce system landscape may appear overwhelming to create, but you will find it fairly easy to draw if you have done the FUSIAOLA analysis correctly and gathered all the information prior to attempting to draw the system landscape.

There are seven things to consider and include from the FUSIAOLA analysis when drawing a Salesforce system landscape.

## What Is the Salesforce Organization Strategy?

A company can either maintain a single environment of Salesforce for use by the entire company or have multiple Salesforce environments, each environment with its own set of users, licenses, data, functionalities, and governor limits allocated and managed independently. We will discuss the approach to choosing an ideal org strategy in detail in Chapter 3.

## What Are the Systems Existing or New That Need to Interact with Salesforce?

The list of systems to be included here should come directly from the list of systems you outlined during the FUSIAOLA analysis. There are many ways of outlining the systems in the diagram. My preference is often to stack them below an integration layer tool, one beside the other in a row. We also recommend indicating within or around each system whether

- To keep or replace the system.

- To integrate with the system or migrate data from the system.

- The system is on-premise, on-cloud, or a hybrid of on-premise and on-cloud.

- Data will be migrated to Salesforce or an external data warehouse or both.

For a visual aid, you can often add a tick mark ✓ against the systems that will remain and a cross ✗ against the systems that will be replaced.[1] The arrows connecting the system to Salesforce or the middleware or another system should indicate if it is one-way sync or bidirectional sync.

## What Are the Specialty Salesforce Licenses That You Will Be Using Beyond the Core Sales, Service, or Platform Licenses?

Salesforce offers a variety of Salesforce licenses related to specialty functions such as Marketing, Quotes Management, and Einstein Analytics, which can be combined with the core Sales Cloud, Service Cloud, or Platform licenses. Most of the specialty Salesforce products seamlessly integrate with the core Salesforce platform similar to a

---

[1] In case you are wondering, how about symbols to indicate new systems? Here is our take on that: Any system without any symbol is assumed to be a new system added in the system landscape. Adding a symbol for every new system in a system landscape could make the diagram unnecessarily busy.

Salesforce AppExchange app which is installed as an add-on package in your Salesforce environment and inherits access to all required records within Salesforce through the add-on app connection.

In exceptional cases, such as in the case of Salesforce Marketing Cloud, integration is configured using a Salesforce-provided connector called the "Marketing Cloud Connect." The "Marketing Cloud Connect" connector is included within the price of the Marketing Cloud licenses and can be configured as a connected app to set up bidirectional integration between Marketing Cloud and your Salesforce environment. We will discuss the most commonly used Salesforce products and a high-level introduction of each product in Chapter 3.

## What Are the AppExchange Products That You Will Leverage to Avoid Custom Development?

In addition to its vast variety of products and thousands of declarative capabilities, Salesforce also has a marketplace for independent third-party vendors who offer prebuilt apps that can be easily downloaded to extend any feature not fully available via Salesforce's license types. The Salesforce marketplace for third-party apps, known as "AppExchange," is similar to the "App Store" for Apple devices and the "Google Play Store" for Android devices.

Although most apps available on AppExchange have subscription costs associated with them, there are several apps available on AppExchange that are completely free. Some of these free apps are developed by Salesforce themselves such as the "Salesforce Adoption Dashboards" which provides a Salesforce administrator and other relevant users with visibility into overall user login history, trending, adoption of key features such as opportunity pipeline, and marketing productivity.

Also, brand name vendors such as DocuSign and QuickBooks, which offer specialized capabilities such as electronic signatures and bookkeeping, respectively, have connectors and adapters available on AppExchange to allow companies with a subscription to their services, with the ability to use their services seamlessly within Salesforce.

Almost all apps on AppExchange are required to be updated regularly to be compatible with the latest version of Salesforce and all its new features. Often the regular updates and maintenance of the apps are offered by the app developers to the Salesforce subscribers at no extra cost.

Hence, as an architect, you need to consider AppExchange as the next best option after exhausting declarative configuration capabilities and before considering coding options in Salesforce to meet business needs.

For your reference, we have shared details about a variety of popular and commonly used apps available on AppExchange in Chapter 3.

## How Many Different Types of Salesforce Community Licenses Are Needed for External (or Any Internal) Users?

Salesforce communities deserve some consideration on their own when designing a Salesforce solution which requires giving access to a high volume of external users or when collaboration with external partner organizations is required or when a significant group of internal users needs to access Salesforce infrequently and for a small set of functions within Salesforce. A Salesforce community is used to provide segregated access to and allow collaboration between external customers, partner companies, and internal employees. A Salesforce environment can support multiple communities and community types, with each serving a distinct purpose and set of users.

A user's access into Salesforce and their respective access to specific information within Salesforce not only vary between access via a core Salesforce platform license and a Salesforce community license but also vary significantly between the various types of Salesforce communities such as Community, Community Plus, Partner Community, and Employee Community.

The assignment of the ideal Community Cloud license to the appropriate users impacts the design for the various user authentication methods needed, data security, visibility, and sharing capabilities.

We will talk a bit more about the Salesforce communities and the different types of communities in Chapter 3.

## What Are the User Authentication/Authorization Tools for Both Internal and External Users to Authenticate into Salesforce?

Having completed the FUSIAOLA analysis, you may already have a list of actors and the different methods of authentication that are needed by each actor. Users can access Salesforce directly using a standard username/password on the Salesforce login page or via the Community Cloud login page or through SSO capabilities supported by an identity and access management system such as Active Directory Federation Services or by using the credentials of a social account such as the user's Facebook account.

We will be discussing in detail the various types of authentication methods and when to use which authentication method in Chapter 7. However, for the purpose of the Salesforce system landscape, we recommend making a note indicating the type of authentication needed by each actor besides the respective actor.

## What Is the Integration Strategy to Integrate Salesforce with Existing or New Systems?

An integration strategy for most companies includes serving two key integration capabilities:

1. Extract-Transform-Load (ETL) large volumes of data.

2. Connect two or more systems for data accessibility across the connected systems.

To support these integration capabilities, the technology industry recognizes two main types of integration tools. They are

1. **ETL Tool**: Supports the process of extracting, transforming, and loading large volumes of data from multiple data sources. They can be used with batch, scheduled, or ad hoc data operations. They can also be used to perform data migration and data archiving activities.

2. **Enterprise Service Bus (ESB)**: A system that provides a homogeneous bus designed to distribute work between connected systems and applications. This middleware environment normally connects systems via an Application Programming Interface or API. Salesforce recently bought MuleSoft, an industry leading ESB provider.

Most integration tools such as MuleSoft and Informatica can support both ETL functions and ESB functions, eliminating the need for multiple integration tools. There are five key benefits of using an ESB tool vs. setting up point-to-point integrations between Salesforce and non-Salesforce systems:

1.  **Orchestration**: Composing of several existing detailed components into an aggregated service. Orchestration will manage the level of service and data. This can be done to achieve appropriate "extensibility" of the underlying components.

2.  **Transformation**: Data transformation is often required to move information from one system to another. The ESB creates a transformation template to move data in one format to another format needed by a consuming system.

3.  **Transportation**: Transport protocol negotiation between multiple formats (such as HTTP, JMS, JDBC). Note: Mule treats databases like another "service" by making JDBC just another transport (or endpoint) where data can be accessed.

4.  **Mediation**: Providing multiple interfaces for the purpose of (a) supporting multiple versions of a service for backward compatibility or, alternatively, (b) allowing for multiple channels to the same underlying component implementation. This second requirement may involve providing multiple interfaces to the same component, one legacy interface (flat file), and one standards-compliant (SOAP/XML) interface.

5.  **Nonfunctional Consistency**: For a typical ESB initiative, this can include consistency around the way security and monitoring policies are applied and implemented. Additionally, the goals of scalability and availability can be achieved by using multiple instances of an ESB to provide increased throughput (scalability) and eliminate single points of failure (SPOFs), which is the key objective for highly available systems.

As a rule of thumb for an architect, we recommend using an ESB tool when

- More than two systems need to be integrated with Salesforce, with complex integration requirements.

- Multiple data transmission protocols are used, such as FTP, HTTP, web service, and JMS.

- Business criteria dictate the message routing to and from external systems based on message content and criteria-based parameters.

Salesforce in addition to its standard API capabilities also provides prebuilt integration features such as **Files Connect,** which allows seamless integration between Salesforce and external files and document management systems such as Quip, Google Drive, SharePoint, or Box.com. With Files Connect, Salesforce users can seamlessly access, share, store, and search for files stored externally within Quip, Google Drive, SharePoint, or Box.com.

In this section, we mainly discussed the use of an ESB tool as the integration strategy. However, in Chapter 6, we will discuss integration strategies with out-of-the-box Salesforce integration capabilities.

So far, we conducted a deep-dive analysis of business needs and discussed the system capabilities needed with the FUSIAOLA analysis. Next, with the system landscape artifact, we discussed how Salesforce fits into the company's technology ecosystem of new and existing systems.

In the next artifact, we will be diving into the inner mechanics of your Salesforce org by discussing how data is stored, retrieved, accessed, and managed within Salesforce.

# Data Model Artifact

Data is the core ingredient of every system, but how data is entered, stored, organized, and utilized within a system determines the performance and efficiency of the system.

In a multi-tenant architecture, such as Salesforce, an optimized data model is extremely significant, because data model inefficiencies in Salesforce can result in performance degradation, leakages or blockages in visibility and sharing, and even data breach when interacting with external users and systems.

To get us started on what an ideal data model artifact looks like, please refer to Figure 2-3.

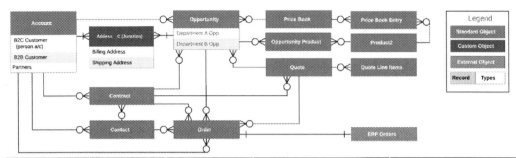

| Object | Object Type | OWD Setting | Record Owners | Estimated # of records |
|---|---|---|---|---|
| Account | Standard | Private | Salesperson | 5 Million |
| Contact | Standard | Public Read-Write | Salesperson | 10 Million (2 x account) |
| Opportunity | Standard | Public Read-Only | Salesperson & Product Specialist (opportunity team) | 15 million (3 x account) |
| Address__C | Custom (Junction) | Controlled by parent | Address book administrator | 10 million (2 x account) |
| Contract | Standard | Private | Officer (sharing rule) | 7.5 Million (50% of opportunity) |
| Order | Standard | Private | Salesperson & Order Manager (sharing rule) | 7.5 million (1:1 contract) |
| Product2 | Standard | Public Read-Only | Product Manager | 100 (all department products) |
| Opportunity Product | Standard | Controlled by parent | Salesperson & Product Specialist (opportunity team) | 15 million (1:1 Opportunity) |
| Price Book | Standard | Public Read-Only | Pricing Manager | 5 (Country Price books) |
| Price Book Entry | Standard | Public Read-Only | Pricing Manager | 500 (Product X Pricebook) |
| Quote | Standard | Private | Salesperson | 15 million (1:1 Opportunity) |
| Quote Line Item | Standard | Private | Salesperson | 45 Million (3 X Quote) |
| ERP Orders | External Object | Public Read-Only | ERP System | 7.5 million (1:1 Order) |

***Figure 2-3.*** *Sample Data Model of an Opportunity and Order Management Application*

Every data model artifact should, at a minimum, specify the following seven details:

1. Objects needed to store and manage data in Salesforce

2. Object types (i.e., whether they are standard, custom, or external objects)

3. Record types within each object

4. Object relationship to other objects

5. The organization-wide default settings for object visibility

6. Owners of the records within each object

7. Estimated number of records per object that can exist at any given period of time

# Objects Needed to Store and Manage Data in Salesforce

One of the best ways to identify the objects that will be used to store and manage data is to start by assessing the standard objects within Salesforce and the purpose served by each standard object within Salesforce. To review which standard objects are available within Sales Cloud or Service Cloud, visit this site: `https://developer.Salesforce.com/docs/atlas.en-us.api.meta/api/data_model.htm` *(please note, in this Salesforce article, the Service Cloud objects are referred to as "support objects").* Salesforce has developed these standard objects and their relationship to each other based on years of industry best practices. It is important that you map your sales and service business process as closely to the out-of-the-box business processes supported by Salesforce, in order to reap the most benefits from standard objects and the out-of-the-box capabilities supported by all standard objects. For example, the Salesforce assignment rules only work with the standard lead object or case object and are not available to use with any custom objects.

The first and most important standard object to start with is the account object. You cannot ignore the account object in Salesforce because Salesforce is an account-based system and is managed as the ultimate parent of most standard objects and custom objects that exist within any Salesforce org. Many of the sharing rules within Salesforce are also determined based on a specific user's access level or ownership of the records within the account object. An account object can relate to a company or an individual. In cases where the account is mapped to individuals such as individual customers, the record type of account is called a "person account." A person account can be enabled for any Salesforce org by opening a case with Salesforce.

The next core object that can be easily mapped with almost any business process is the contact object, which houses the details of individuals such as customers who are related to one or more accounts *(e.g., employees of customer companies).*

The account and contact objects are universally available standard objects across all Salesforce license types. Although there is a significant overlap among the standard objects available with Sales Cloud vs. Service Cloud licenses, the availability of many standard objects of Salesforce depends entirely on the Salesforce licenses that you have available within your org. So a key determinant for an optimized data model with efficient use of standard objects is to have the right Salesforce licensing model. We will discuss the various products and licensing models of Salesforce and the key distinctions in standard objects available within most of the products in Chapter 3. But for the purpose of this artifact, here are some of the other key standard objects that should be considered before creating custom objects:

- Lead

- Opportunity

- Order

- Contract

- Case

- Product

- Asset

- Quote

- Pricebook

A key thing to note about Salesforce standard objects is that the standard objects and the standard fields within the standard objects cannot be modified or deleted. You can always add new custom fields and not use the standard fields within the standard object if they are not standard required fields of that standard object. Also, the relationships between two standards objects cannot be modified or deleted. You can always have additional lookup relationships between two standard objects. You cannot create a custom master-detail relationship between two standard objects because one of the limitations of the standard objects is that standard objects cannot be on the detail side (i.e., child object) of a master-detail relationship.

Salesforce does not penalize you with any data storage limits or any restrictions if you do not use any or all of the standard objects available to you. But if you do use any of the standard objects, your data needs to play by the rules of that standard object. For example, if you use the opportunity standard object, then certain fields on the opportunity object such as "Stage" (i.e., opportunity stage) are required fields when you create or update an opportunity. Also, for opportunities with products, the opportunity amount field is automatically set to the sum of all products associated with that opportunity, and the amount field cannot be directly edited by users unless the opportunity has no products associated with it.

Due to some of these conditions and limitations associated with using standard objects, an architect can justifiably consider creating custom objects, instead of using a set of standard objects. The other justifiable reason for considering custom objects is when the architect has exhausted all data management options with standard objects and the data exhibits characteristics that cannot be accommodated by any available standard object. We will discuss the different object types in the next section.

# Object Types

In simple terms, objects created by Salesforce are called standard objects, objects created by you within Salesforce are called custom objects, and any objects you create that map to data stored outside your Salesforce org, in an external system, are called external objects.

We discussed standard objects in the previous section, so here we will discuss the considerations related to using custom objects and external objects.

The following are some considerations of creating and using custom objects:

- Every custom object name should be **unique** among all standard or custom or external objects existing in your Salesforce org and is automatically assigned a suffix of "__C" to distinguish itself from all standard objects.

- A **sharing rule object** is automatically created for each custom object that does not have a master-detail relationship with another object. The sharing rule object manages any sharing rules that are applied to the custom object, such as a criteria-based sharing (CBS) rule, allowing sharing the object records with another user when a certain user-defined sharing criterion is met by the record. All sharing objects inherit the same name as the custom object but are appended with the suffix "__Share" instead of "__C" that is appended as a suffix to custom object names.

External objects are similar to custom objects, except that the data lives in an external system outside your Salesforce org. External objects are a great way to extend the Salesforce data model beyond Salesforce by connecting with externally stored data without having to bring in the data or store the data into Salesforce. Each external object that you create relies on a data mapping configured by you that maps the Salesforce data with the data stored in a data table on the external system. Each of the external object's fields maps to a table column on the external system.

The following are some considerations of creating and using external objects:

- Every external object name should be **unique** among all standard or custom or external objects existing in your Salesforce org and is automatically assigned a suffix of "**_X**" to distinguish itself from all standard objects.

- External objects can only maintain lookup relationships with any standard and custom objects within Salesforce. The lookup relationships for external objects can be one of two types: external lookups and indirect lookups. (Both are discussed in a later section of this chapter.)

- Formulas and roll-up summary fields in standard or custom objects cannot reference fields on external objects.

- You cannot assign default values to custom fields created in external objects.

- You cannot create any of the following custom fields in external objects:

  - Auto-number (available only with the cross-org adapter for Salesforce Connect)

  - Currency (available only with the cross-org adapter for Salesforce Connect)

  - Formula

  - Location

  - Master-detail relationship

  - Picklist and multi-select picklist (available only with the cross-org adapter for Salesforce Connect)

  - Roll-up summary

  - Text (encrypted)

  - Text area (rich)

- You cannot use the following standard features of Salesforce with external objects:

    - Activities, events, and tasks

    - Approval processes

    - Attachments

    - Field history tracking

    - Merge fields

    - Notes

    - Record-level security (sharing)

    - Record types

    - Schema Builder

    - Validation rules

    - Workflow rules

- When you deploy an external object that is connected via OAuth 2.0, from a sandbox org to a production org, you will need to update the authentication provider each time you deploy.

# Record Types Within Each Object

Often during data modeling, you may identify multiple sources of data exhibiting similar characteristics that requires you to reuse an existing standard or custom object that you are already using. An example of this situation is when you want to store data about partner companies and B2B customer companies both in the account object.

This is a classic scenario for creating a record type of common object where two types of data need to be stored. Record types can be perceived as different flavors of the same object, partitioned from each other based on differences in business processes and user visibility needs. You can expose different fields to different users via different record types of the same object. All fields in the different record types of a single object are still stored together in the same object. However, the record types allow you to provide different user experience requirements due to differences in business processes. Another key use of record types is to present different values in a picklist field to different users without creating redundant or duplicate picklist fields on an object. Picklist values are often critical within an object since they are used to capture information such as record status, record stage, user preferences, and record choices. Duplicating these fields can cause significant data integrity and data reporting issues.

Records within one record type can also be switched to another record type *(if warranted by the business needs)*. This level of flexibility makes record types a critical design element when designing the data model for Salesforce.

The following are some considerations of creating and using record types:

- Business and person accounts require at least one active record type. Person accounts are account records to which a special kind of record type is assigned by Salesforce. Person account record types allow contact fields to be available on the account and allow the account to be used as if it were a contact. A default person account record type named "Person Account" is automatically created when person accounts are enabled for your org. You can create multiple person account record types after having the initial person account enabled by Salesforce in your Salesforce org. Users can change a "person account" record type to another "person account" record type or a business account record type to another business account record type through the UI. But a person account record type can only be changed to a business account record type and vice versa programmatically.

- A user can be associated with several record types. For example, for a user who creates opportunities for both B2C and B2B sales, then both the B2C and B2B opportunity record types can be made available to the same user when creating new opportunities.

- You need to update any sharing rules associated with some record types if you want to apply the same sharing rule to other record types of the same object. For example, let's say you have a record type called "B2C Opportunity" and you created a criteria-based sharing rule that shares all opportunity record types with your sales team. Now if you also have another record type called "B2B Opportunity" that you would also like to share with the same sales team, then you will need to update the sharing rule to include the "B2B Opportunity" record type in the criteria; else, it will not be shared automatically with the sales team.

- Deactivating a record type doesn't remove it from any user profiles or permission sets. Deactivating a record type only means that no new records can be created with that record type. However, any records that were previously created for that record type are still associated with it, and so are any page layouts associated with that record type.

- When converting, cloning, or creating new records, these additional considerations apply to objects with multiple record types:

  - When converting a lead, the new account, contact, and opportunity records use the default record type for the owner of the new records. The user can choose a different record type during conversion.

  - When cloning a record, the new record has the record type of the cloned record. If the user's profile doesn't have access to the record type of the cloned record, the new record adopts the user's default record type.

  - When a user creates a case or lead and applies assignment rules, the new record can keep the creator's default record type or take the record type of the assignee, depending on the case and lead settings specified by the administrator.

# Object Relationship to Other Objects

An object standard or custom can have the following types of relationships with other objects:

**Master-detail relationship**

- Associating one object with another in a hierarchical relationship such that one object is a master *(also known as parent object)* and the other is a detail object *(also known as child object)*. The parent object in such an association dictates the behavior of the child object including accessibility to the child object.

- Detail and subdetail records inherit security settings and permissions from the master record. You can't set permissions on the detail record independently.

- The owner of the master object record automatically inherits ownership of the detail object records associated with it; ownership cannot be changed.

- The records in a detail object cannot have any sharing rules exclusively applicable to itself. All sharing rules for a detail record are inherited from its master record.

- A master record must exist and is required to create and store any detail record.

- Deleting a detail record moves it to the Recycle Bin and leaves the master record intact; deleting a master record also deletes related detail and subdetail records. Undeleting a detail record restores it, and undeleting a master record also undeletes related detail and subdetail records. However, if you delete a detail record and later, separately, delete its master record, you cannot undelete the detail record, as it no longer has a master record to relate to.

**Lookup relationship**

- Links two objects together. Lookup relationships are similar to master-detail relationships, except they do not support sharing or roll-up summary fields.

- Can be required, prevent deletion, and cascade delete if set up.

**Many-to-many relationships**

- Created by creating a custom object with two master-detail or lookup relationships. Such a custom object that sits between two objects is called a "junction object."

**Hierarchical relationship**

- A special lookup relationship is available for only the user object. It lets users use a lookup field to associate one user with another that does not directly or indirectly refer to itself. For example, you can create a custom hierarchical relationship field to store each user's direct manager.

The following types of relationships only apply to relationships between external objects and standard or custom objects:

**External lookup relationship**

- An external lookup relationship links a child standard, custom, or external object to a parent external object.

- The standard external ID field on the parent external object is matched against the values of the child's external lookup relationship field. External object field values come from an external data source.

**Indirect lookup relationship**

- Links a child's external object to a parent standard or custom object.

- When you create an indirect lookup relationship field on an external object, you specify the parent object field and the child object field to match and associate records in the relationship. Specifically, you select a custom, unique external ID field on the parent object to match against the child's indirect lookup relationship field, whose values come from an external data source.

# The Organization-Wide Default Settings for Object Visibility

Organization-wide sharing default settings set the baseline accessibility for each of your standard or custom objects across all users in your Salesforce org. You can set the organization-wide sharing default settings for any object to one of the following:

- **Private**

    When this setting is enabled for the object, only the record owner, and users higher in the role hierarchy, can view, edit, and report on those records.

- **Public Read-Only**

    When this setting is enabled for the object, all users within your Salesforce org *(i.e., internal as well as external users with access)* can view and report on records but not edit them. Only the owner, and users above that role in the hierarchy, can edit those records.

- **Public Read/Write**

  When this setting is enabled for the object, all users within your Salesforce org (i.e., internal as well as external users with access) can view, edit, and report on all records.

- **Controlled by Parent**

  *(only applicable to child objects in a master-detail relationship)*

  When this setting is enabled for an object that is a child object in a master-detail relationship with another object, then the user accessing this child object is granted the same access as the user's access to the parent object.

- **Public Read/Write/Transfer**

  *(only applicable to the lead object and case object)*

  When this setting is enabled for the lead object or the case object, all users can view, edit, transfer, and report on all lead and case records.

- **Public Full Access**

  *(only applicable to the campaign object)*

  When this setting is enabled for the campaign object, all users can view, edit, transfer, delete, and report on all campaign records.

We will be discussing more on the need for visibility and sharing using organization-wide default sharing settings in Chapter 5. However, this sharing setting needs to be identified in the data model artifact because it is the only security setting that determines the object-level visibility and security within Salesforce.

# Owners of the Records Within Each Object

Ownership of records within each object is an important detail that needs to be identified within a Salesforce data model because, in Salesforce, record ownership determines the visibility and security of data at a record level. Record ownership determines which users can access which records and record types related to the object.

The ownership-based record-level visibility and sharing capabilities within Salesforce are supported by three key elements:

1. An **owner field** is automatically created in every object, except for a child object in a master-detail relationship.

2. A **sharing rule object** is created for each custom object and already exists for standard objects, which defines which users and groups can access records.

3. A **group membership object** manages access to records via sharing rules granted to a group of users through private and public groups, queues, the role hierarchy, and the territory hierarchy.

We will be discussing more on visibility and sharing at a record level based on ownership-based sharing (OBS) in Chapter 5. An important skill is identifying the record owners for records within each object. During the design of the data model, identifying which user can see what data allows you to detect any large data volume concerns. This concern is called an "ownership data skew." Data skew occurs when a single user owns more than 10,000 records of a single object. We will be discussing more on the concerns related to large data volumes in the next section and also in Chapter 4.

# An Estimated Number of Records Per Object That Can Exist at Any Given Period

You need to identify the volumes of data stored in each Salesforce object. Storing and managing large data volumes in Salesforce requires additional care. A large data volume design requires special consideration regarding ownership, sharing, queries, and role hierarchies.

When large data volumes are stored or managed in Salesforce, it leads to significant performance degradation of your Salesforce org, including slower SOQL queries, more time-consuming searches, and slower rendering of list views.

As of this writing, Salesforce considers large data volumes to occur when

- There are more than 50 million records stored in the account object.

- There are more than 20 million records stored in the contact object.

- There are more than 100 million records stored in any single custom object.

- The total number of internal users within a single Salesforce org exceeds 10,000 users.

- A single user within Salesforce is the owner of more than 10,000 records within a single object.

- 100 GB of record data storage capacity is reached, not including files and attachments.

There are several approaches to mitigate large data volumes within Salesforce. Most approaches start by identifying the objects with a potential for accumulating large data volumes over time, which is key to prescribing the appropriate measures for curing system performance of Salesforce.

With the preceding considerations, you should be well equipped to draw Salesforce data models. However, as we discuss the core concepts of Salesforce in the following chapters of this book, you will be able to create more productive and more detailed artifacts, including the optional artifacts we mentioned at the beginning of this chapter.

# Summary

In this chapter, we covered

- The three key artifacts that you as a Salesforce architect must produce for every solution. These consist of the FUSIAOLA analysis, the system landscape, and the data model.

- The FUSIAOLA analysis decomposes the business requirements into functions and features, users and user groups, other systems interacting with the solution, integration methods between the other systems and Salesforce, authentication and authorization methods for users and systems to gain access into the solution, objects within Salesforce that will store various data records created for the solution, the Salesforce licenses needed for users, and finally the assumptions made in designing the solution.

- Business requirements must be decomposed to determine the functions and features by categorizing them into one of three technical contexts. The three technical contexts are data context, business logic context, and interface context.

- Users and user groups can be grouped together based on four attributes, which are information role attribute, business function attribute, internal vs. external attribute, and role hierarchy index attribute.

- Other systems interacting with the solution can be existing systems or new systems that need to be set up as part of the final solution.

- Integrations between existing and new systems and Salesforce need to be designed for each system based on its interaction level with Salesforce.

- Authentication and authorization needs to be designed for each user group and system requiring access into the Salesforce solution.

- An object model design in Salesforce determines how data is stored, organized, and utilized in Salesforce for optimal use and efficiency of the solution.

- Assumptions should be documented to justify your design considerations that cover missing or implicit details relevant to the solution.

- A system landscape artifact should be developed based on seven enterprise-level considerations.

- A data model artifact should be developed based on seven enterprise-level considerations.

# CHAPTER 3

# Salesforce Application Architecture

Let's dive straight into the design thinking needed to design a Salesforce application. In this chapter, we cover

- Salesforce's licensing model and how to choose the right licenses

- Comparisons of the common Salesforce products

- How to choose the right features of Salesforce and when to use declarative vs. programmatic capabilities to design an application

- The order of execution of Salesforce events

- Considerations and strategies for a multi-org vs. a single-org environment of Salesforce

- Different ways to extend Salesforce capabilities by utilizing third-party apps available in Salesforce's AppExchange marketplace

- When to consider managing functionalities off the Salesforce platform and how to integrate with off-platform services to work seamlessly with Salesforce

## Salesforce Licenses

Salesforce's licensing model can be complex and nonintuitive at first. Choosing the appropriate licensing model is crucial to design a Salesforce solution since it almost entirely determines what any user can or cannot do within Salesforce. Different Salesforce licenses enable or restrict access to different Salesforce features and objects.

© Dipanker Jyoti and James A. Hutcherson 2021

D. Jyoti and J. A. Hutcherson, *Salesforce Architect's Handbook*, https://doi.org/10.1007/978-1-4842-6631-1_3

At its core, Salesforce offers five different license types:

- Org-level licenses

- User-based licenses

- Permission set–based licenses

- Feature-based licenses

- Usage-based entitlements

---

Salesforce regularly updates and changes product names, features, and limitations. It is vital to work directly with your Salesforce account executive or program architect before purchasing licenses.

---

# Org-Level Licenses

Org-level licenses are also often referred to as Salesforce editions.[1] This is the type of license that a company needs to select for the first time. The org-level licenses determine the infrastructure resources such as storage and API access assigned by Salesforce to your company. The editions also determine the level of SaaS or PaaS functionalities that will be available to that environment (org) of Salesforce. Salesforce offers five org-level license editions. For business use, typically, the editions start with the Essentials Edition (ES), and each edition above that is an upgrade from thereon. The only exception to editions is the Developer Edition (DE), a free edition available to anyone with features similar to the Enterprise Edition (EE) licenses. The Developer Edition is primarily meant for use by developers and third-party vendors who intend to build apps for Salesforce's AppExchange ecosystem (more on AppExchange later in this chapter) or anyone just interested in exploring Salesforce for free.

The five org-level licenses available from Salesforce, in the order of least robust to most robust, are

1. Essentials Edition (ES)

2. Professional Edition (PE)

3. Developer Edition (DE)

---

[1]https://help.salesforce.com/articleView?id=overview_when_you_buy.htm&type=5.

4.   Enterprise Edition (EE)

5.   Unlimited Edition (UE)

See Figure 3-1 for an illustration of the five org-level licenses.

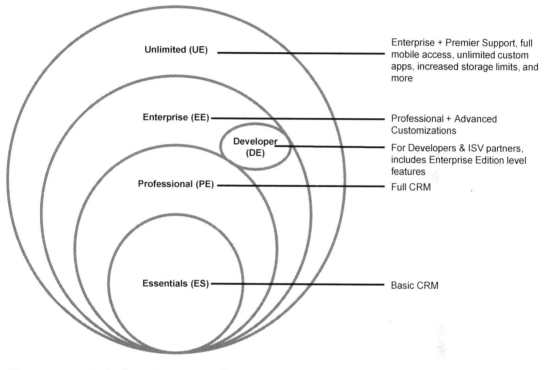

***Figure 3-1.*** *Salesforce License Editions*

For a more detailed comparison of the editions, please refer to `www.salesforce.com/editions-pricing/sales-and-service-cloud/`.

Here are some key points to consider when choosing the right edition of Salesforce:

- An org-level edition license is required for every org of Salesforce, and every Salesforce org can only belong to one edition of Salesforce.

- The edition applies to the entire org and all licenses within that org.

- You can switch from a lower edition of Salesforce to a higher edition, but you cannot downgrade from a higher edition to a lower edition. (Example: You cannot switch from a Professional Edition to an Essentials Edition.)

# User Licenses

Just like an org-level license, user licenses determine to which each user within your org has access. A user license is required for each user accessing your org.

There are specifically six specific types of user licenses:

1. Chatter licenses

2. Salesforce licenses

3. Salesforce platform licenses

4. External Identity licenses

5. External Apps licenses

6. Customer and Partner Community licenses

## Chatter Licenses

Chatter licenses are licenses, available with all standard Salesforce licenses, that only give the assigned user access to Salesforce's collaboration feature known as "Chatter" similar to the user experience within Facebook or LinkedIn. Chatter licenses are meant for one thing and one thing only, that is, collaboration with other Salesforce users.

There are three types of Chatter licenses[2]:

1. Chatter External

2. Chatter Free

3. Chatter Only

### Chatter External Licenses

These licenses are meant for external users such as prospects, customers, partners, and anyone outside of your organization's domain. Users with these licenses do not have access to any Salesforce objects or data stored within your Salesforce org. They can only see and post messages within chatter groups that they are invited.

---

[2]https://help.salesforce.com/articleView?id=users_license_types_chatter.htm&type=5.

## Chatter Free

As the name suggests, Chatter Free licenses are free user licenses that can be assigned to any internal user within your organization's domain that does not need a paid user license to use Salesforce but needs to collaborate with all Salesforce users within your org. These users can access basic Chatter items such as people, profiles, groups, and files posted in chatter posts, but they cannot access any Salesforce objects or data. However, Chatter Free users can be given moderator permissions to moderate any chatter group(s).

## Chatter Only License (Also Known as Chatter Plus)

Contrary to general belief, Chatter Only licenses are not free and are for internal users only. In addition to all functionalities available via the Chatter Free licenses, users with this license have the following additional access:

1. View-only access to account and contact objects.

2. View and edit up to ten custom objects.

3. View reports and dashboards.

4. Be assigned as an approver and approve an approval process of Salesforce.

5. Be assigned to tasks by other users.

6. Create/view/edit their own events, activities, and tasks.

7. Add any records they access to within chatter groups that they are part of.

8. Use Salesforce CRM content, ideas, and answers.

# Salesforce Licenses

Salesforce licenses are only available for internal users within your enterprise. They provide access to Salesforce's SaaS-based Customer Relationship Management (CRM) products, which primarily include Sales Cloud, Service Cloud, and Lightning CRM Cloud. In order to access any standard CRM application within Salesforce, these licenses are required.[3]

---

[3]https://help.salesforce.com/articleView?id=users_license_types_available.htm&type=5.

The Lightning CRM Cloud license includes all Sales Cloud and Service Cloud features. The Service Cloud license includes most features of Sales Cloud except for a few features and standard objects that are only available with Sales Cloud licenses *(or the Lightning CRM licenses)* such as quotes and sales contracts. However, Service Cloud has many more features and standard objects that are not available in Sales Cloud, such as entitlements, work orders, and service contracts. A good resource to identify which objects are available with Sales Cloud vs. Service Cloud is the data model section within Salesforce's officially published *SOAP API Developer Guide.*[4]

In addition to the Sales, Service, and Lightning CRM Cloud licenses, Salesforce offers add-on products that can be paired either with a Sales Cloud or a Service Cloud license. Some common add-on products requiring at least the Sales Cloud license are Salesforce CPQ, Pardot, and Financial Services Cloud, and the add-on product requiring at least the Service Cloud license is Salesforce Field Service Lightning. For a detailed list of all add-ons that can be paired with Salesforce licenses, please refer to Salesforce Add-on Pricing sheet on Salesforce's official website.[5]

## Salesforce Platform Licenses

Salesforce platform licenses are also only available for the internal users within your enterprise. They provide access to the platform of Salesforce with access limited to the core standard objects (also known in the industry as "Hero" objects) of Salesforce. These core objects are accounts, contacts, cases, activities, tasks, events, content, and documents. Salesforce platform licenses come in two types of offerings: Lightning Platform Starter and Lightning Platform Plus.

Only cases related to internal users are allowed, and any cases related to external users are contractually prohibited.

The main distinction between the two platform offerings is the limit on the number of custom objects that can be created with each type. With the Lightning Platform Plus license, you can create up to 110 custom objects, whereas with the Lightning Platform Starter license, you can only create up to ten custom objects. These custom objects are in addition to the standard core objects available with both options.

[4]https://developer.salesforce.com/docs/atlas.en-us.api.meta/api/data_model.htm.
[5]www.salesforce.com/content/dam/web/en_us/www/documents/pricing/all-add-ons.pdf.

## External Identity Licenses

External Identity licenses offer a Customer Identity and Access Management (CIAM) solution specifically to manage the identity services of external users. It is a standalone license offered by Salesforce to allow your external users to authenticate via standard username/password, passwordless logins, or social sign-on or even act as a single sign-on service for the external apps exposed to them.

The External Identity license provides access[6] to the following standard objects (mostly in read-only mode): accounts, assets, contacts, documents, individuals, and files. Salesforce allows the creation of up to ten custom objects with this license type.

## External Apps Licenses

Salesforce's External Apps licenses are similar to the Salesforce platform licenses but for external users of your enterprise. Salesforce has contractual restrictions that prohibit assigning the earlier indicated Salesforce licenses or the Salesforce platform licenses to any user external to your enterprise. For external users who need access to your Salesforce platform capabilities and not to the Salesforce CRM capabilities, you can assign External Apps licenses to these external users. We will talk about the Salesforce CRM capabilities in a later section when we talk about Customer and Partner Community licenses.

External App licenses can be assigned uniquely for each user as a named user license or as usage-based entitlements, which are based on the number of user logins per month. More on user license types covered a bit later in this chapter.

Similar to earlier indicated Salesforce platform licenses, External Apps licenses are available in two types of offerings: Lighting External Apps and Lightning External Apps Plus. The distinction between the two types of offerings is identical to the distinction between Lightning Platform Starter and Lightning Platform Plus offerings of Salesforce platform licenses. However, it is important to note that External Apps licenses cannot be purchased and utilized independently. External Apps licenses are dependent on having at least a Salesforce or Salesforce platform or External Identity license in the org.

---

[6]https://help.salesforce.com/articleView?id=users_license_types_external_identity. htm&type=5.

## Customer and Partner Community Licenses

Needless to say, Customer and Partner Communities are licenses for external users such as your customers and partners, providing them access to the standard and custom applications that you wish to expose to them for support and self-service. As of this writing, Salesforce has renamed their Community Cloud product to "Experience Cloud."[7]

---

Salesforce has renamed their **Community Cloud** product to **Experience Cloud**.

---

The most popular community license offerings are Customer Community, Customer Community Plus, and Partner Community. The best way to look at these three options is to see the Customer Community having the least number of features/capabilities compared to the other two. Customer Community Plus has all the Customer Community license capabilities plus additional capabilities such as advanced sharing and external users' access to standard Salesforce reports and dashboards. Partner Community licenses provide all capabilities/features available via Customer Community Plus licenses plus additional features, including access to additional standard objects that are only available to external users via Partner Community, such as leads, opportunities, and campaign objects. Figure 3-2 highlights a high-level comparison of the three community license types.

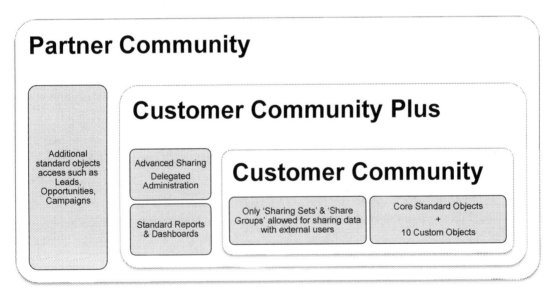

***Figure 3-2.*** *High-Level Comparison of Experience Cloud Licenses*

---

[7]www.salesforce.com/products/community-cloud/overview.

For further reading on Salesforce community licenses, we would highly recommend the book *Practical Guide to Salesforce Communities* by Philip Weinmeister (Apress, 2018). Here, once again, it is important to note that, similar to External Apps, Experience Cloud licenses are dependent on having at least a Salesforce or Salesforce platform or External Identity license in the org.

---

Experience Cloud (formerly known as Community Cloud)licenses are dependent on having at least a Salesforce or Salesforce platform or External Identity license in the org.

---

# Permission Set Licenses

Permission set licenses were first introduced in the winter 2014 release. The primary objective of permission set licenses was to allow the assignment of add-on licenses to a single user. Add-on product offerings such as *Salesforce Field Service Lightning, Salesforce CPQ, Salesforce Health Cloud,* and *Salesforce Financial Services Cloud* can be added in addition to your Salesforce licenses.

In Figure 3-3, we have provided our point of view to help visualize the Salesforce licenses discussed so far and some of the common Salesforce product add-ons for Sales and Service Cloud.

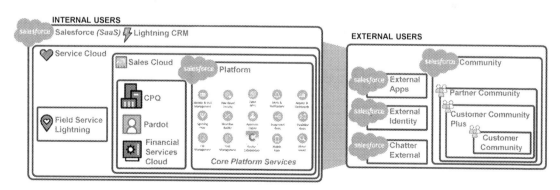

***Figure 3-3.*** *Salesforce Licenses and Common Add-On Permission Set licenses*

---

**Note**    Figure 3-3 is only a point of view on common Salesforce licenses. As Salesforce is evolving its products, the point of view is subject to change.

---

For specific details on licenses and add-ons, please refer to Salesforce's official website. Salesforce also used to publish a license comparison pdf document, the URL for which keeps changing. To find this document, we recommend a quick search online with the following keywords: *Salesforce User License Comparison PDF*.

# Feature Licenses

Finally, Salesforce has 11 features that are not available as part of any licenses indicated previously. These feature licenses predate the arrival of permission set licenses, which is a much elegant way of assigning add-on capabilities to users. We do not anticipate Salesforce introducing any new feature licenses in the future, but it is important for an architect to acknowledge that these feature licenses need to be assigned for these features to be accessible by the user. Overlooking a feature license assignment can stop a user from running a Lightning Flow or accessing knowledge articles. When troubleshooting user access, an architect must be aware of the feature licenses assigned to the user. The good news is, as of the date of this writing, there are only 11 feature licenses. These are presented in Table 3-1.

***Table 3-1.*** *11 Salesforce Feature Licenses[8]*

| Feature License | What Does It Enable the User to Do? |
| --- | --- |
| Chatter Answers User | To access "Chatter Answers." This feature license is automatically assigned to high-volume portal users who self-register for Chatter Answers. |
| Flow User | To run Lightning Flow. |
| Knowledge User | To access Salesforce Knowledge. |
| Chat User | To access chat. |
| Marketing User | To create, edit, and delete campaigns, configure advanced campaign setup, add campaign members, and update their statuses with the Data Import Wizard. |
| Offline User | To connect offline. |

(*continued*)

---

[8]https://help.salesforce.com/articleView?id=users_feature_licenses_available. htm&type=5.

***Table 3-1.*** (*continued*)

| Feature License | What Does It Enable the User to Do? |
| --- | --- |
| Salesforce CRM Content User | To access CRM content stored within Salesforce. |
| Service Cloud User | To access the service console within Service Cloud. |
| Site.com Contributor User | To edit content published on Site.com Studio. |
| Site.com Publisher User | To create and style websites, control the layout and functionality of pages and page elements, and add and edit content on Site.com Studio. |
| WDC User | To access work.com objects and features. |

## Usage-Based Entitlements

Salesforce offers a usage-based licensing (*also commonly referred to as "login-based licenses" for products such as Salesforce communities and External Apps*) model as an alternative to purchasing a named license for each and every user in the org. With usage-based entitlements, a company purchases lump-sum credits for a number of logins per month for their users or for a number of transactions per month, such as in the case of data.com[9] (*i.e., Salesforce's data quality and data integrity management service*). With usage-based entitlements, a company can overallocate these licenses to any number of users. However, users with these licenses get access to Salesforce on a first-come-first-served basis until the number of logins per month or the transaction limits allocated are reached for that month.

Usage-based entitlements are most popular with assigning Salesforce Experience Cloud (formerly known as Community Cloud) licenses. From the external user's perspective, the experience is no different whether they are assigned a named user license or a usage-based entitlement license. When deciding whether to assign a named user license or a usage-based entitlement. For users accessing Salesforce more than three times per month, usage-based licenses may not have any cost savings over a named user license.

---

[9]https://help.salesforce.com/articleView?id=data_dot_com_clean_clean_overview.htm&type=5.

**Tip**    Assign a usage-based license where you have a large volume of one-time uses or very low use assignments. This is common for customer communities and service communities. A rule of thumb to follow is to assign a usage-based entitlement to any user that logs into Salesforce three times or less per month.

## Platform vs. CRM Licenses

Table 3-2 outlines the key considerations and limitations of platform vs. standard CRM licenses of Salesforce.

***Table 3-2.*** *Comparisons Between Platform, Sales, and Service Cloud Licenses*

| Product Type | Considerations | Limitations |
| --- | --- | --- |
| Platform | Cheapest license for internal users. Access to Hero objects + up to 110 custom objects. Access to internally generated standard cases and work orders. Account teams can be enabled and used. | No Bulk API or Streaming API. No access to external cases and external work orders. No access to campaigns, leads, opportunities, orders, products, pricebooks, assets, contracts, quotes, entitlements. No opportunity teams or case teams. No forecasting. No omni-channel. No live agent. Can use but cannot create workflows, approval process, Process Builder, flows, or any Apex code. |

(*continued*)

*Table 3-2.* (*continued*)

| Product Type | Considerations | Limitations |
|---|---|---|
| Sales Cloud | Includes everything available with platform licenses. Access to all standard CRM objects and features except for entitlements and service contracts. Access to sales contracts, quotes. Omni-channel only available for leads, order, and any custom object with no parent object. Territory management feature. Opportunity split feature. Required for add-ons such as CPQ, Pardot, and Financial Services Cloud. | No access to entitlements, service contracts. Omni-channel not available for cases, contact requests, chat, social posts. SOS feature not available. |
| Service Cloud | Includes everything available with platform licenses. Access to all standard CRM objects and features except for quotes and sales contracts. Full omni-channel capabilities. SOS feature available (in Classic only). Required for add-ons such as Field Service Lightning. | No access to quotes, sales contracts. No territory management. No opportunity splits. |
| Lightning CRM | Most expensive license for internal users. Includes everything available with platform and Sales and Service Cloud licenses. Up to 2000 custom objects allowed. | None. |

In addition to the comparisons indicated in Table 3-2, you should familiarize yourself with the following Salesforce products:

- **Experience Cloud (formerly known as Community Cloud**: Used to provide access to external users

- **Marketing Cloud and Pardot**: Designed to manage B2C and B2B marketing efforts

- **Field Service Lightning**: Adds features to Service Cloud specific to outbound service resources

- **CPQ**: Developed to support the configuration, pricing, and quoting process

- **B2B and B2C Commerce Cloud**: Supports the presentation and transactions associated with online storefronts

- **Tableau CRM Analytics (previously known as Einstein Analytics)**: Provides advanced data analytics

- **Financial Services Cloud**: Integrates financial functionality, such as accounting

- **Health Cloud**: Incorporates both patient cares and medical operations

- **Nonprofit Cloud and Education Cloud**: Provides support for grants managements and education-related features such as admissions and registration

- **Quip**: Enables collaboration

- **Work.com (Including the New Version with Pandemic Support)**: Designed to support an ever-changing working environment

- **Heroku**: Delivers a PaaS to create, deliver, and manage on the cloud

- **MuleSoft**: Provides an integration platform

# Salesforce Application Design Choices

Salesforce has hundreds of out-of-the-box features that can be configured to design a business application out of the box. However, as an architect, you should at least be familiar with the 18 most common declarative options and the 16 most common programmatic options available to design any application on the Salesforce platform.

In Chapter 2, we talked about assigning one among three technical contexts to each business requirement. Once again, the three contexts are interface context, business logic context, and data context. Figure 3-4 presents a quick reference to the declarative and programmatic options available to address requirements belonging to one or more technical contexts.

Common Declarative options:

1. Page Layouts
2. Lightning App
3. Record Types
4. Workflow
5. Process Builder
6. Flow
7. Assignment rules
8. Escalation Rules
9. Approval Process
10. Formula Fields
11. Validation Rules
12. Roll-Up Summary Fields
13. Sharing Rules
14. Custom Objects
15. Custom Fields
16. Platform Events
17. Canvas
18. Salesforce Connect

Common Programmatic options:

1. Visual Force Page
2. Lightning Component
3. Lightning Web Components
4. Apex Class
5. Triggers
6. Metadata API
7. Tooling API
8. SOAP API
9. Rest API
10. Streaming API
11. Bulk API
12. User Interface API
13. Batch Apex
14. Queueable Apex
15. Scheduled Apex
16. SOQL/ SOSL

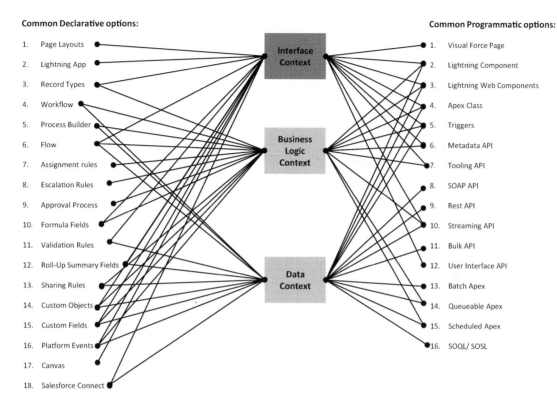

***Figure 3-4.*** *Application Design Options Based on the Technical Context of Requirements*

Now let's discuss each option in a bit more detail.

# Common Declarative Options

Salesforce offers many declarative options to develop an application. These options are often called "point and click," "drag and drop," or "low code/no code" configuration. This approach should be the first option selected by an architect, as it provides a faster development turnaround, reduces the overall cost of development, and allows "nonprogrammers" to create and manage enterprise-class applications. Table 3-3 presents various declarative options with a description and the technical context of their use: interface context, business logic context, and data context.

***Table 3-3.*** *Declarative Development Options Available in Salesforce*

| Declarative Options | Description |
| --- | --- |
| Page layouts | Page layouts control the display and organization of the user interface, including buttons, fields, any Visualforce pages embedded within the page, custom links, and related items for each object. They also help determine which fields are visible, read-only, and required. Each page layout can be assigned directly to one or more user profiles, which defines the view of that object detail for the users in the assigned profile.<br>*Technical context for this option:* **Interface context** |
| Lightning app | A Lightning app is a collection (i.e., folder) of record pages and user features that work together to serve a particular user function. Lightning apps can be branded and customized along with including utility bars at the bottom of the page and custom design the navigation of other tabs and related sub-tabs.<br>*Technical context for this option:* **Interface context** |
| Record types | Record types allow configuring different business processes, picklist values, and page layouts for different users that use the same object differently (e.g., opportunities for different business lines).<br>*Technical context for this option:* **Interface context and/or business logic context** |
| Workflow | A workflow rule is a set of business logic defined using an if/then criterion that executes when a specified data change (user-defined criteria) occurs in Salesforce or is triggered at a specified recurring time. With workflow, users can create new tasks, send emails, update fields, send an outbound message to another system, and initiate a flow.<br>*Technical context for this option:* **Data context and/or business logic context** |
| Process Builder | Process Builder can be used to do everything that can be done using workflow EXCEPT FOR sending outbound messages (i.e., declarative web service messaging from Salesforce to an external system). Additionally, Process Builder provides a graphical drag/drop interface to design the business processes related to each object. Compared to workflow rules, Process Builder can also update child records, post to Chatter, auto-submit records in the approval process, and invoke Apex classes.<br>*Technical context for this option:* **Data context and/or business logic context** |

*(continued)*

***Table 3-3.*** (*continued*)

| Declarative Options | Description |
| --- | --- |
| Flow | Flow can be easily defined as the most declarative way of creating code through a graphical drag and drop user interface. A single Lightning Flow is an application that automates a business process by collecting data and executing actions within your Salesforce org or directly in an external system from within Salesforce. It is the most powerful declarative tool among all and compared to workflow rule and Process Builder. This is a great choice when the business logic is complicated or it requires accommodating an if/then data logic and something that also requires user interaction. However, a flow can be an overkill if a single or couple of fields need to change or the business logic is straightforward.<br>*Technical context for this option:* **Any or all three** |
| Assignment rules | Assignment rules can only be used with leads and/or case objects. It defines the rules and assigns a lead or a case to the appropriate user or a queue that manages leads or cases.<br>*Technical context for this option:* **Business logic context** |
| Escalation rules | Escalation rules can only be used with the CASE object. It defines the criteria under which a case gets escalated to a supervisor of the current case manager. It could be based on case status, case field changes, or time-lapse in case status changes. Escalation rules are primarily useful when certain service-level agreements need to be met by support agents.<br>*Technical context for this option:* **Business logic context** |
| Approval process | Approval processes can be set up to automate any record approvals needed in Salesforce. An approval process specifies each step of approval, including from whom to request approval and what to do at each step of the approval process (e.g., discounts higher than 25% might require the approval of a senior manager).<br>*Technical context for this option:* **Business logic context** |
| Formula fields | Formula fields are READ-ONLY fields, the value of which is evaluated based on the value of other existing fields (e.g., calculate totals, concatenate two or more fields to create a combined text, calculate dates including current date, etc.).<br>*Technical context for this option:* **Interface context and/or business logic context** |

*(continued)*

***Table 3-3.*** (*continued*)

| Declarative Options | Description |
| --- | --- |
| Validation rules | Validation rules verify that the data a user enters for a record meets various data criteria needed for data quality, such as required fields, data logic such as no past dates allowed or amount not greater than another amount field, and so on. A validation rule can contain a formula or expression that evaluates the user-entered data in one or more fields and returns a value of "True" or "False."<br>*Technical context for this option:* **Data context and/or business logic context** |
| Roll-up summary fields | Roll-up summary can ONLY BE USED on the master object of objects connected with each other via a master-detail relationship. Roll-up summary fields calculate values from related child object records (e.g., display the sum of invoice amounts for all related invoice custom object records in an account's invoices-related list).<br>*Technical context for this option:* **Interface context and/or data context** |
| Sharing rules | Sharing Rules are user access control features defined within Salesforce that dictates a specified users access to the data based on record ownership rules, based on specific data criteria, sharing record with a group of users, different roles and their subordinates, users and their subordinates in a different territory.<br>Sharing rules can be defined to provide read-only or read/write access to any record.<br>*Technical context for this option:* **Data context and/or business logic context** |
| Custom objects | Custom objects are the key to extending Salesforce beyond the standard object capabilities. Every custom object automatically gets assigned a page layout out of the box that renders a user interface. In addition to the user interface, it inherits many of the platform capabilities available to all objects within Salesforce. For this reason, a custom object can be used to serve any technical context.<br>*Technical context for this option:* **Any or all three** |
| Custom fields | Salesforce allows you to create 23 different types of custom fields for any object. The choice of custom field not only determines the data type that is acceptable for input but also provides several other capabilities such as the ability to generate auto-numbers and the responsiveness to open hyperlinks in a separate window. Custom fields are also an option to address any technical context.<br>*Technical context for this option:* **Any or all three** |

(*continued*)

***Table 3-3.*** (*continued*)

| Declarative Options | Description |
| --- | --- |
| Platform events | Platform events allow you to connect Salesforce to a remote system(s) based on the publish/subscribe event-driven architecture. In an event-driven architecture, a message is published to an event bus, and subscribers of that message connected to the event bus can consume the data. The subscribers can be a Lightning app within your org or an external remote system. There are two types of platform events that can be configured within Salesforce, that is, Change Data Capture events and Standard Platform events. With "Change Data Capture" events, you can publish change events, representing any changes occurring to Salesforce records within your org. Changes include record creation, updates to an existing record, deletion of a record, and undeleting a record. With Standard Platform events, you can set up an action that publishes a set of predefined data within a platform event object. Any data stored within the platform event object is then published to the event bus. *Technical context for this option:* **Any or all three** |
| Canvas | Canvas is Salesforce's capability to integrate with a remote application via a Data Virtualization pattern (for more details on data virtualization integration, refer to Chapter 6). Canvas is a set of tools that utilizes JavaScript APIs to expose the remote application seamlessly within your Salesforce org as part of your Salesforce user interface. *Technical context for this option:* **Interface context** |

(*continued*)

***Table 3-3.*** (*continued*)

| Declarative Options | Description |
| --- | --- |
| Salesforce Connect | Salesforce Connect can be configured to access data from external sources, along with the Salesforce data within your org. With Salesforce Connect, you can display data from external systems as external objects within Salesforce. External objects are similar to custom objects, except that they map to data located outside your Salesforce org. Salesforce Connect maintains a live connection with the external data stored in the external system such that the data reflected in the external objects within your Salesforce org is up to date.<br>With Salesforce Connect, you can<br><br>• Query data in an external system.<br><br>• Create, update, and delete data in an external system.<br><br>• Access external objects via list views, detail pages, record feeds, custom tabs, and page layouts.<br><br>• Define relationships between external objects and standard or custom objects to integrate data from different sources.<br><br>• Enable Chatter feeds on external object pages for collaboration.<br><br>• Run reports on external data.<br><br>• View the data on the Salesforce mobile app.<br><br>*Technical context for this option:* **Interface context and/or data context** |

# Common Programmatic Options

Salesforce also offers many programmatic options to develop an application. These options extend the "out-of-the-box" functionality with custom code. The programmatic option should only be used if the solution cannot be performed declaratively or to not increase the complexity of the solution. Table 3-4 presents various programmatic options with a description and the technical context of their use: interface context, business logic context, and data context.

***Table 3-4.*** *Development Options Available in Salesforce*

| Programmatic Options | Description |
|---|---|
| Visualforce page | A Visualforce page is similar to a standard web page, but includes additional features to access, display, and update any data from the Salesforce org. Pages can be referenced and invoked via a unique URL specifically assigned to each Visualforce page created.<br>*Technical context for this option:* **Interface context** |
| Lightning components | A Lightning component is a UI framework (i.e., "Aura" framework) that allows for developing single-page applications for mobile and desktop devices. Unlike Apex classes, Lightning components have decoupled code resources for reusability and better code execution on the browser or the mobile app (i.e., client-side application).<br>*Technical context for this option:* **Any or all three** |
| Lightning web components (LWC) | Lightning web components are custom HTML elements built using HTML and modern JavaScript. Lightning web components and Lightning components can coexist and interoperate on a page.<br>*Technical context for this option:* **Any or all three** |
| Apex class | An Apex class contains the programmatic code to execute behaviors and manage the state of any object within Salesforce. Similar to Java, an Apex class is a template or blueprint from which objects are created. An Apex class can also be written to act as a controller, which is a set of instructions that specify what the Salesforce server should do when a user or remote system interacts via an interface. Controllers can be standard controllers that contain the same functionality and logic used for standard Salesforce pages; or a developer can build custom controller classes or controller extensions using Apex to override existing standard functionality, to customize the navigation through an application, to use callouts or web services, or if you need finer control on how information is accessed from a page.<br>*Technical context for this option:* **Any or all three** |

*(continued)*

***Table 3-4.*** (*continued*)

| Programmatic Options | Description |
| --- | --- |
| Triggers | Triggers are Apex scripts written related to any object, where users need to perform custom actions before or after changes are saved for any records such as insertion of new record, updates to existing records, or deletions of existing records. There are two types of triggers: before triggers and after triggers. A before trigger is used to update or validate record values BEFORE they're saved to the database. On the contrary, after triggers are used to access field values that are set by the system (such as a record's ID or LastModifiedDatefield) after the record has been saved in the database and to make changes to related records.<br>*Technical context for this option:* **Any or all three** |
| Metadata API | Metadata API can be used by users to retrieve, deploy, create, update, or delete customizations within any org using the Force.com IDE or Ant Migration Tool or an external code scripting tool such as Microsoft VS Code. The most common use is to migrate changes from a sandbox or testing org to the production environment. Metadata API is intended for managing customizations and for building tools that can manage the metadata model, but not the data itself.<br>*Technical context for this option:* **Interface context and/or business logic context** |
| Tooling API | With Tooling API, you can build custom development tools or custom apps to use with Salesforce. Tooling API is similar to Metadata API, such that you can access and update the Salesforce metadata with it, except that the SOQL queries used with Tooling API can retrieve smaller pieces of metadata. Smaller retrieves of metadata can improve performance, hence making Tooling API a better fit than Metadata API for developing interactive applications that connect with your Salesforce org. You can use Tooling API to add features and functionality to your existing Lightning Platform tools.<br>*Technical context for this option:* **Interface context and/or business logic context** |

*(continued)*

***Table 3-4.*** (*continued*)

| Programmatic Options | Description |
|---|---|
| SOAP API | Salesforce's SOAP API provides programmatic access to your org's information using a simple, powerful, and secure Application Programming Interface. Users and external systems can use SOAP API to create, retrieve, update, or delete records, such as accounts, leads, and custom objects. With more than 20 different calls, SOAP API also allows users to maintain passwords, perform searches, and more.<br>*Technical context for this option:* **Data context** |
| REST API | Salesforce's REST API can be used for field-level changes especially when users are using Salesforce via mobile applications and heavy UI-based web applications. Rest API is best for making field changes when the total number of records to be updated is less than 20 in a single call. For large data volume updates, users can also use Bulk API which uses the REST protocol similar to REST API for integration. With Rest API, external systems as well as mobile and web applications can access all Salesforce objects that are accessible via SOAP API.<br>*Technical context for this option:* **Data context** |
| Bulk API | Bulk API is based on REST principles and is optimized for loading or deleting large sets of data. You can use it to query, queryAll, insert, update, upsert, or delete many records asynchronously by submitting batches. Salesforce processes batches asynchronously in the background.<br>*Technical context for this option:* **Data context** |
| User Interface API | User Interface API is mainly used to replicate all or part of a Salesforce user interface based on some criteria and/or permissions defined for a non-Lightning Experience app. User Interface API even provides endpoints to perform CRUD operations on the data presented with the layout allowing users to edit, update, and delete data. The common use case for User Interface API is to replicate all or part of the Salesforce user interface within a custom mobile or web app. I do not recommend using User Interface API for any data extraction or data uploads because User Interface APIs are contextual to the page displayed.<br>*Technical context for this option:* **Interface context** |

(*continued*)

***Table 3-4.*** (*continued*)

| Programmatic Options | Description |
| --- | --- |
| Batch Apex | Developers can create Batch Apex to build complex, long-running processes that run on thousands of records on the Lightning Platform. Batch Apex operates over small batches of records, covering the selected record changes and breaking the processing down to manageable chunks. Developers use Batch Apex primarily for archiving solutions that run on a nightly basis looking for records past a certain date and adding them to an archive or build a data cleansing operation that goes through selected objects on a nightly basis and updates them if necessary, based on custom criteria.<br>*Technical context for this option:* **Business logic context** |
| Queueable Apex | Queueable Apex are programmatic actions (i.e., jobs) that can be queued for execution, along with a job ID that can be monitored for execution status. Another benefit of Queueable Apex is the ability for developers to use non-primitive data types, such as sObjects or custom Apex types. Those objects can be accessed when the job executes, which cannot be used in asynchronous Apex (i.e., when using future methods in an Apex class). Queueable Apex also allows for chaining multiple jobs by chaining one job to another job by starting a second job from a running job. Chaining jobs is useful if you need to do some processing that depends on another process to have run first.<br>*Technical context for this option:* **Data context and/or business logic context** |
| Scheduled Apex | Scheduled Apex jobs can be used to invoke Apex classes to run asynchronously at specific times using the scheduling interface.<br>*Technical context for this option:* **Data context and/or business logic context** |
| SOQL/SOSL | Similar to the industry-known Structured Query Language (SQL). Salesforce Object Query Language (SOQL) is the query language that can only be used within Salesforce to query any/all data within Salesforce. "Salesforce Object Search Language" (SOSL) is a search language that can be used within Salesforce to perform a text-based search for data within your Salesforce org.<br>*Technical context for this option:* **Data context** |

# Order of Execution Within Salesforce

It is one thing to choose a Salesforce declarative or programmatic option based on the technical context, but it is also important to understand the order in which Salesforce executes each option. Chapter 1 talked briefly about the client-side execution vs. server-side execution in Salesforce and how the Apex runtime engine processes user requests.

Salesforce executes a standard set of events in a particular order each time a server-side call is made to create or update a record within the Salesforce database. This order of events determines which option is run first and which are run later. Each event in the order needs to execute entirely before Salesforce can execute the next event. Figure 3-5 illustrates the order of events followed by Salesforce when committing a record to the database.

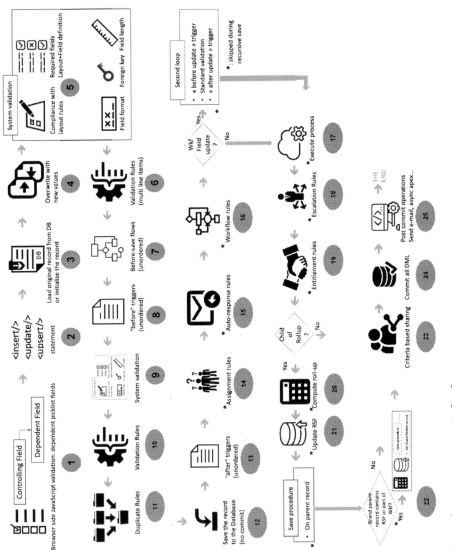

*Figure 3-5.  Order of Execution in Salesforce*

1.  **JavaScript Validation**: Dependent picklist field validation will run on the browser side and will be enforced only if there are any depended fields configured for the record on the transaction.

2.  **DML Statement**: The DML statement will start.

3.  **Record Load**: The original record is loaded from Salesforce; this will cross-check in both the existing and new records.

4.  **Record Overwrite**: The new values are overwritten in the old record.

5.  **System Validation (first-run)**: Validations performed by system to enforce the integrity of field types (e.g. number fields do not have special characters), page layouts and the uniqueness of indexed fields such as external Id's.

6.  **Validation Rules (first-run)**: User-defined validation rules run if multiline items were created, such as quote line items and opportunity line items.

7.  **Before Triggers**: Before-save flows are executed. Before triggers are executed; usually, before triggers are used to perform logic in the records that are being processed. Triggers run in bulk mode with up to 200 records per transaction.

8.  **System Validation (second-run)**: System validations will be performed using layout rules, required fields, field format rules, and foreign keys.

9.  **Validation Rules (second-run)**: Custom validation rules are enforced in this step; note that changes done in the before trigger will affect the result of the validation rules.

10. **Duplicate Rules**: Executes duplicate rules. If the duplicate rule identifies the record as a duplicate and uses the block action, the record is not saved and no further steps, such as after triggers and workflow rules, are taken.

11. **Save Record**: Saves the record to the database but doesn't commit yet.

12. **After Trigger**: After triggers are executed; usually, after triggers are used to perform login in other records besides the ones being processed. Triggers run in bulk mode with up to 200 records per transaction.

13. **Assignment Rules**: Assignment rules are triggered.

14. **Auto-Response Rules**: Auto-response rules are executed.

15. **Workflow Rules**: Workflow rules are triggered. If there is an update, the following actions will run again: before-update triggers, standard validations, and after-update triggers.

16. **Execute Flows**: Flows are executed; if the flow performs a DML action, the record will go through the save procedure again.

17. **Escalation Rules**: Escalation rules run.

18. **Entitlement Rules**: Entitlement rules run.

    a. If the record contains a roll-up summary field or is part of a cross-object workflow, performs calculations, and updates the roll-up summary field in the parent record. The parent record goes through the save procedure.

    b. If the parent record is updated and a grandparent record contains a roll-up summary field or is part of a cross-object workflow, performs calculations, and updates the roll-up summary field in the grandparent record. The grandparent record goes through the save procedure.

19. **Criteria-Based Sharing**: Criteria-based sharing is evaluated and calculated.

20. **Commit DML**: The record is committed into the database.

21. **Post-Commit Operations**: Post-commit operations are triggered (send emails).

# Salesforce AppExchange

AppExchange by Salesforce is a storefront that offers apps, bolt solutions, flow solutions, Lightning data, and components that can be installed into a given Salesforce instance to accelerate the time to market for small enhancements to full applications.

AppExchange makes it easy to improve the Salesforce software. **Apps** provide turnkey solutions that can be installed as managed or unmanaged packages. A managed package is created by an Independent Software Vendor (ISV) and is installed as a locked package and updated by the ISV. The application can be changed, and the update is pushed to your instance automatically. An unmanaged package is also installed from AppExchange, but is unlocked and can be modified by users in the instance. Updates are not pushed automatically, as the solution is open to changes, some of which may not be supported by the solution. The managed package is considered a first-generation managed package (1GP). As you might expect, Salesforce has introduced a second-generation managed package (2GP) that provides a new way to build modular applications managed using your version control system.[10]

With 2GP, Salesforce offers a packaging designed for internal business apps called the unlocked package. The unlocked package uses a version control system to create, distribute, and deliver source-driven development.

Regardless of the type of package you select, AppExchange should be considered as a viable option to create fully custom applications. An app installed from AppExchange provides the following advantages without adding normal license or feature restrictions, such as the number of object limitations:

- Faster deployment

- Better customer service

- Available documentation

- Regular updates

- Quality assurance and security

**Bolt solutions** allow the ISV or internal developer to create solutions quickly using declarative capabilities within Salesforce and package them to be reused. This design can save organizations time and money. Bolt solutions can also combine any of the following solutions: community templates, flow categories, and custom apps.

**Flow solutions** take advantage of no code Lightning Flows that can package predefined business processes. Flow solutions are similar to bolt solutions, as they can be combined to enhance existing apps.

**Lightning data** are packages that are used to enhance and add data to your Salesforce data. The data is offered by third-party companies such as Dun & Bradstreet. The solution can fill out missing fields or add missing associated records such as email addresses and account contacts.

---

[10]Salesforce (2020). Second-Generation Managed Packages | Salesforce DX Developer Guide | Salesforce Developers. Retrieved on October 21, 2020, from `https://developer.salesforce.com/docs/atlas.en-us.sfdx_dev.meta/sfdx_dev/sfdx_dev_dev2gp.htm`.

**Components** are available Lightning components (both Aura and LWC) that can be loaded and used to enhance your Lightning experience, process, and integrations. The components are loaded for use with the App Builder Canvas app.

No matter the solution you are using, AppExchange is an option that should be considered. Many of the solutions are free or very low cost and can add functionality quickly.

# Considerations for Using Off-Platform Systems Instead of Salesforce

As an architect, you need to recognize when Salesforce is not the right choice and to make the decision to select an off-platform solution. Whether you are looking for a backup and archive solution or a payment gateway or an enterprise data warehouse, the best solution is using an off-platform solution. Here are a few things to consider:

- Do you have large data volumes (LDVs)? Data volumes that are in the tens to hundreds of million records can cause significant performance issues.

- Are you looking for an off-line backup or archival solution? By default, these solutions should be off-platform.

- Do you have unstructured data or need a Big Data solution? Salesforce has a solution, but often, a Big Data application is better off-platform.

- Do you need two-phase commit transaction processing where you need to ensure the atomicity property of the transaction? This means that a transaction updates two or more independent databases, and all need to be confirmed before the transaction can complete for any of the databases. Salesforce does not support this requirement natively.

- Does your solution need to support an external ERP or financial system? These solutions are often off-platform and require integration. They are not candidates for solutions in Salesforce.

- Do you need to process payments? The payment gateway and the payment processing application are external and are not candidates for solutions in Salesforce.

- Do you have a highly branded web application? Often, it is better to keep the solution off-platform.

- Do you have legacy applications or specialized solutions? The investment to move these applications into Salesforce may not make sense.

- Does the organization have a cloud-based infrastructure environment such as AWS or Azure? It is advisable to use an application rationalization framework to identify candidates for Salesforce. Look at TCO, business value and fit, business need, and time to market.

# Salesforce Org Strategy Considerations

An "organization" or "org" in the Salesforce ecosystem refers to a single production environment of Salesforce partitioned and provisioned for your company. Having said that, a company can subscribe to multiple Salesforce orgs (Salesforce production environments) for valid reasons. A few reasons for having multiple orgs of Salesforce over a single org of Salesforce are as follows:

- Risk of exceeding governor limits within a single org can be mitigated by having multiple orgs, as each org will have its own set of governor limits.

- Logical separation of data and business functions to support regulatory and compliance requirements or business complexity.

- Risk of large data volumes within a single org can degrade the system performance.

- Organization-wide default settings related to object-level security and role hierarchy can be different and uniquely set for each org in multiple orgs.

- Licensing needs to be considered separately for each org; common users in multiple orgs will need to have multiple licenses with respect to each org.

- Deploying a common set of configurations or code across multiple orgs cannot be done within an org-based development approach since sandboxes related to each org can only be used to deploy within the same org.

Often the answers to the preceding reasons are not apparent at the beginning of a project. There are pros and cons for each strategy, and it is important to choose an org strategy that best suits the enterprise needs. Table 3-5 illustrates some of the pros and cons of having a Salesforce single-org vs. multi-org strategy.

***Table 3-5.*** *Single-Org vs. Multi-org Strategy*

| Organization Strategy | Pros | Cons |
|---|---|---|
| **Single-org** | Cross-business unit collaboration. | Org complexity could become a barrier to progress. |
| | Salesforce Chatter shared in the organization. | Potential to hit specific org limits, such as number of custom tabs, objects, and code lines. |
| | Aligned processes, reports, dashboards, and security – consolidated customization. | Org-wide settings could become difficult to govern and manage. |
| | Ability to share data. | Time to market and innovate could be impacted by the number of teams rolling out new functionality. |
| | Unified reporting | More teams updating shared configuration and code means more regression testing is needed as complexity increases over time. |
| | Single login to access multiple business functions. | Fewer sandbox environments reduce testing capabilities. |
| | 360 view from a central point of view – overall reports possible. | Local administration is difficult. |
| | Interfaces are easier to maintain. | Can violate adherence to industry compliance standards such as EU GDPR privacy laws requiring logical separation of data and user visibility. |

*(continued)*

***Table 3-5.*** (*continued*)

| Organization Strategy | Pros | Cons |
|---|---|---|
| **Multi-org** | Logical separation of data. | Harder to get a clear global definition of processes and data. |
| | Reduced risk of exceeding org limits. | Less reuse of configuration and code. |
| | Org-wide settings are easier to be governed and managed since Lower data volumes within a single Org – potentially improves performance. | Solutions for shared common business requirements need to be deployed into multiple orgs. |
| | Improved time to market and freedom to innovate. | Inferior collaboration across business units (no shared Chatter). |
| | Fewer teams impacted by shared updates. | Duplicated administration functions required. |
| | Reduced complexity within a single org. | Increased complexity for single sign-on. |
| | More sandbox environments mean more testing capabilities. | Merging/splitting orgs and changing integration endpoints is very difficult. |
| | Local administration and customization possible. | The administration is extensive for configurations that cannot be deployed by automated processes (deployment strategy needed). |

When implementing a multi-org strategy, there are various approaches to setting up and managing the multiple Salesforce organizations. The following strategies are the three most common ways in which multi-orgs can be set up:

- **Independent Multi-org Strategy:** In this type of setup, each Salesforce org is set up independently with no connection or links maintained with any other Salesforce org.

- **Master-Child Multi-org Strategy:** In this type of setup, a master organization is treated as the centralized parent org with all other Salesforce organizations being connected to this parent org using the Salesforce to Salesforce[11] feature that allows seamless integration and exchange of data among the connected Salesforce organizations. The master Salesforce org manages the master records for all accounts and contacts and distributes a subset of all related data to each linked Salesforce org that acts as the child organization to the master org.

- **Decentralized Multi-org Strategy:** In this type of setup, each Salesforce org is connected to all other coexisting Salesforce organizations, without any one Salesforce org acting as the master. Each Salesforce org maintains the master copy of all records and data stored within its own org, and each organization is directly linked to other Salesforce organizations using the Salesforce to Salesforce feature that allows seamless integration and exchange of data among the connected Salesforce orgs.

You should certainly choose and identify the ideal org strategy within your system landscape so that the stakeholders can evaluate the context, value, and considerations for managing a single org of Salesforce vs. a multi-org strategy.

# Chapter Summary

In this chapter, we learned about

- The five distinct license types within Salesforce

- The six types of user licenses

- Comparisons of the Salesforce community products

- Considerations and limitations of platform licenses vs. CRM licenses

- Considerations for common declarative and programmatic design choices for application design

---

[11]*Once the Salesforce to Salesforce feature is enabled for an org, it cannot be disabled.*

- Order of execution of all events within Salesforce

- Salesforce AppExchange and the various types of components available on AppExchange

- The nine considerations for using off-platform systems instead of Salesforce

- Key considerations for using a single-org vs. multi-org strategy

- Three common approaches to implement a multi-org strategy

# CHAPTER 4

# Salesforce Data Architecture

The amount of data that we consume each day is overwhelming. According to Jeff Desjardins, founder and editor of Visual Capitalist, the world has an estimate of 44 zettabytes of data.[1] A zettabyte is 1,000 to the power of 7 or 1 with 21 zeros. Fortunately, most architects do not need to manage data that large, but the size of the data we manage is still staggering.

The study of data is a scientific discipline. At its core, data has two broad categories: qualitative and quantitative. Quantitative descriptions use numbers and things you can measure objectively described as discrete or continuous outcomes. Qualitative descriptions use items that cannot be measured directly described as nominal, ordinal, and binomial. If we look at data from a more abstract perspective, we find that data is much more than its core descriptions. The best way to describe data is to look at it as a continuum. Russell Ackoff (1989) described data as the symbols, information as processed data, knowledge as being communicated by instruction, understanding as being conveyed by explanations, and wisdom as the value gained for the exercise of judgment, as shown in Figure 4-1.[2]

---

[1]Desjardins, J. "How much data is generated each day?" Visual Capitalist, April 15, 2019, www.visualcapitalist.com/how-much-data-is-generated-each-day/.

[2]Ackoff, R. L. "From Data to Wisdom." *Journal of Applied Systems Analysis*, Volume 16, 1989, p. 3–9.

© Dipanker Jyoti and James A. Hutcherson 2021
D. Jyoti and J. A. Hutcherson, *Salesforce Architect's Handbook*, https://doi.org/10.1007/978-1-4842-6631-1_4

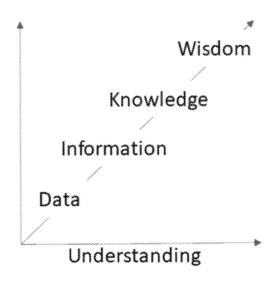

***Figure 4-1.***  *Ackoff Knowledge Continuum*

So how does all of this theoretical discussion fit into the topic of Salesforce data architecture? Our job, as Salesforce architects, is to structure the data with an understanding of its use, its various categories, and its ultimate value to the organization. Understanding different data considerations, constructs, implications, and patterns is the heart of data architecture. In this chapter, we focus on three main areas of data architecture: **data modeling**, **large data volumes (LDVs),** and **data migration**.

In this chapter, we cover

- The importance of data architecture as it relates to the overall instance design

- The high-level data modeling concepts needed to select the right design as it relates to business processes, data movement, and optimization

- The best practices, considerations, and tools used to manage a large data volume (LDV) environment

- Determining the right data lifecycle management in the Salesforce approach to improve performance and maintain compliance

- Evaluating data migration strategy, considerations, and appropriate tools

# Why Is Data Architecture Important?

The primary role of any system in terms of managing data is to

- Intake data from the user or another system through a user interface or system interface.

- Store data within its storage component or another system's storage component.

- Process data based on clearly predefined business logic.

- Return results from processing the data to the user or another system through a user or system interface.

A simple example of data management is when you use a calculator. To use a calculator, you enter the numbers by using the user interface. The calculator intakes the numbers that you want to calculate. The calculator also requires you to choose the business logic that you want to apply to the numbers entered, such as add, subtract, multiply, or divide. During this intake process, the calculator stores all the data entered by you in its memory and starts processing the data based on the predefined business logic chosen by you (i.e., add, subtract, multiply or divide). Finally, it returns the results of the processed data by displaying the final result on its user interface.

Salesforce uses a strongly typed object-oriented programming language called *Apex*. Every functionality in Salesforce, even if it is configured out of the box using clicks, is built using Apex as the codebase.

In an object-oriented programming language, data is collected, processed, and stored in a logical grouping called an *object*. For example, all data related to a customer account, such as account name, address, phone number, website details, and account status, are managed and stored in an account object. Just like a file folder, objects logically separate a specific type of data within the system from another type of data.

For instance, a typical sales record for a clothing distributor may consist of the following:

- **Customer Company Name**: ABCD Inc.

- **Customer Contact Name**: Joe Smith

- **Customer Company Phone Number**: (555) 555-5555

- **Customer Contact Email Address**: joesmith@abcdinc.com

- **Customer Is Interested in**: 2000 blue V-neck T-shirts, 3000 polo T-shirts with collar

- **Contact's Role at the Company**: Decision maker

- **Customer's Previous Purchases**: 3 purchases

  - **Purchase-1**: 2000 denim jeans

  - **Purchase-2**: 500 winter jackets

  - **Purchase-3**: 100 hats

- **Customer's Service Requests**: 1 new request and 1 pending request and 1 completed request

  - **New Request**: "Need product catalog for the summer season."

  - **Pending Request**: "Need to return previously ordered 100 hats, along with the full refund."

  - **Completed Request**: "Processed a refund for 100 denim jeans for $2000, returned from the total delivered in Purchase-1."

From an initial look of the preceding sales data, it may seem more straightforward to store all of the sales details in a single document and manage all changes related to this customer by accessing and updating that single file. However, things could get complicated very quickly when hundreds of new opportunities are created for multiple customers and often by multiple sales team users selling and servicing a typical customer daily.

When using a system like Salesforce, all data is logically stored and managed within objects (i.e., data groups). Each object uses a unique object identifier, and this object identifier for each data record uses a link to one object with another to synchronize the intake processing and representation of data in a unified view. Figure 4-2 illustrates a data object model that would be appropriate to store and manage the preceding data within Salesforce.

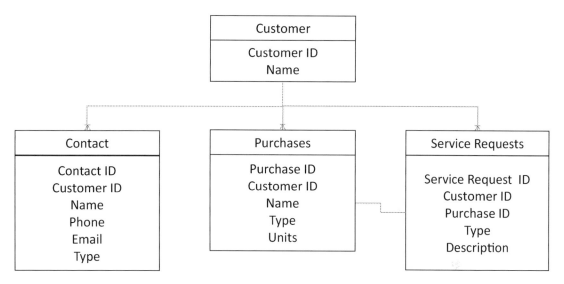

***Figure 4-2.*** *Salesforce Data Object Model to Store the Sales Data*

# Data Modeling in Salesforce

In Chapter 2, we introduced the data model artifact that described the seven attributes used in Salesforce to describe how data is managed (refer back to Chapter 2 for specific details related to each attribute):

1. Objects needed to store and manage data in Salesforce

2. Object types (i.e., whether they are standard, custom, or external objects)

3. Record types within each object

4. Object relationship to other objects

5. The organization-wide default settings for object visibility

6. Owners of the records within each object

7. Estimated number of records per object that can exist at any given period

# Data Model Techniques and Considerations

Data modeling is more than just using standard objects and creating or relating custom objects. Data modeling starts with giving your data a structure. Still, it continues with understanding the business process and the data visibility for the users and stakeholders. The data model is a holistic design that needs to support the business vision, business reporting, KPI measurements, security requirements, and application performances. Often, these **requirements conflict with each other, and trade-offs need consideration**. As a Salesforce architect, you need to understand and design your data model to support these conflicting requirements. The following list provides a few considerations to review for every Salesforce data model:

- **What is the overall goal(s) of the Salesforce environment?** Often, Salesforce supports multiple business functions with different applications, all using the core Salesforce "standard" objects and a defined set of custom objects. Understanding each business use case is critical before the presentation of the final design.

- **How will the business use the data in Salesforce to report business trends, outcomes, and KPI predictions?** Starting with the final reporting requirements often changes the overall data model design to support the requirements.

- **Does the user need to see data on the detail page or in a related list?** Traditional and academic database normalization does not work well in Salesforce. You need to understand how the application is used and consider the user experience (UX) and the page layout and presentation (UI).

- **Will your data model support declarative business logic?** The design of the data model can also impact your ability to create an application declaratively or programmatically. Many businesses are expecting no/low code solutions.

Let's dive a little deeper into some of the data model considerations.

# Top-Down Consideration with Bottom-Up Requirements

**Vision/Process/Challenges/Pain Points:** Before you start the data model design, work with the executive team to understand the overall vision for Salesforce. Identify the business pain points each of the stakeholders has in the current environment and capture the business processes they use. Identify the challenges they have and the potential impact of those challenges in Salesforce.

**Reporting and KPI:** Often, Salesforce supports business processes and collects data to report and measure success. It is essential to understand the expected reporting requirements. Often, reporting is left to the end of a project, only to find out that the data model needs to be changed to support the reports. Starting with reporting and dashboards can provide valuable business insight, but it can also reduce the technical debt incurred by not knowing the reporting requirements early.

**Security:** Understanding the overall security landscape of the business and the detailed requirements reduces efforts on both the data model design and the visibility and sharing of data within the Salesforce instance.

**Performance:** There are three high-level ways to measure the speed of the design: intake, processing, and reporting. The first measurement, intake, is the speed in collecting data. It is crucial to understand how the system collects data used by the business process. User frustration increases if they are required to jump from object to object to collect data, causing data quality issues. The processing of data is also a consideration. Business processes that require complex, custom-built methods run slower and are challenging to maintain and update. The last performance measurement is reporting and how the initial and processed data can be extracted and reported.

**Business Process:** The data model design often dictates which process tools can support the business. Costly changes occur if the data model does not consider the processes used in the design. The most basic example is the use of *roll-up* fields. If a lookup relationship field is used instead of a master-detail relationship, then the roll-up summary solution requires a programmatic approach to support the business requirement. This example also demonstrates the need to understand the security required, as the use of the master-detail relationship field opens the access of the data.

## Choices and Compromises

Often, architects need to evaluate conflicting requirements and the various considerations to find the one solution that maximizes the application. Not one approach or solution is perfect. Often, you need to compromise one consideration for another to improve the overall solution for the client. Figure 4-3 shows how your choices might look. Your job is to find the best mix of choices to produce the best solution for the client. It is essential to explain your recommended choices and compromises.

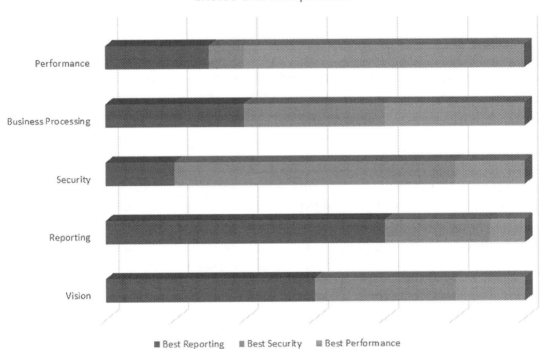

**Figure 4-3.** *Choice and Compromise – Consideration of Choices*

Let's look at two user stories to see how different decisions can impact the outcome(s) of the design choice.

## User Story: Same-Day Shipping

**AS A** shipping manager, **I WANT** to track the percentage of orders placed today shipped for all the warehouses **SO THAT I** can generate a critical KPI report showing same-day shipping per quarter.

# Approach Options: Normalized or Denormalized

Several approaches can solve this story. One approach, using a **"flat file" or a denormalized structure**, is to use one object to capture the data needed to collect the information. Another option would be to normalize or break the process into two different objects. The first object would collect the order, and the second object would track the actual shipments for all warehouses. The object designs would look something like what is shown in Figure 4-4.

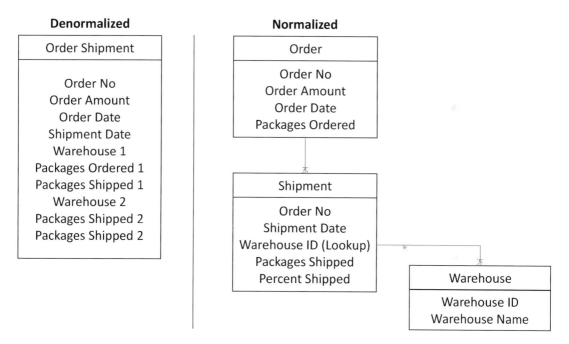

***Figure 4-4.*** *Denormalized Data Model vs. Flat Data Model - Order Shipment*

For this example, let's look at two considerations:

- **Analytics Requirements**: A real-time report showing the percentage of same-day shipments per quarter

- **User Experience (UX) Requirements**: Ability to capture the shipment dates

## Architecture Choice: Normalized

The focus of this user story was the analytics or reporting requirements. Therefore, it makes sense to store the warehouse data in its object. Additionally, the consideration of both the data capture and UX allows the warehouse object to collect the data as it happens.

Let's look at a second user story.

## User Story: Lead Contact Information

**AS A** marketing manager, **I WANT** to quickly enter contact information from a lead **SO THAT I** can quickly find the contact number for a given lead when I look at the lead detail page, reports, lists views, and highlight elements.

## Approach Options: Normalized or Denormalized

Again, the approach would be to use either a normalized or denormalized design. The first object would collect the lead, and the second object would track the contact number. The object designs would look something like what is shown in Figure 4-5.

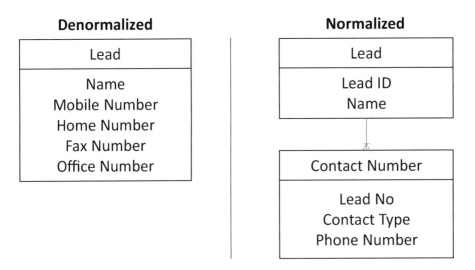

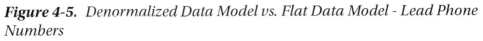

***Figure 4-5.*** *Denormalized Data Model vs. Flat Data Model - Lead Phone Numbers*

Let's look at the same two considerations:

- **Analytics Requirements**: For this story, the analytic need is not a consideration.

- **User Experience (UX) Requirements**: Ability to capture information and to display data on the detail page, report, list view, and highlight element.

### Architecture Choice: Denormalized

The focus of this user story was the information capture and UX requirements. Therefore, it makes sense to store the lead data and the phone data in the same object. This approach supports both the data capture and UX requirements.

# Cardinality: Salesforce Options

Salesforce offers only a few data relationship options, which are one-to-one, one-to-many, and one derived option for many-to-many relationships. These primary data cardinals are the foundation of all data designs. It is critical to understand the impact each approach has on the data model design decisions.

# Selecting the Best Type of Relationship

Salesforce allows either a **lookup relationship** or a **master-detail relationship** between two data objects. Each option should be considered and selected to maximize the ultimate solution. Table 4-1 shows high-level considerations for your decision.

**Table 4-1.** *Differences Between Lookup and Master-Detail Relationships in Salesforce*

| Consideration | Lookup | Master-Detail |
|---|---|---|
| Object dependents | Loosely coupled. | Tightly coupled. |
| Number of relationships per object | 40 in total including count of master-detail (can increase to 50 on request). | Only 2. |
| Parent required | No. Records can be orphaned or reparented. | Yes. No orphans. Deletion of reparenting only. |
| Sharing | Independent. | Inherited from parent. |
| Cascade deletes | No – Standard object.Selectable – Custom objects (delete is not allowed for >100,000 records). | Yes. |
| Many-to-many | Not recommended as lookup since it does not mandate a relationship record on both sides by default. | Yes, sharing requires including both related objects. However, ownership is controlled by the first M-D field or primary master object. |
| Self-relationships | Yes. | Only one M-D. No M:M allowed. |
| External object | Yes. | No. |
| Indirect lookup (external child object to standard or custom SF object) | Yes. | No. |
| Hierarchical | On user object only. | No. |
| Roll-up summary | With code or AppExchange app. | Yes. |

# Revisiting Cardinality in Salesforce

Relationships in Salesforce are managed by connecting the parent records with one or more child records. The relationships can use either a lookup field or a master-detail field. The relationships can be between a single object (called self-relationship), standard objects, custom objects, both standard and custom objects, and external objects. Objects can have direct, indirect, or hierarchical relationships. Relationships can be one-to-one (1:1), one-to-many (1:M), or many-to-many (M:M). See Figure 4-6.

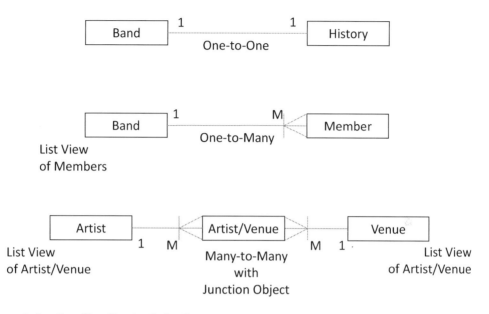

**Figure 4-6.** *Cardinality in Salesforce*

# Other Data Modeling Considerations

Salesforce offers several standard data models depending on the "cloud" solution you recommend to your client. Each "cloud" is composed of the objects used in the software as a service (SaaS) offering. At the time of this writing, **Salesforce listed 871 different standard objects supported for all of its "cloud" products**. At the core of the most popular "cloud" licenses (Sales and Service), Salesforce provides standard objects that are the heart of the overall design. **These objects are often called the "Hero" or core objects. These objects include the account, contact, opportunity, lead, and case objects**.

In Figure 4-7, you can see the relationship between each object. The lead object is a dotted line in that it is typically converted from a single lead record to records into the account, contact, and (or) lead objects. From these base objects, Salesforce adds the 866 additional objects to create the various standard SaaS "cloud" practices.

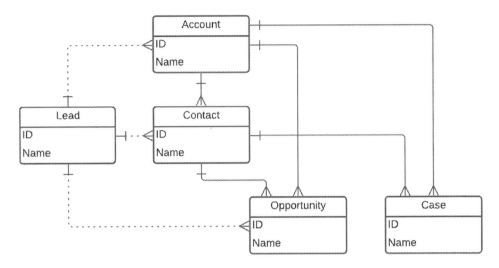

***Figure 4-7.*** *Salesforce Standard or Core Objects*

Architects should know how standard objects create a scalable data model that supports all business processes with an appropriate level of customizations (click vs. code) while considering performance for large data volumes. Let's look at the object types available in Salesforce.

**Custom Objects**: These objects are created by the administrator or architect to store information that is unique to the business or requirements of the design. A custom object has similar attributes and characteristics of Salesforce standard objects, including standard and custom fields, field history tracking, relationships, custom links, search layouts, page layouts, object limits, and sharing.

**External Objects**: These objects are similar to custom objects, except that they map to data outside of Salesforce. An external object uses an external data source definition to connect to the external system. Usually, this is the Salesforce Connect optional product. External objects are searchable and appear the same to Salesforce users. Salesforce sharing rules do not control access to the data; permission sets or profiles control access to the data. Limits come from the external host system.

**Storage Considerations**: Salesforce has storage limitations. Because of these limits and the availability of external objects, an architect understands these options. (See specific license information for details.)

# Large Data Volume Architecture

Salesforce defines a large data volume or LDV as

> *an imprecise, elastic term. If your deployment has tens of thousands of users, tens of millions of records, or hundreds of gigabytes of total record storage, you have a large data volume. Even if you work with smaller deployments, you can still learn something from these best practices.*[3]

This definition leads me to more questions than it answers. In fact, in practice, the actual definition of LDV is even more elusive. LDV impacts the full spectrum of interaction with Salesforce from importing and exporting data; establishing sharing and visibility; using data in the UI, reports, and list views; and performing business rules and processes. The size of the data is not a one-size-fits-all assumption. It is also nuanced in how to use data volume. An architect's role is understanding how to identify an LDV, what causes it, and, most importantly, how to mitigate its impact on your Salesforce instance performance.

Why should we be concerned with large data volumes? It is all about performance. Consider the following performance topics for any modern system:

1.  What is the performance of the UI/UX?

2.  Is the efficiency of the underlying database optimized?

3.  Will API throughput meet or exceed requirements?

4.  Will you have data migration issues during the data lifecycle?

## What Causes LDV Issues?

The access to and the presentation of data is a vital feature provided in Salesforce. To support this critical feature, Salesforce uses a data model that creates a pivot table to index fields, enforce unique fields, and manage foreign keys.[4] Salesforce also establishes

---

[3]Best Practices for Deployments with Large Data Volumes, `https://resources.docs.salesforce.com/226/latest/en-us/sfdc/pdf/salesforce_large_data_volumes_bp.pdf`. Salesforce.com update, August 20, 2020.

[4]"Multitenancy and Metadata Overview | Best Practices for Deployments with Large Data Volumes | Salesforce Developers." Salesforce Developers Documentation, developer.salesforce.com/docs/atlas.en-us.salesforce_large_data_volumes_bp.meta/salesforce_large_data_volumes_bp/ldv_deployments_concepts_multitenancy_and_metadata.htm.

tables to manage sharing and group access; see Chapter 5. Additionally, Salesforce uses an underlying database to support its multi-tenant design called the Lightning Platform Query Optimizer. The query optimization runs automatically to create indexes, select the best table to run queries, order data, create key values and joins, and establish execution plans to minimize database transactions.[5] Because of the complexity of the design, large data volumes can impact overall performance. Let's look at the potential causes of poor database performance in Salesforce.

## Object Size

One of the first factors used to identify large data volumes is within its name. Yes, you guessed it. Look at the volume or data size of an object. Although Salesforce does not have any published numbers, a reasonable rule of thumb is as follows[6]:

- >50 M account records

- >20 M contact records

- >100 M custom records

- >10 K users

- >100 GB record data storage

These volumes are not definitive. Rather, they are indicators that an LDV impact might occur. Let's look at the ">100 M custom records" example. For this rule of thumb, the assumption is that the custom object is going to be used to capture associated data, and its associated relationship easily reduces the volume with a simple query. Remember that LDV is multifaceted. Let's dig a little deeper.

**Object Size Growth**: Another consideration is the potential growth of an object volume. If our 4 million contacts are expected by 20% per month for the next 36 months, we have more than 23 million contacts in 36 months.

---

[5]"Multitenancy and Metadata Overview | Best Practices for Deployments with Large Data Volumes | Salesforce Developers." Salesforce Developers Documentation, developer.salesforce. com/docs/atlas.en-us.salesforce_large_data_volumes_bp.meta/salesforce_large_data_volumes_ bp/ldv_deployments_concepts_multitenancy_and_metadata.htm.

[6]Large Data Volumes: Technology & Best Practices (December 15, 2012). T. K. Holmes. Salesforce. com.

**Tip**  Examine the data growth for several years and consider current and future growth expectations. A good rule of thumb is to look at 2–3 years minimum, with a maximum of 5 years.

**Hint**  Present Value * (1 + Percent Growth)$^n$ = Future Value

**Why does the object volume matter?** What can impact its performance? In Salesforce, every record has an owner. A specific user (internal or external) or a queue (a group of users) owns a record. Additionally, a list of data or a report is the primary user experience. As a data volume grows, so does the number of system resources required to manage and present the data. Let's look at a few crucial perspectives.

## Record Ownership

In Salesforce, every record must have an owner. The owner can be a single user, or it can be a "queue" of users. Salesforce mandates this design to support the security and visibility requirements inherent in the design. The owner of a record has full access to the record. To keep data secure and only allow appropriate users access to that record, Salesforce also provides a *system object* to manage the sharing rules associated with that record. A system object is not visible directly in the Salesforce UI. However, it is available to the business logic in terms of both declarative and programmatic controls used to manipulate the associated data.

## Record Relationships

Every record in Salesforce is related to several other objects. At the system level, the relationships include the owner, created by, last modified by, sharing, and other business process relationships. These relationships are either a master-detail type or a lookup type.

129

**Master-Detail Relationship (Tightly Coupled Relationship)**: Utilizing the master-detail form of relationship provides a powerful way to model containment, where one parent object record acts as a container for other child records. Here are a few considerations:

- The platform automatically cascades the deletion of child records when the deletion of the parent occurs and enforces the need for a parent reference upon the creation of a child record.

- By default, the platform prevents users from moving the child records to another parent by editing the relationship field. However, you can disable this validation and permit this by selecting the reparenting option for child records.

- With the use of roll-up summary fields, it also becomes possible to build calculated fields based on values of the child record fields.

- You can define up to three levels of master-detail relationships.

**Lookup Relationship (Loosely Coupled Relationship)**: Utilizing the lookup type of relationship allows you to model connections between related records that are optional and may also have other relationships not necessarily in ownership or containing aspects of their parents. Keep in mind the following points when using lookup fields to define relationships:

- The deletion of a parent record does not result in a cascade delete of related child records; Salesforce Support can enable this feature.

- Unlike with master-detail, you can elect for the platform to enforce referential integrity during the creation of the field by utilizing the *Don't allow deletion of the lookup record* that's part of a lookup relationship option.

- Currently, the roll-up summary fields are not supported when using a lookup relationship.

- Lookup fields of either kind are automatically indexed by the platform, making queries, in some cases, faster.

**External Lookup**: External lookup is a relationship that links a child standard, custom, or external object to a parent external object. The external lookup relationship field is a standard external ID field from the parent external object matched against the values of the child ID.

**Indirect Lookup**: Indirect lookup is a relationship that links a child's external object to a parent object. The lookup is a custom, unique, external ID field on the parent object matched against the child's indirect lookup on an external data source.

**Hierarchical Lookup**: Hierarchical lookup is a relationship available for only the user object to support user lookups for both direct and indirect relationships.

## Data Skews

The primary factor associated with data skew is the aligning of many relationships with a single record or owner. In other words, if you load tens of thousands of leads or accounts to one user or if you associate tens of thousands of contacts with a single account in Salesforce, you are creating a data skew. Three factors impact Salesforce performance: **record locking, sharing performance, and lookup skew**. Let's look at each factor.

**Record locking** occurs when a change occurs to a given field on a record. Salesforce locks the affected record and the parent record to maintain data integrity. Without record locking, it would be easy to have data out of sync and inaccurate during and directly after an update. The record lock does not take long to resolve for a single record. But, if the record locking happens across many records simultaneously, then the impact of the record lock is exponential. Additionally, if the record lock blocks an update, the system retries the transaction, thus slowing the system performance. Here are special considerations to avoid locking:

- Use a Public Read or Read/Write OWD sharing model for all nonconfidential data loading.

- To avoid creating implicit shares, configure child objects to beings "Controlled by Parent."

- Configure parent-child relationships with no more than ten thousand children to one parent record.

- If you have occasional locking errors, retry logic might be sufficient to resolve the problem.

- Sequence operations on parent and child objects by ParentID and ensure that different threads are operating on unique sets of records.

- Use compression using gzip for responses to reduce network traffic and HTTP keep-alive to improve performance.

- Tune your updates for maximum throughput by working with batch sizes, timeout values, Bulk API, and other performance optimization techniques.

---

Salesforce introduced improved batch management in the Winter '21 release to support LDV data loads.

---

**Sharing performance** is impacted when a change is made that causes a cascaded impact across many records. This performance impact is highly visible in a situation where a parent or child record is changed and the system has to iterate through tens of thousands of potentially affected records. The sharing recalculation happens every time a criterion is changed that could or would change the sharing requirement, such as ownership and criteria-based sharing rules. Having a large number (greater than 10,000) of child records associated with a single owner causes this performance issue.

**Lookup skew** is when an extensive set of records are associated with one record within a lookup object. Behind the scenes, Salesforce needs to identify and lock any associated lookup record. Process, workflow, and validation exacerbate lookup skew for a given object.

# Addressing LDV Issues

Salesforce highlights five approaches to understanding and resolving LDV issues[7]:

- Divisions

- Force.com Query Plan

- Skinny tables

- Indexes

- Database statistics

---

[7]Best Practices for Deployments with Large Data Volumes, `https://resources.docs.`
`salesforce.com/226/latest/en-us/sfdc/pdf/salesforce_large_data_volumes_bp.pdf`
Salesforce.com, updated on August 20, 2020.

Let's look at each approach.

**Divisions:** Divisions can partition an organization's data into logical sections, making searches, reports, and list views smaller and faster. Note: Submit a case to enable this feature.

**Force.com Query Plan:** Salesforce offers a tool in the Developer Console to review and evaluate the performance of queries in large data volumes. The goal is to optimize queries using selective and indexed fields and to speed up performance over large volumes. **Note**: Enable this feature in the Developer Console.

**Database Statistics:** Salesforce performs a nightly process to collect statistics from the database. This process happens automatically. The outcome is improved index objects. An architect can use this knowledge to tune the query design to take advantage of these automatic calculations and indexing files. **Note**: The statistics is calculated by Salesforce automatically.

**Skinny Tables:** Salesforce can create skinny tables (denormalized, flat files) that combine frequently used fields and remove joins. Skinny tables can resolve specific long-running queries for objects with millions of records. Skinny tables resolve long-running reports, slow list views, and SOQL queries that time out. **Note**: Submit a case to enable this feature.

**Custom Indexes:** Salesforce creates custom indexes to speed up queries. They can be helpful for SOQL queries that need to use non-indexed fields. **Note**: Submit a case to enable this feature.

## A Final Word on Account Skews, Ownership Skews, and Lookup Skews

The impact on organizational performance is the lack of adherence to account and ownership skew guidelines. Let's restate them here:

**Ownership Skew:** Guidance states that one user or one queue should own less than 10,000 records for each owner.

- *Mitigation Option:* Place the user in a separate role at the top of the hierarchy. Keep the user out of public groups.

**Account Skews**: Guidance states that any single account should have less than 10 K child records.

- *Mitigation Option:* Split the account into smaller (fewer children) accounts and use a parent account to consolidate information.

**Lookup Skews**: Guidance states that any single object should have less than 10 K child record lookups.

- *Mitigation Option*: Split the parent object record into smaller (fewer children) records and use a parent account to consolidate information.

**Here are other mitigating options for data skews:**

- Avoid records with many child records.

- Use triggers instead of workflows.

- Picklists instead of lookup.

- Schedule maintenance updates at non-peak times to avoid record locking.

# Data Lifecycle Management in Salesforce

Even with recent acquisitions, Salesforce does not provide end-to-end enterprise-class data lifecycle management out-of-the-box tools. As an architect, it is critical to implement a data lifecycle plan that addresses at least three primary objectives: data migration, data backup, and data archiving. Figure 4-8 presents a nominal approach to data lifecycle management in Salesforce.

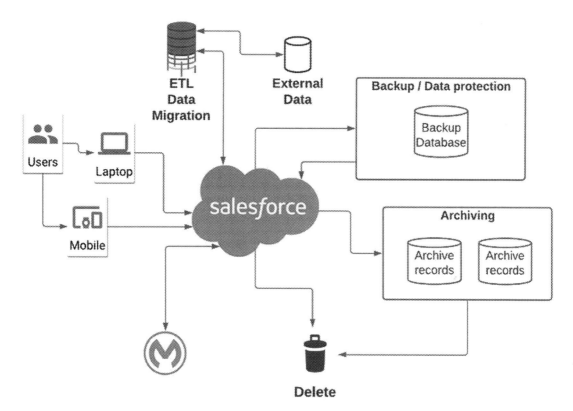

***Figure 4-8.*** *Salesforce Data Lifecycle: Backup and Archiving Approach*

# Data Migration

Migrating data into Salesforce is straightforward with the available REST and Bulk Data API. Additionally, there are several tools available to Salesforce administrators, including DataLoader, DataLoader.io, and data wizards. These tools take advantage of Data APIs provided by Salesforce to import, update, upsert, and delete data in specific objects. Simple data migration into a single object is pretty straightforward. Before we start, let's look at a few requirements to migrate data into Salesforce. Table 4-2 presents a comparison between common data loading tools.

***Table 4-2.*** *Common Data Migration Tools Comparison*

| Data Migration Tool | Features | When to Use |
|---|---|---|
| DataLoader – included with standard license | • Standalone application.<br>• Supports bulk data loads.<br>• Supports auto-scripts. | This tool is suited for small to medium data migration efforts or when overnight process is needed. DOS batch routines can be used. |
| DataLoader.io – basic features built-in to UI | • Web-based options.<br>• Supports bulk data loads.<br>• Option to purchase enhanced features. | This tool is well suited for administrator data management. It supports advanced data management features with scheduling. |
| Data wizard – internal feature | • Step-by-step tool for users and administrators.<br>• Limited to CSV files. | This toll is used by end users and admins to perform basic data managements such as loading leads and contacts. |

# Types of Data Manipulation Operations Available for Data Migration

The lifecycle of data migration starts with the creation or insertion of data into a Salesforce object. The next step in the lifecycle is to update the data as required over time. Salesforce offers an operation that can insert and update in the same operation called upsert.

**Insert**: The insert operation creates a new record in an object and commits it to the database. This operation is the fastest and should be used for new data.

**Update**: The update operation identifies the related record using a primary or foreign key to change one or more fields in the record. This operation is slower because it must look for existing records to update.

**Upsert**: The upsert is a combined operation that either creates or updates a record when the record matches the primary or foreign key. The operation provides a single process but has a cost of a slower transaction. Using the upsert operation, you can either insert or update an existing record in one call. The upsert operation determines whether a record already exists using the record's ID as the key to match records, external ID field, or idLookup attribute set to true. This produces at least one of the following three outcomes:

1. If the key does not match, then a new record is created.

2. If the key matches once, then an existing record is updated.

3. If the key matches multiple times, then an error is generated, and the operation fails.

A record is inserted or updated based on how it is related to existing records if a relationship has already been defined between the two objects, using either a lookup or master-detail relationship, which is considered a foreign key ID. Note: Updates cannot make changes to the related object using the same operation.

A data migration plan can also require the removal or deletion of existing data. Salesforce offers three delete operations to support this requirement. Before we look at the available delete operation, we need to understand the impact a delete can have on the direct and related records. If a record is a master record in a master-detail relationship, the process deletes the related record if allowed. (For more information on what can stop a deletion, please refer to the Salesforce referential integrity rule). Salesforce also provides an operation to restore soft deletes and related records. The process relies on the availability of items remaining in the trash bin. The delete operations are as follows:

**Delete**: The delete operation is a soft delete of records. Recovery of data is possible.

**Hard Delete**: The "hard delete" operation is a permanent deletion that removes the record and any related records concerning referential integrity.

**Mass Delete**: The "mass delete" operation is only available for custom objects. If the entire custom object requires removal, use truncation instead.

## Data Migration Process

Data migration is the process of moving from one system to another. It uses the simple data manipulation operations described, but it requires a more deliberate approach. At the base level, data migration follows seven steps:

1. Identify the data you want to migrate. Determine the state of the data and how you want to use it in the new org.

2. Create templates for the data. Build the loading template to gather all of the required fields and relationships. Don't forget historical data elements like created date and created by users. Also, look at special requirements such as record types and picklist values.

3. Prepare your data. Look for duplicates and wrong or missing data. If required, clean the data to provide the best data in the new organization. Be careful with leading zeros and case-sensitive record ID.

4. Populate your data into the templates. To catch issues before you migrate the data, organize the data, and load the template.

5. Prepare the destination org for use and testing. Consider adding information from the legacy system that can improve your data. Adding an external ID can help troubleshoot issues and make future updates easier.

6. Migrate the data using appropriate operations; if possible, turn off business processes, workflows, triggers, and sharing recalculation before you start. Also, consider loading a test in a sandbox environment first to make sure the template works as expected.

7. Validate the data. After the data is loaded, run tests to make sure you had a successful migration. Make sure the number loader equals the number of new or updated records. Spot-check for added validation.

Data migration is often much more complicated than a single object update. In these cases, the structured and unstructured data includes many legacy objects with complex or normalized data. When this happens, the process is much more complicated, but the necessary steps still hold. The interaction is more of a consideration. As an example, the data may require a series of data loads to support the ultimate solution. Here we need to add a step to understand the order of operations and both the upstream and downstream implications. As an example, you may need to load the users into the system first to obtain the unique Salesforce ID to associate the user to the created by ID. In Salesforce, you can only add the "createdBy" ID as a system input during the creation of an initial record. If you tried to update the record later, your update would fail.

# Complex Data Migration

Having the right tools is essential for a complex project. Data migration is not different. The architect must review the requirement and suggest the right tools for the job. It could be a simple tool like DataLoader, or it could be a sophisticated ETL (Extract-Transform-Load) solution such as Informatica.

---

### DATA MIGRATION APPROACH FOR ETL - MNEMONIC

(CS-DEV) "See as a developer":

**C**: Cleanse data.

**S**: Standardize data.

**D**: Dedupe data.

**E**: Enhance data via ETL.

**V**: Validate data.

---

# ETL (Extract-Transform-Load)

ETL is a process using three distinct but interrelated steps (extract, transform, and load) and is used to synthesize data from multiple sources. There are fundamental steps used to implement an ETL solution and data migration flow. A necessary ETL process falls into four distinct stages. Yes, ETL translates into four (4) steps. They are as follows:

1. Data extraction

2. Data cleansing

3. Data transformation

4. Data loading

Step 2, data cleansing, is added into the process, as it is required to prepare data for the transformation.

# Data Extraction and Data Cleaning

The main objective of the extraction and cleaning process is to retrieve all the required data from the source data systems. Make sure to consider the impact the act of extraction has on the performance, response time, and locking within the source systems. Data cleansing and scrubbing is the detection and removal of inconsistent, insufficient, or duplicate data. The goal of cleansing is to improve the quality and usability of data extracted from the host system before loaded into a target system.

Most data migrations include more than one system and more than one source data for each object. It is essential to consider the following:

- Review and identification of significant data issues, such as duplicates and troublesome or missing data.

- Evaluation of data formatting. The originating system may use a different date format. As an example, Excel uses a base numbering system to create and manipulate dates.

- Enrich your data during the cleansing process. This process improves the transformation and usefulness of the data in the new environment.

- Clean the data with the destination system in mind. Focus on the fields and objects used in both the transformation and destination systems.

- Review how the workflow might change the data as it migrates into the system and include all of the required fields.

- Data issues come in many forms, such as misspelled, incorrectly capitalized, duplicated, and missing or null. It can also include reference errors with contradictory values, referential integrity errors, or summarization errors. Use the cleansing stage to resolve these errors.

# Data Transformation and Verification

The transformation step is the point in the ETL process where the data is being shaped, aligned, and "transformed" to be ready to load into the new system. It is also the point where there is a detailed knowledge of the new data model and how incoming data transforms during the load. It is also the time to define the order of operations for the data to be loaded. The transformation happens in steps, and the new relationships are created.

Equally important is the verification process. This part of the ETL process includes the testing and evaluation of the outcomes. In its simplest form, the verification includes a "checksum" count or summarization for a given transformation that can be used as a test if the expected number of users, opportunities, and accounts is loaded. This checksum helps to confirm that all records have been processed and included in the transformation.

Depending on the complexity of the transformation, an architect creates an intermediate area or staging area where the transformation takes place. Spreadsheets, SQL-based databases, or external transformation solutions, including using scripts for recurring data migration processes, can support the staging process. Let's look at a few options:

**Microsoft Excel Spreadsheets**: For simple transformations, Excel is an easy tool to create tables of CSV files for capturing structured data and adding transformations such as accountID, OwnerID, and RecordTypeID. The process works well for transformations that are limited to single object lookups. Once your process requires a multistep transformation, the Excel option starts to break down quickly.

**Microsoft Access, MySQL, or SQL Server DB**: As the transformation complexity increases, the need to build tables and cross-reference tables to support the transformation also increases. An off-the-shelf database option provides the architect with the ability to create transformations to support a complex requirement. The downside is that it assumes the availability of the tools and the knowledge and experience with the selected DB to create the transformation application. Often, this approach requires a substantial amount of work to create a solution with the appropriate amount of testing and validation.

**Informatica and Jitterbit**: This type of third-party solution allows the architect to focus on the transformations without building the application to manage and run the process. They usually have predefined mapping and transformation tools that significantly reduce the time required to implement the required processes. The downside to this option is the initial cost of the tool. You should expect to pay for the tools and processes created to make your work easier.

Regardless of the approach, the transformation step needs to address any or all of the following steps and outcomes:

- **Formatting Data**: Transform data to specific data types and lengths.

- **Required Field Population**: Adding required information to base data to support data validation requirements in the destination system.

- **Deduplication**: Delete or merge duplicate records.

- **Cleaning**: Normalizing the data to a standard for given values such as gender, addresses, and picklist values.

- **Foreign Key Association**: Create key relationships across tables.

- **Translating Data Fields**: Translate data coming from multiple sources into values that make sense to business users.

- **Parsing Complex Fields**: Transforming complex fields into individual fields.

- **Merging/Combination of Data**: Merging data from multiple fields as a single entity, for example, product, price, type, and description.

- **Calculated and Derived Values**: Aggregate or calculate field values for the ultimate load.

- **Summarization**: Convert external data in multidimensional or related tables.

## Data Loading

The last step is to "load" the data into the new instance. It is imperative to remember that loading data into a system like Salesforce has two perspectives. The first is the impact that a "large data" load has on the system, and the second is the limitations with the loading of data. Let's look closer at each point.

**Large Data Impacts**: Salesforce supports a broad set of capabilities including sharing, validations, and processes that can burden the system during a "large data" migration into the environment. It is essential to review and understand the destination environment. Here are a few system-level items to consider before loading data:

- If possible, change affected objects and related objects to Public Read/Write security during the initial load to avoid sharing calculation overhead.

- Defer computations by disabling Apex triggers, workflow rules, and validations during loads; consider using Batch Apex after the load is complete instead of during the data load.

- Minimize parent record locking conflicts by grouping the child records by parent in the same batch.

- Consider the order of data loads for large initial loads; populate roles before sharing rules:

  - Load users into roles.

  - Load record data with owners to trigger sharing calculations in the role hierarchy.

  - Configure public groups and queues, and then let those computations propagate.

  - Then add sharing rules one at a time while letting computations for each rule finish before adding the next one.

- Add people and data before creating and assigning groups and queues:

  - Load the users and data.

  - Load new public groups and queues.

  - Then, add sharing rules one at a time, letting computations for each rule finish before adding the next one.

**Data Limitations**: As we all know, Salesforce has system governor limits to protect the instance. As such, these limits come into play during the load phase. If you are using the API to load data into Salesforce, you must consider both the daily API limit and the query size limits. Make sure to plan your migration using these guideposts.

**Data Loading Tools**: Salesforce supports several data migration tools, including data wizard, Java-based Salesforce DataLoader, MuleSoft DataLoader.io, and API-based third-party applications.

# Data Backup

On July 31, 2020, Salesforce discontinued its recovery services for production instance owners. That said, the service was not tenable, as it cost $10,000 and took more than six weeks to recover your lost data. This may sound shocking, but data in the cloud is not risk-free. It is critical to have a plan and to use it regularly. A good architect will have a data architecture that includes data backup and archiving plan.

Out-of-the-box Salesforce provides the ability to create backup files of the instance data on a weekly or monthly basis, depending on your edition. The data is saved as CSV files and file blobs and consolidated into zip files. The system administrator downloads them one zip file at a time. This data is only visible for a couple of days; Salesforce does not store the data long-term. Salesforce does not have any extraction tools to recreate your data. WARNING: This is not a viable option for enterprise data management.

We recommend that you invest in a third-party backup and recovery service such as OwnBackup.com. We do not have a relationship with the company other than limited exposure to the solution and the high ratings it has on Salesforce AppExchange. Do your homework.

Data backup includes two sides of the data management coin: the backup or extraction of data from your org and the recovery or the replacement of data into your org after a disaster. Any data backup solution needs to provide services in both directions. Recovery services are the most critical part of the solution. We remember back when on-prem solutions used a magnetic tape to store copies of data as a backup. More often than not, when the company tried to recover the data, the tape was severely damaged, or the process did not work.

Make sure that your backup strategy includes using both the data and metadata API to perform full, incremental, and partial backups. It should also provide security safeguards to secure data. The restore features should support all of the following:

- Recover from data corruption.

- Quickly restore one, a few, or all records in an object quickly.

- Support mass restore and rebuild all associated and related data.

- Recover metadata.

- Restore process and automation seamlessly.

- Restore system, process, and data integrations.

# Data Archiving

An essential aspect of data management within Salesforce is to develop a data archiving strategy to offload from the active Salesforce instance. Salesforce provides minimal setup tools to archive data from Salesforce. See the "Data Backup" section.

Data archiving is only valuable if it is usable. Useful data archiving is accessible, organized, retrievable, and intelligently retained. In the past, archives were thought of as long-term, infrequently accessed data and mostly ignored and never used. This approach is wasting one of the most valuable assets a company can have: its data. A useful data archiving plan looks at four main areas:

1. Organize the archive data for understanding.

2. Make the archive accessible to the business.

3. Establish processes to retrieve data elements and summaries.

4. Retain valuable data, not trivial.

# Salesforce Big Object

The cost of data and file storage in Salesforce can be expensive when compared to external options. That said, Salesforce does offer a solution for storing vast amounts of data to provide holistic views for data, such as customers and partners, storing audit and tracking data, and near-real-time historical archives. The solution is called Big Objects. Salesforce uses standard Big Objects to manage the FieldHistoryArchive, which is part of the Field Audit Trail projects. Salesforce now allows an architect to use the same non-transactional database for custom solutions.

The archive requirement is a great use case for this data option. Using custom applications to extract data from Salesforce relational database objects, you can create archive data to support the archiving plan listed in the preceding text. The Big Object is not available to the user experience as other objects are, and a custom interface is required to update and extract the data in the Big Object. That said, several AppExchange applications are available to support these requirements.

**Features of Big Object:**

- It uses a horizontally scalable distributed database.

- It is a non-transactional database.

- It can process hundreds of millions or even billions of records efficiently.

**Limitations of Big Object:**

- Data deleted programmatically, not declaratively.

- You cannot use standard Salesforce sharing rules.

- You must use custom Lightning and Visualforce components rather than standard UI elements, home pages, detail pages, and list views.

- You cannot have duplicate records in Big Objects.

- You cannot encrypt Big Object data.

# Chapter Summary

In this chapter, we learned

- That data moves through a continuum from data to knowledge, as understanding improves.

- That data management includes intake, storage, processing, and presentation throughout its lifecycle.

- The importance of the data architecture as it relates to the overall instance design and that data modeling is more than the creation of an Entity Relationship Design (ERD).

- That high-level data modeling concepts are needed to select the right design as it relates to business processes, data movement, and optimization. Your data model selection requires choices and compromises to optimize it from your organization.

- That large data volume (LDV) management involves using the tools provided and the knowledge to apply them appropriately. Understanding what causes LDV issues makes solving them more manageable.

- That data lifecycle management involves more than operational data. It starts with the initial migration and continues through backup and restore and data archival.

- That using available Salesforce resources, such as Big Objects, can solve difficult data lifecycle issues.

# CHAPTER 5

# Salesforce Security Architecture

Salesforce security encompasses several significant areas to provide security, access, and visibility of data across a given instance. Security is a foundational element of the overall Force.com design. You must understand the interworkings of system security and data sharing within the Salesforce platform.

In this chapter, we review three main areas of security architecture, including **platform security**, **record-level access mechanics**, and **internal and external user visibility and sharing**.

In this chapter, we cover

- The importance of the Salesforce security architecture as it relates to visibility of and access to data within a Salesforce instance

- How Salesforce grants access to data behind the scenes

- The impact of the Salesforce license on the instance security

- How to manage the platform to control security, access, and visibility

- The use of public groups to expand and manage access and visibility

- The declarative and programmatic platform security features that can be used to meet record-level security requirements

- The use of teams and territories to extend sharing to broader groups of users

- How implicit sharing can impact record sharing

- Making the optimal sharing and visibility options available

© Dipanker Jyoti and James A. Hutcherson 2021
D. Jyoti and J. A. Hutcherson, *Salesforce Architect's Handbook*, https://doi.org/10.1007/978-1-4842-6631-1_5

# Why Is Security Architecture Important?

In 2020, the world dynamics changed that forced virtually every business to adapt quickly to support remote workers and to grant access to systems and data from beyond the confines of the corporate private network. The role of the security architecture was tested like never before.

Security is often aligned along three principles: confidentiality, integrity, and availability, or CIA for short. **Confidentiality** is an evaluation of how well an organization keeps its data private. Salesforce manages confidentiality with organization-wide defaults, roles, profiles, and permission sets which limit who has access to data and, more importantly, who does NOT have access to given data. **Integrity** is the safeguards used to keep the data safe and reliable. Salesforce supports digital signatures and certificates, encryption, intrusion detection, hashing, auditing, version control, and strong access and authentication controls to maintain integrity. **Availability** looks at the reliability of the systems and the timely access given to authorized users. Salesforce has established a high standard for system reliability and uses countermeasures to protect its users against denial-of-service attacks, natural disasters, and general human error through deploying redundant systems, using well-managed update procedures, and using DR and DOS protection solutions.

A primary role of any system, including Salesforce, is the security of and the access to data. The data that your company creates, stores, and uses is a precious resource. Your role, as an architect, is to design a solution that protects it from exploitation and unauthorized access by external and internal individuals. Safeguarding your data can help protect against brand erosion, loss of consumer confidence, financial damage, and reputation harm. Additionally, data security laws require organizations to maintain compliance with these rules. Security includes several attributes and features, including

- **Authentication, Authorization, and Access Control**:
  Authentication, along with authorization, is the first line of defense for data security, and it protects the system against data breaches. Chapter 7 covers this topic in detail.

- **Backups and Recovery/Archive and Deletion**: Developing a plan and using it to manage your data with backups and recoveries and clear archival and deletion will further protect your data against system failure, disaster, data corruption, or breach. When information is no longer useful or has lost its value, it must be removed and archived or deleted. It is essential to establish guidelines that support your legal requirements. Often, it is as necessary to delete data as it is to retain it. Work within company guidelines and legal regulations in your industry. Remember the process of deletion also requires erasure. Make sure you have made the information irretrievable.

- **Encryption**: Salesforce offers two types of data encryption: classic encryption and shield platform encryption. Classic encryption uses a special kind of custom text field, which uses a 128-bit Advanced Encryption Standard (AES) algorithm. Classic encryption supports masking and uses permission-based access to read encrypted fields. Shield platform encryption offers a broad set of encryptions from the field level to processes and across standard objects. Shield platform encryption uses a 256-bit Advanced Encryption Standard algorithm. It also supports the management of encryption key permission and HSM-based key derivation.

---

**Note**   The Advanced Encryption Standard or AES is a symmetrical algorithm that uses a series of rounds that include substitution, shiftrows, mixColumns, and addroundrows. AES is faster than traditional encryption with flexible key length to limit effectiveness of cyberattacks.

---

- **Tokenization**: Tokenization substitutes confidential data with random characters that are not algorithmically reversible. The relationship between the field value and its token values is stored in a protected database lookup table instead of a mathematical algorithm.

## Three Pillars of Salesforce Security Strategy

*Salesforce uses three guiding principles to keep everyone on task when it comes to cybersecurity; nail the basics, engineering, and business agility, and raise the security bar.*[1]

---

[1]Salesforce Approach to Security, June 3, 2020. `https://org62.my.salesforce.com/sfc/ p/#000000000062/a/0M0000000QQz/09TOkGo5uHou_DAeEjb8nwOe85bLIKTXYK.ruNAHn1O`.

In the first pillar, Salesforce implements threat detection and vulnerability management and identity and access management. In the second pillar, Salesforce uses a secure development lifecycle that includes a security-focused framework. In the final pillar, Salesforce utilizes and innovates PKI and certificates, detection, and platform security. Salesforce also ties into the Salesforce ecosystem through its architects to keep security in front of the mind.

The Salesforce security features limit the exposure of data to the unauthorized. As an architect, you need to implement security controls suitable for the sensitivity of your given data. Salesforce security protocols protect your data from unauthorized access from outside your company and inappropriate access from internal users. Let's look at a few areas where Salesforce offers security features for you to consider:

- **Security Infrastructure**: Salesforce provides advanced technology for cybersecurity. Salesforce uses Transport Layer Security (TLS) technology to protect client data using server authentication and classic encryption.

- **Phishing and Malware**: Salesforce continually monitors email attacks, including phishing and malware attacks. In addition to your internal security team, you can report incidences and obtain continuous updates in real time on security@salesforce.com. Salesforce Trust is an inherent service.

- **Redirects to External URLs**: Salesforce protects from malicious links by alerting users when an untrusted link redirects the URL outside the Salesforce domain. Your administrator can manage and update trusted URLs.

- **Auditing**: Salesforce offers extensive auditing features, including user login history, field-level tracking, and metadata change history. This feature allows an administrator to monitor changes and potential security breaches.

- **Security Health Check**: Health Check is a wizard that can be run to identify and fix potential vulnerabilities in your security settings. The Health Check tool presents a summary score showing how your instance compares to a security baseline.

# Platform-Level Security: Access and Visibility

Salesforce created its security model to support a broad spectrum of security, access, and visibility requirements among its customers. The security model starts with controls associated with **objects** and associated **fields** and then the **records** created within a given object.

## Object, Field, and Record Levels

The Salesforce object can be a standard object provided as part of the SaaS solution or a custom object created by the customer to support unique requirements on the platform. Salesforce controls access to an object with its organization-wide default settings and the profile and permission set given to a specific user or group of users.

Organization-wide default (OWD) settings classify how the users of the system access an object. The OWD should be set to support the most restrictive level of access you expect for the user with the least access. In other words, set the OWD to limit the most restricted user in the system. If you want everyone who uses the system to see every record on a given object, set the OWD to "Public" for that object. However, to restrict the data for any record in the object, set the OWD to "Private" for that object.

---

**Note**   You cannot use sharing rules to restrict access. Sharing can only be used to grant more access to a broader group of users.

---

Salesforce offers three primary OWD settings: **Public Read/Write**, **Public Read-Only**, and **Private** for both standard and custom objects. The names are self-explanatory. Public Read/Write means that anyone can view and create records in those objects. Public Read-Only means anyone can view records in those objects, but not create new records. Private means that no one except for the owner of the record can view the record. Salesforce supports two additional options: Public Full Access for the standard campaign object and Read/Write/Transfer for the lead and case standard objects. The Salesforce standard price object uses no access and view only and uses OWD settings to support their use.

---

**Note**   Record ownership can be either the user or queue assigned to have the right to access a record. Ownership privileges include (1) view and edit, (2) transfer, (3) changing ownership for a record, and (4) deleting a record.

---

A **decision tree** for determining the OWD set includes three questions:

1. Which user or group of users has the most restriction on viewing and creating records of data in the object?

2. Should the user from the first question be prevented from seeing any of the records in the object? If yes, set the OWD to Private.

3. Should the user from the first question be prevented from editing a given record? If yes, set the OWD to Public Read-only; else, set the OWD to Public Read/Write.

An object comprises any number of records that include a defined set of standard and custom fields. The object OWD determines if a user has access and visibility to a given field defined for a given object. This is called field-level visibility. The object permissions control access at the object level and are managed in profiles and permission sets. The controls include allowing and not allowing each of the following: **Read, Create, Edit, Delete, View All, and Modify All**.

Access to individual records for a given object is controlled by the sharing model or the ownership of the record. As previously stated, a given record is visible based on either the OWD, ownership, or sharing rules applied.

**Grant Access Using Hierarchies**: Salesforce role hierarchy automatically grants access to records owned by users below them in the hierarchy by default. Salesforce standard objects cannot be changed. However, custom objects can remove this automatic sharing by controlling their selection during object creation and management.

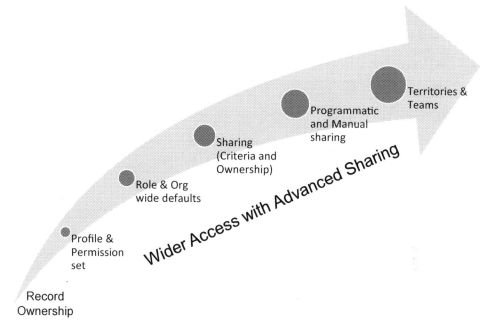

***Figure 5-1.*** *Approach to Sharing – Access to Records Expands with Each Feature*

# Sharing

Salesforce facilitates the management of record sharing through a set of declarative and programmatic features and tools, as shown in Figure 5-1. It is essential to understand how sharing approaches can be applied to obtain an optimal solution. This section looks at how Salesforce builds access from the most restrictive OWD to the required solution. A sharing architecture can control both the precision and the access to a given set of data in your environment.

# Record Owner

Record ownership is the starting point for visibility and sharing within Salesforce. Record ownership allows a given user to view the assigned record per the user profile and assigned permission sets. The entire record access infrastructure is built around record ownership.

Ownership-based sharing architecture uses three key components to support data sharing across the platform:

- Each record has an owner, except "detail records" in master-detail relationships.

- Object share tables are used to define which users and groups should receive access to records.

- Group membership tables grant users access to records through groups, queues, role hierarchy, and territory hierarchy.

The owner listed on the record is used to create an AccountShare record. We will talk about each of these components in more detail later in the chapter.

Record owners can be either a named user or a queue. Queues can prioritize, distribute, and assign records to groups of users. Queues are used to route lead, order, case, and custom object records to a group of users to perform the business process.

Role hierarchy works the same with queue members, where users higher in a role hierarchy can access a given record. Users in a queue or the role hierarchy can view records in a list view, as shown in Table 5-1. Typically, such users will take ownership of the record and remove it from the queue.

*Table 5-1.* *Record Ownership Considerations*

| Approach | Description and Considerations |
|---|---|
| Record or queue ownership | • Must be a single user or queue. <br> • Profile setting overrides access at field/object level. <br> • Queue helps distribute and assign members. <br> • Higher roles can take ownership of a record. |

**LDV considerations**   If a user has more than 10,000 records, they should not have a role. (If needed, it should be the highest level.)

# Permission Sets

A permission set extends "permissions" given to a user or group of users without extending the permission to all of the users associated with a profile. Creating a permission set provides access to objects, fields, and controls not included in the user's profile. The permission set can include settings and permissions that give users access to various tools and functions like those found in the user profile.

Permission sets are managed, adding and removing, from the user detail page. Permission sets can be created with an associated license or without a license. Additionally, some permission set features require a permission set license to be created. This license typically adds functionality not included in the base Salesforce license.

Session-based permission sets support features, settings, and tools for a specific user session. Such permission sets allow access under given circumstances or situations. An architect creates solutions using this feature for advanced requirements. Here are a few examples:

- **Proximity:** Access to information only when in the proximity of a room, building, location, or IP address.

- **Limited Authentication:** Access to service only while remotely approved.

- **Private or Confidential Access While Using VPN:** Activates when users authenticate into your environment using a token.

- **Occasional Access Required:** Uses flow to confirm the running user and activate permission during runtime.

- **SOAP API Activation:** Allows API to set permission.

- **Self-Activates Permissions:** Uses flows to activate and deactivate permission.

**Permission set groups** are available to manage and organize permission sets for groups of users. These groups allow you to bundle permission sets that can then be assigned to users. Any changes in a single permission set will then propagate to all assigned permission set groups. Salesforce also supports muting or limiting permission. Table 5-2 presents the major considerations of permission sets.

***Table 5-2.*** *Permission Set Considerations*

| Approach | Considerations |
|---|---|
| Permission set | • Like profiles, but users can have more than one permission set.<br>• Permission set group can improve performance.<br>• Make sure the license limits are considered.<br>• Every user profile is automatically associated with a permission set. This permission set stores the profile's user, object, and field permissions.<br>• Can be used to assign access to Apex class methods.<br>• Salesforce will resolve "broken permissions," where access to a parent record already exists.<br>• Cannot assign Default App with a permission set. |

# Profile

Profiles define how a given user accesses objects and the data and what they can do within the Salesforce instance, as shown in Table 5-3. Like the permission set, a profile identifies the permissions that are assigned to a user. However, the user can only have one profile assigned.

***Table 5-3.*** *Profile Considerations*

| Approach | Major Considerations |
|---|---|
| Profile | • CRUD rights on record/field.<br>• View All or Modify All ignores sharing rules at an object level.<br>• Preferable to add View All Data or Modify All Data at org level.<br>• Field level available.<br>• Manage permissions in permission set groups with a muting permission set. |

The profile is used to assign page layouts, record types, custom apps, connected apps, and tab settings associated with a set of users. It also defines the field-level security for each object and the administrative setting and general user permissions for the Salesforce instance.

Beyond that, a profile assigns many of the system-level permissions including login IP range, Visualforce page access, external data access, named credentials, custom metadata type access, custom settings, flow access, service presence status access, and custom permissions. The profile also establishes the session settings, password policies, and login hours.

## Organization-Wide Defaults

Organization-wide defaults (OWDs) establish the sharing baseline for all standard and custom objects in the Salesforce instance, as shown in Table 5-4. The primary settings include **Controlled by Parent, Private, Public Read-Only, Public Read/Write, Public Read/Write/Transfer** *(for cases and leads)*, and **Public Full Access** and **View-Only** *(for campaigns)*.

***Table 5-4.*** *OWD Considerations*

| Approach | Major Considerations |
|---|---|
| Org-wide defaults | • Setting: Public Read/Write, Public Read, Controlled by Parent, and Private.<br>• The default level of access to records : Set to the most restrictive level required and then add permissions to add access to other users.<br>• OWD is the only way to restrict user access to a record.<br>• Settings can be changed but require sharing recalculated. |

Salesforce requires OWD settings for both internal and external users. External OWDs are a separate group of settings for external users. Salesforce uses the design to simplify sharing rule configuration and improve recalculation performance. External settings cannot be more permissive than internal settings.

## Role Hierarchy

Role hierarchy, OWD, and sharing settings are used to determine the levels of access users placed higher in the hierarchy will receive. Roles above their assigned role in the role hierarchy are allowed access to records and associated reports for data of users below them in the hierarchy. The "Grant Access Using Hierarchies" option can be disabled for a custom object. The role for the associated account record determines who has access to cases, contacts, and opportunities, regardless of who owns those specific records. Table 5-5 presents the major considerations of role hierarchy.

***Table 5-5.*** *Role Hierarchy Considerations*

| Approach | Major Considerations |
|---|---|
| Role hierarchy | • Allows managers to have the same access to records as subordinates regardless of OWD settings. |
| | • Org limit is 500 roles, but this can be increased by Salesforce. The best practice is to keep them under 25,000 for non-portal roles and 100,000 roles for portal roles. |
| | • Best practice is to limit to no more than ten levels of branches. |
| | • Peers to not guarantee access to each other's data: Peers require sharing rules, teams, or territory management. |
| | • Moving the user to another role requires sharing rule recalculation. |
| | • Custom objects have "Grant Access Using Hierarchies" to prevent inheriting access. |

**Note**    The role assigned with reporting acts differently. It allows the users in the role access, but not the senior role in the hierarchy.

**Important**    Spend the time to understand role hierarchy as it is the foundation of the entire sharing model.

## Sharing (Criteria and Ownership)

Sharing rules are used to create exceptions to your OWD settings, as shown in Table 5-6. The sharing rule extends access beyond the role hierarchy. There are two types of sharing rules: those based on record owner (ownership based) and those based on field values in the record (criteria based).

***Table 5-6.*** *Sharing Rule Considerations*

| Approach | Major Considerations |
|---|---|
| Sharing (criteria and ownership) | Ownership-based sharing (OBS) rules:<br>• Based on record owner only.<br>• Private contact records do not apply.<br>• Use case(s): Service needs access to sales data, but not in the role hierarchy, or peer access for those in the same role or territory or access to other groups (public groups, portals, roles, and territories).<br>Criteria-based sharing (CBS) rules:<br>• Sharing based on a field value (criteria) using the sharing record.<br>• Record ownership is NOT considered. |

**Note**    Sharing rules are not available if the OWD is set to Public Read/Write.

## Ownership-Based Sharing (OBS) Rules

An ownership-based sharing rule opens access to records owned by specific users. For example, a company's managers need to see records owned by managers in a different role hierarchy. The sharing rule could give the other role hierarchy manager access to the record owned by another manager using owner-based sharing.

## Criteria-Based Sharing (CBS) Rules

A criteria-based sharing rule opens access to records based on field values. For example, you have a custom object with a custom picklist field. A criteria-based sharing rule could share all records in which the field is set to a specific value with all managers in your organization.

**OBS Limits**    No more than 1,000 OBS rules per object.

**CBS Limits**   No more than 50 CBS rules per object. These limits are restrictive and must be considered. Salesforce can increase this limit, but the requirement must be justified and not solved with other options.

# Manual and Programmatic Sharing

Often, the business requirements related to sharing and visibility go beyond options available with ownership, permission sets, profiles, and sharing rules. When this happens, you will need to consider broad-based sharing such as teams and territories, or you will need to implement manual or programmatic sharing.

## Manual Sharing

Manual sharing is used to grant users access to specific records when other automated methods are not available or if the sharing is a one-off action required by the record owner or role hierarchy user.

**Note**   Manual sharing is available only in Salesforce Classic. Several AppExchange apps are available to add manual sharing in Lightning.

Care should be taken with manual sharing, as it can also grant access to a given record, including all of its associated records. For example, manually sharing an account record grants access to associated records in the opportunity and case objects. Salesforce limits manual sharing to (1) the record owner, (2) users higher in the role hierarchy (where it is allowed in OWD), and (3) a system administrator.

**Note**   Manually created share records are deleted when the record owner changes, including shares associated with related object records.

Manual sharing allows the record owner to share records with other users and a broad selection of group types, including **manager groups, manager subordinate groups, public groups, personal groups, roles, roles and subordinates, roles and internal subordinates, roles and internal and portal subordinates, territories, and territories and subordinates**.

## Programmatic or Apex-Managed Sharing

Apex-managed sharing allows developers to share records programmatically. Apex-managed sharing users can only use sharing with the "Modify All Data" permission. The sharing access is maintained across record owner changes. An Apex sharing reason is required to create an Apex sharing record. The Sharing reason is a developer note justifying the need for the apex sharing.

Table 5-7 presents the major considerations of both manual and programmatic sharing.

***Table 5-7.*** *Manual and Programmatic Considerations*

| Approach | Major Considerations |
|---|---|
| Manual and programmatic | Manual sharing:<br><br>• Record owners can give read and edit permissions to other users and groups of users.<br>• Manual sharing is removed each time the record owner changes. It does not add as it is already provided with the OWD.<br>• Manual shares can be created programmatically.<br>• The "row cause" uses "manual share."<br>• All share records with a row cause defined to "manual share" can be edited by the Share button (Classic only), even if created programmatically.<br><br>Programmatic or Apex-managed sharing:<br><br>• Programmatic sharing (Apex sharing) allows you to use code (Apex or other) to build sophisticated and dynamic sharing settings when it cannot be met by any other means.<br>• If created programmatically with the row cause description as "manual share," then the shared record is managed with the Share button. As such, it is deleted upon owner transfer.<br>• The "Modify All Data" permission is required to add, edit, or delete sharing that uses an Apex sharing reason.<br>• Deleting an Apex sharing reason will delete all sharing on the object that uses the reason.<br>• Objects are limited to ten Apex sharing reasons.<br>• Metadata API can create Apex sharing reasons. |

# Teams

Teams are a particular sharing process specifically for a limited set of Salesforce standard objects, including accounts, opportunities, and cases. The record owner assigns team members. Team members are defined into roles and given a level of access, such as read-only access or read/write access. Table 5-8 presents the major considerations of teams.

***Table 5-8.*** *Team Considerations*

| Approach | Major Considerations |
| --- | --- |
| Teams | • The group working on an account, opportunity, or case. |
| | • Gives read-only access or read/write access. |
| | • Owners, users higher in the hierarchy, and administrators can add team members. |
| | • Read/write access members can add other members. |
| | • Creating a team member creates two records: a team record and an associated share record. |
| | • Only one team per record (if more needed, use programmatic sharing). |
| | • A team object is not a first-class object, meaning you cannot create custom fields, validations rules, or triggers. |

**Note**   Users with a high level of access will have that access regardless of the access given in the team role.

# Territories

Territory management is an account object sharing system that grants access to accounts based on the characteristics of the account records. It is an advanced sharing strategy to extend further access to records not supported with other sharing options.

**Note**   Territory sharing only supports accounts and master-detail related objects.

A territory is a collection of accounts that gives a user access to the account record regardless of who owns the account record. The access level is configured to grant read, read/write, or owner-like access to the account records in that territory. Account records and users can exist in multiple territories. Territories exist in a hierarchy that can set up with nested levels. Account records are added to a territory either manually or with assignment rules that assign account records to territories automatically. Account record assignments can be added via an API.

The key benefits of territory management include (1) the ability to use account criteria to expand a private sharing model; (2) the support for complex and frequently changed organization structures; (3) the support for transferring users between territories, with the option to retain related opportunities; and 4) territory-based reporting for higher-level users. Table 5-9 presents the major considerations of territories.

***Table 5-9.*** *Territory Considerations*

| Approach | Major Considerations |
| --- | --- |
| Territories | A single dimensional hierarchy which can be structured by business units in a hierarchical structure to grant access. |
| | • When enabled, both the role hierarchy and territory hierarchy must be managed. |
| | • Territories exist only on account, opportunity, and respective master/detail children. |
| | • The best practice is to have no more than ten levels of branches in the hierarchy. |
| | • If the assignment rules or membership for territory is changed, sharing rules using that territory as the source will be recalculated. |
| | Account territory sharing rules (when enabled): |
| | • Only available for accounts marked with the territory. |

# Divisions

Division management is a field-level attribute that identifies which division a given record belongs. Divisions allow you to split your Salesforce data into logical business-level segments. This segmentation can greatly improve searches, reporting, and UI presentations. Division is also helpful in managing large data volumes that are segmenting across different parts of the business. Table 5-10 presents the major considerations of divisions.

***Table 5-10.*** *Division Considerations*

| Approach | Description and Major Considerations |
| --- | --- |
| Division | • Must be enabled with a Salesforce service ticket.<br>• Users are assigned a default division that is applied to newly created records.<br>• User permissions impact divisional separation and each time a division is created, it needs to be assigned to each user manually.<br>• Improves searching by limiting the result set to the division level.<br>• Reduces LDV issues by segmenting data into smaller subsets. |

# Access to Data Behind the Scenes

As a Salesforce architect, you should know how to grant users an appropriate level of access to the data in your Salesforce instance. Data access in Salesforce uses two main access categories: object-level access with field-level access and record-level access.

---

**Note**   Salesforce does not have a field-level sharing rule. Rather, Salesforce uses OWD permissions for field-level access.

---

Object-level access verifies a user has access to a particular object, the specific actions the user can perform, and the specific fields the user can see. Object-level access is managed via the user profile or the given permission set. Object-level access can restrict users with object permissions, such as "Read," "Create," "Edit," and "Delete," and field-level security to limit visibility. It can also open up access for users with object settings such as "View All" and "Modify All" object permissions.

Record-level access is called "sharing" in Salesforce. Record-level access determines which records a given user can see for a particular object. As shown in the preceding text, sharing uses organization-wide defaults, role hierarchy, sharing rules, manual sharing, programmatic sharing, teams, and territory hierarchy.

It is crucial to understand how Salesforce calculates and grants access because sharing record access with users can quickly become complicated and changing your sharing configuration impacts the performance of the system.

# Access Grants and Record Access Calculations

Salesforce determines record accessibility each time a user views a record to grant data visibility. Record access is granted using many different factors such as ownership, role hierarchy, sharing rules, implicit sharing, and so on. For enterprise-class Salesforce implementations, the sharing architecture is complex and requires extensive sharing calculations to maintain. Salesforce does not perform these calculations in real time. Instead, Salesforce calculates and populates a sharing record each time a record is changed.

Salesforce uses access grants to confirm the type and level of access a user has to specific object records. Access grant also specifies the sharing means responsible for providing the record access to the user, such as the sharing rule, teams, roles, and so on. There are four types of access grants:

- **Explicit Grants**: Where the record is shared directly with the user of the group

- **Group Membership Grant**: Based on membership

- **Inherited Grant**: Gained through the hierarchy

- **Implicit Grant**: Built-in sharing based on parent/child

# Salesforce Access Grants Are Stored in Three Different Tables

Salesforce grants access to records with three different tables: object record tables, sharing tables, and group maintenance tables. The record access calculation reviews the various sharing options to determine the required sharing records to be created in each of the three tables (objects). Let's look at each type in Table 5-11.

***Table 5-11.*** *Behind-the-Scenes Sharing and Group Tables*

| Table Type | Use of the Table Related to Sharing |
| --- | --- |
| Object record table | The object tables store the actual records for a specific object. The object indicates which user, group, or queue owns each record. |
| Sharing table | The sharing table stores the data that supports explicit and implicit grants. Most objects have an object sharing table. The exceptions include objects with Public Read/Write OWD, the detail side of a master-detail relationship, and select objects like activities and files. |
| Group maintenance table | The group maintenance tables store supporting group membership and inherited access grants. Supporting group membership and inherited access grants are created for each user, group, or queue aligned to the record. These grants are established in advance when you create or change the group (or role or territory) members. |

Salesforce uses the three tables to determine if the accessing user has the proper grant to gain access. Salesforce begins with the object record ownership. It then looks at the sharing table. It then looks at the group maintenance table. Salesforce uses SQL statements that are subsequently appended to find the access grant. If a grant is found, the additional SQL statements are not completed. This process uses the available resource efficiently. The SQL statement begins with matching the record ID in the object and object sharing table. If that does not find a response, the SQL statement is amended to expend the search in the object sharing and group maintenance tables using the user ID or group ID.

The granting method is different between the two processes. The first SQL statement uses sharing rows to grant access. The process checks if the user ID that is seeking access is listed within any row of the object's sharing table. The second SQL queries the group maintenance table, specifying who belongs to each group. These tables store membership data for every group, including system-defined groups. Salesforce creates two types of system-defined groups, role groups and RoleAndSubordinates groups. If the organization has external OWDs enabled, a third system-defined group, RoleAndInternalSubordinates, is created.

# The Impact of License on Security

Unlike standard Salesforce licenses, high-volume community users are not in access grant tables with sharing rules because they do not have roles or public groups. Only users with licenses that support roles are included in sharing rules.

**Licenses**: Full Sharing Model, High-Volume Portal (HVP), Chatter Free

- **Full Sharing** may not be turned on for all modules, but exists.

- **HVP** does NOT utilize the sharing model. Instead, it uses a foreign key (FK) between HVP and the account/contact lookup. Customer Community users are included as HVP licenses, not Partner Community and Community Plus licenses.

- **Chatter Free**: Collaboration-only, including Chatter, people, profiles, groups, files, chatter desktop, and limited Salesforce apps. No access to standard or custom object – so no sharing.

# Platform Security

Security within Salesforce is categorized into two levels:

1. **Application-Level Security**: Areas of security that can be managed, configured, and controlled at each Salesforce instance level, by any Salesforce administrator, and as per the security needs of the enterprise.

2. **Infrastructure-Level Security**: Areas of security at an infrastructure level of Salesforce, which is exclusively controlled and managed by Salesforce. Salesforce provides this level of security to all customers equally as part of their multi-tenant architecture offering. Individual Salesforce users or Salesforce administrators do not have access to this level of security and cannot modify or configure these security options.

Figure 5-2 illustrates the various security features at an application level as well as the security features managed by Salesforce at an infrastructure level.

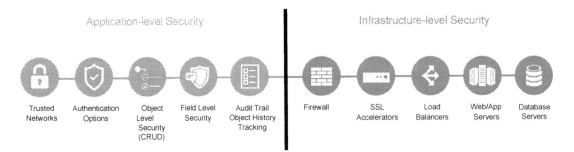

***Figure 5-2.*** *Salesforce Security Levels*

To stay within the scope of this book, we will focus only on application-level security. We will not cover infrastructure-level security since an architect, or any end user, does not have much control over Salesforce's infrastructure-level security.

For more details on infrastructure-level security, please refer to Salesforce's infrastructure and sub-processor level documentation available at `www.salesforce.com/content/dam/web/en_us/www/documents/legal/misc/salesforce-infrastructure-and-subprocessors.pdf`.

Although we will talk more in detail about each of the application-level security features, at a high level, application-level security features are as follows:

1. IP range restrictions and enforcement of VPN-based access

2. Multiple user authentication options

3. Organization-wide default settings

4. Sharing rules

5. Profiles and permission sets

6. Objects and field-level security

7. Field Audit Trail

8. Setup Audit Trail

9. Event monitoring

10. Data encryption

Regarding industry standard security and regulatory compliance and adherence, Salesforce has an exhaustive and ever-growing list of regulatory and security compliance certifications for its core platform and core products. Figure 5-3 illustrates a few of the essential regulatory compliance certifications that are covered by Salesforce out of the box.

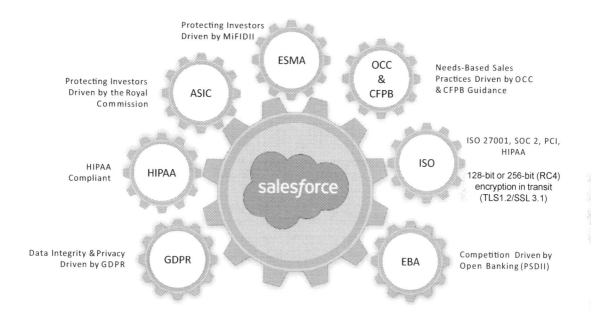

***Figure 5-3.*** *Salesforce Security and Regulatory Compliance and Adherence*

For more details, refer to `www.salesforce.com/content/dam/web/en_us/www/documents/legal/misc/salesforce-security-privacy-and-architecture.pdf`.

# Standard (Out-of-the-Box) Salesforce Audit and Event Monitoring Capabilities

Salesforce provides several standard audit and event monitoring tools as part of its security infrastructure. Let's look at a few crucial features.

## User Login Monitoring

Salesforce administrators can monitor all login attempts for their orgs and any enabled portals or communities activated from their managed orgs. The login history page shows up to 20,000 records of user logins for the past six months and can also be downloaded in a CSV or zip file format. The downloadable file can contain more than 20,000 records, which is a limitation when viewing the login history page, which can only show 20,000 records at any given time.

## Field History Tracking

With standard out-of-the-box capabilities, administrators can choose up to 20 fields for any standard or custom object to track and display the changes made to those fields in a history-related list of each object. Field history data is retained for 18 months from within the Salesforce org and up to 24 months when accessing the field history via the API.

## Monitor Configuration and Setup Changes

Audit trails and debug logs can be set up to track all changes to configuration or code made by any user of the org. The debug logs are categorized into nine categories of functionalities within Salesforce and can provide seven debug levels.

For more details about standard debug logs in Salesforce, please refer to https://help.salesforce.com/articleView?id=code_setting_debug_log_levels.htm&type=5.

## Transaction Monitoring and Policies

Transaction Security is a framework that intercepts real-time Salesforce events and applies appropriate actions and notifications based on security policies that an administrator has set up in the org. When any security policy is triggered, the administrator or any user can receive a notification.

# Data Encryption and Data Security Options

There are several methods to encrypt and secure data within Salesforce. Table 5-12 illustrates the description, use case, and pros and cons of different encryption methods available in Salesforce.

***Table 5-12.*** *Salesforce Data Encryption and Security Option*

| Option 1 | **Encrypted Custom Fields** |
| --- | --- |
| Description | Standard functionality: Field contents are encrypted via 128-bit AES encryption; user perm required to view the actual data within Salesforce; keys are manageable within Salesforce. |
| When to use | The exact data values are needed for the use of some functionality in salesforce.com and can be seen by select, logged-in end users. |
| Pros | • Encryption and key management are native functionality.<br>• Can be included in reports, search results, validation rules, Apex scripts. |
| Cons | • Not available for standard fields.<br>• No search, filtering, use in workflow, mobile.<br>• Limited to 175 characters.<br>• Fields still accessible by administrators.<br>• ECFs are always editable, regardless of whether the user has the correct perm. |
| **Option 2** | **Data Masking** |
| Description | Only part of a sensitive piece of data is stored in Salesforce (e.g., the last four digits of a SSN or credit card number). |
| When to use | Typically with call centers: Some part of the sensitive information is needed in the case management or identity verification process for a caller; end users should never know the whole value. |
| Pros | • Sensitive data is "de-sensitized" before it gets to Salesforce and rendered benign while still being able to support the business process. |
| Cons | • None, if this is the proper use case and the unmasked values can still support their needed function. |
| **Option 3** | **Data Transformation** |
| Description | Sensitive information is programmatically transformed before it is stored in Salesforce (e.g., credit ratings above 750 are translated to "Tier 1"). |
| When to use | Some derived meaning of the original values is needed in Salesforce. |
| Pros | • Sensitive data is "de-sensitized" before it gets to Salesforce and rendered benign while still being able to support the business process. |

*(continued)*

***Table 5-12.*** (*continued*)

| Cons | • If the transformation changes often, this approach can present additional work to change the algorithm. ECFs are always editable, regardless of whether the user has the correct perm. |
| --- | --- |
| **Option 4** | **Storing a Hashed Value in Salesforce** |
| Description | Sensitive data is hashed to a benign value by the customer before being stored in salesforce.com. |
| When to use | The hashed value is needed for integration or to otherwise tie information in Salesforce back to the information stored elsewhere; users and business processes do not ever need to see the real values. |
| Pros | • Customer can fully control/maintain the hash on their infrastructure.<br>• Sensitive data never exists in Salesforce in any manner. |
| Cons | • Requires implementation on customer infrastructure (hashing agent, hardware).<br>• Real values are not leveraged via any Salesforce functionality. |
| **Option 5** | **Mashups** |
| Description | Sensitive data remains inside the customer network or other approved platforms; UI rendered as needed using an iframe; data is never transmitted to or stored in Salesforce. |
| When to use | Users only need to temporarily view sensitive data in the context of the business processes and screens implemented in Salesforce. |
| Pros | • Data never leaves the customer or secure network/platform.<br>• The customer has ultimate control of and responsibility for who sees the data and how they see it. |
| Cons | • Real values are not leveraged via any Salesforce functionality.<br>• Can require SSO or additional changes to these systems to be readily frame-able.<br>• Usability and page load performance can take a hit.<br>• The customer is fully responsible for DR, failover, scalability, performance, and so on. |

*(continued)*

***Table 5-12.*** (*continued*)

| Option 6 | Web Service Callout |
|---|---|
| Description | Sensitive data remains inside the customer network or other approved platforms; data only rendered as needed using Visualforce (to guarantee it is not persisted in Salesforce). |
| When to use | The system storing the sensitive data has an externally callable web service and not a suitable mashup UI. |
| Pros | • The customer has ultimate control of and responsibility for who sees the data and how they see it.<br>• Possibly the best UI/UX. |
| Cons | • The callout requires a custom in-line Visualforce component or page.<br>• Real values are not leveraged via any Salesforce functionality.<br>• Can require SSO or additional changes to these systems to be readily frame-able.<br>• Usability and page load performance can take a hit.<br>• The customer is fully responsible for DR, failover, scalability, performance, and so on. |
| Option 7 | Encryption Appliance/DRO |
| Description | An appliance whose primary function is to encrypt outbound data sits inside the customer network; all data passed over the Internet is encrypted before transmission. |
| When to use | The loss of functionality/limitations with ECFs is not acceptable to the customer, and they are willing to host a solution. |
| Pros | • Supported product (nee Navajo, not GA).<br>• Data is fully encrypted when it gets to the Salesforce servers. |
| Cons | • Additional hardware, setup, administration, and maintenance resources and costs.<br>• Customer/partner is fully responsible for DR, failover, scalability, performance, and so on.<br>• Some Salesforce functionality is still lost. |

# Salesforce Shield

Although Salesforce provides a multitude of security controls and features out of the box as part of its product licenses, Salesforce also has a dedicated product for enhanced security requirements called Shield. Salesforce Shield addresses the need to protect, monitor, and retain critical Salesforce data via platform encryption (for data at rest), event monitoring (with Transaction Security), and Field Audit Trail. Hence, Salesforce Shield includes three core services:

- Platform encryption
- Event monitoring with Transaction Security
- Field Audit Trail

## Platform Encryption

Shield platform encryption leverages an HSM-based key management service and AES encryption standards with 256-bit keys. With this level of encryption, an enterprise can encrypt any sensitive data at rest across the entire Salesforce org. The main distinction between standard Salesforce encryption and Shield platform encryption is that the Shield platform encrypted fields are available with most field types. Additionally, encrypted fields are searchable and can be used within any Salesforce automation tool such as workflow rules, validation rules, and so on.

You can learn more here:

`https://help.salesforce.com/articleView?id=security_pe_overview.htm&type=5`

## Event Monitoring

Shield's event monitoring capability enables an enterprise to monitor detailed performance, security, and usage across the Salesforce org. Shield tracks login history, transaction security, and event logs. Each interaction is tracked and accessible via the API. Event monitoring data can be also imported into any data visualization or application monitoring tool like Einstein Analytics or Splunk or New Relic.

Learn more here: `https://trailhead.salesforce.com/content/learn/modules/event_monitoring`.

## Field Audit Trail

With Field Audit Trail, you can retain data history for forensic-level compliance and more significant operational insights into your business. Field Audit Trail available with Shield allows you to track up to 60 fields for each object of Salesforce, compared to the standard Salesforce audit trail, only allowing 20 fields to be tracked for any object. The field tracking history can be retained for up to 10 years using Shield.

Learn more here: `https://help.salesforce.com/articleView?id=field_audit_trail.htm&type=5`.

# Security for External User Experiences and Salesforce Portals

In terms of security for external user interaction via Salesforce communities, Salesforce provides the following options out of the box.

## Clickjack Protection in Communities

This feature secures the user's browser interaction by disallowing any browser behavior that redirects the user from Salesforce to unauthorized or malicious websites.

## Cross-Site Scripting (XSS) Prevention

Salesforce implements the Content Security Policy (CSP) standard, which is a W3C industry standard, allowing Salesforce to control the source of every content that can be loaded onto the community pages. Salesforce provides two different levels of CSP security, depending on the level of security vs. content flexibility needed.

# Using Groups to Manage Access and Visibility

A group is a collection that can include individual users, other groups, or all the users in a particular role or territory. It can also contain the associated subordinate users in the role or territory hierarchy. Groups, by themselves, do not affect access and visibility. Instead, groups are used to improve sharing by creating a collection of users to be used by the sharing rules.

Groups also can select subordinates in a role, so it traverses the hierarchy in the opposite direction of sharing related to role hierarchy. This feature is quite handy for granting access to an extended group of users. Groups use role hierarchy to identify users to include in the collection. The users are identified by member type. The following member types are available: users, public groups, roles, roles and subordinates, roles and internal subordinates, portal roles, internal and portal subordinates, portal roles and subordinates, Customer Portal users, partner users, and personal groups. Table 5-13 presents the major considerations of public groups.

***Table 5-13.*** *Public Group Considerations*

| Approach | Major Considerations |
| --- | --- |
| Public groups | • Collection of users, roles, and territories that have functions in common. |
| | • Groups can consist of |
| | • Users, Customer Portal users, partner users |
| | • Roles, roles and internal subordinates, roles and internal and portal subordinates |
| | • Portal roles, portal roles and subordinates |
| | • Territories and territories and subordinates |
| | • No more than five nested public groups allowed. |
| | • No more than 100,000 public groups. |
| | • Groups plus sharing rules are needed for data access. |
| | • Grant Access Using Hierarchies can be used to support limiting role access to sensitive data. |

**Note**   **Personal groups** are intended only to create and manually add to given records they want to be shared with a group.

# Implicit Sharing Can Impact Record Sharing

Many sharing behaviors are built into the Salesforce design. This kind of sharing is called implicit sharing. It is not configured; it is defined and used by the system to support collaboration among different users. Implicit sharing automatically happens and cannot be changed or overcome. Parent and child implicit sharing are described as follows.

**Parent implicit sharing** gives read-only access to account records when a given user has access to a related record of the parent account. It applies for all records in the contacts, opportunities, and cases associated with that account record. This grant happens for all users with shared access to the child records; they do not have to own the child record.

Additionally, the privileged user will also see the account name in the shared related objects, but not the account details. The name visibility rolls up to the parent account as well. This implicit share happens on all other objects, including custom objects. The sharing table automatically saves all users with the sharing value with a RowCause equal to "ImplicitParent."

**Child implicit sharing** gives access to the child records (contact, opportunity, and case objects) of a parent account record for the owner of the related account record. This implicit share is carried to both account sharing rules and account team access. If the parent account owner is changed, all of the implicit shares need to be recalculated. The "Controlled by Parent" feature removes this implicit sharing.

# Community Sharing for External Users

Sharing information to external users extends the Salesforce instance to a large group of users. Creating deliberate sharing protocols will keep your information secure. External users are users, including authenticated website users, Chatter external users, community users, Customer Portal users, high-volume portal users, partner portal users, and Service Cloud Portal users. It can also include guest users and unauthenticated users. This section reviews different ways to manage the security of your instance.

# External Organization-Wide Defaults

**External organization-wide defaults** facilitate the support for different sharing settings for internal and external users. External OWDs can simplify sharing rules and speed up sharing calculations. The external OWD is limited to a subset of objects, including account, contact, case, opportunity, lead, asset, campaign, individual, order, user, and custom objects.

External OWD must be equal to or more restrictive than Internal OWD. External OWD settings include Controlled by Parent, Private, Public Read-Only, and Public Read/Write. Sharing rules can extend the sharing model but are limited to 50 sharing rules per object. Sharing is ownership based by default. Sharing sets are used to give access to records owned by others.

## Sharing Sets

A sharing set grants access to external users associated with a record using either the user's account or contact ID. Sharing sets are only available for external users.

Sharing sets work differently than other Salesforce sharing methodologies. The sharing approach utilizes the created community user derived from a contact record connected to an account. Remember how to create a community user? A sharing set uses these variables: User.ContactID and Contact.AccountID. A sharing set creates the sharing table entry based on the assigned variable.

Sharing sets are limited to the core standard objects and custom objects. The option to create a sharing set is only available for custom objects that are related to a contact or account. The external OWD for the object must be private.

## Share Groups (for Internal Users)

High Volume Portal (HVP) users do not have roles and cannot be added to the role hierarchy. Thus, the sharing of records owned by HVP users needs a unique sharing tool. This tool is the share group. A share group is associated with a sharing set, and there can only be one share group per sharing set. The grant creates full read/write access.

## External Role Hierarchy

External users do not have the same role hierarchy as standard Salesforce users. The scope and type of role are controlled by the license type used. Let's look at the license options and the related role options.

**Customer Community** licenses do not support roles, and role-based sharing will not work. Public groups and manual sharing are not allowed.

**Customer Community Plus** licenses have three role types: user, manager, and executive. Public groups and manual sharing are allowed.

**Partner Community** licenses have three role types: user, manager, and executive. Public groups and manual sharing are allowed.

Here are a few considerations related to external roles:

- Community user hierarchy is linked through an associated account record or ownership.

- Role hierarchy visibility allows reporting and regular roll-up views.

- External account roles are created with the creation of the first user associated with the account.

- Community Plus and Partner Community have one default role. Up to three roles are available.

- By default, 50,000 roles are creatable, with more available if needed.

# Making Optimal Decisions

This chapter presented many different concepts related to platform security, sharing, and visibility. Table 5-14 is designed to give you a series of access and visibility requirements with potential optimal solutions.

***Table 5-14.*** *Potential Optimal Solutions for Various Security, Sharing, and Visibility Scenarios*

| Requirement | Environment Settings | Solution(s) |
|---|---|---|
| Two in a box: A role-based user wants access to another role to assist | Private OWD, role based | Ownership-based sharing rule: Edge case, trusted user set. |
| User needs access to different department data (records) | Private OWD, role based | Ownership-based sharing rule: Common use case, other teams needing access. |
| Core team (a group of different roles) on account | Private OWD, role based | Teams: Only one team per account needed. |
| Manager access to subordinates | Private OWD, role based | Role hierarchy: Supports access to subordinate records. |

*(continued)*

***Table 5-14.*** (*continued*)

| Requirement | Environment Settings | Solution(s) |
|---|---|---|
| Limited privilege: The team cannot modify team member | Team button access | Remove button from the layout. |
| Buddy support: Allow access to the same profile | Private OWD, role based | Teams  (notwithstanding the preceding text). |
| Add specialist to an opportunity | Private OWD, role based | Teams: Manually added.Trigger: If always known. |
| Two teams need access to the same account | Private OWD, role based | Territory management: Account team is too granular. |
| Separate unit needs access to account for specific opportunity team. Unit is a shared resource | Private OWD, role based | Territory management: Unit of users is supported with a sub-territory if TM is used for teams. |
| One-off-basis access to account | Private OWD, role based | Teams: A native aspect of teams. |
| Department needs access to given business unit data | Private OWD, role based | Ownership-based sharing rule:Sharing rule using a group, a branch of role, or a role and subordinate. |
| VIP customer directly managed by a manager and editable by the manager and above | Private OWD, role based | Ownership and role hierarchy. |
| Only the manager can set account as VIP customer | Private OWD, role based | OWD private, profile with RecType. |
| Only the given actor can set up and enable product | Private OWD | OWD: Permission set to add, create, and edit products. |
| Only active products available for purchase by the customer | Community | OWD private, create PB, share using role. |

(*continued*)

***Table 5-14.***  (*continued*)

| Requirement | Environment Settings | Solution(s) |
|---|---|---|
| Customer can view own account and contact | Community | Customer can access their own account and contact records, based on implicit sharing. |
| Customer can create and view cases | Community | Add the Case tab and set visibility to read, create, and edit with permission or permission set. |
| Customer can view the shipment status | Community | Add the Shipment__c tab and set visibility to read with permission or permission set. Update Manage Community for tab. |
| Only a given actor can  create and manage leads and convert into opportunities | Private OWD, role based | Permission set (convert leads permission) with permission for account, contact, and opportunity. |
| Lead only visible to the owner | Private OWD, role based | OWD private |
| The lead owner can change the "Visible to All" flag to allow other CRs to manage | Private OWD, role based | OWD on lead is private.Profile.Criteria-based sharing rule on field. |
| Sr. user wants a monthly summary report on shipment orders for all regions | Private OWD, role based | Role above shipment owners, running user settings. |
| (a) Internal case created by an employee (b) Internal case visible only to VP and CIO and above (c) Internal case not visible by manager | Private OWD, role based | OWD private.Employee = create and edit.Manager = no access.VP/CIO = read. |
| When needed, given actor involves partner manager or partner user on opportunity | Partner Community | External OWD = private.On-demand can use manual sharing of opportunity. |

(*continued*)

***Table 5-14.*** (*continued*)

| Requirement | Environment Settings | Solution(s) |
|---|---|---|
| Partner company wants to collaborate among partner teams on deals, shipments, and update opportunities owned by any member of the partner | Partner Community | External OWD.Create partner roles. Create a sharing set for a partner company and partner team. |
| Global partner has franchises. The owner wants to see all customers managed by franchises | Partner Community | External OWD.Create partner roles. Create a sharing set for a partner company and partner team. |
| All partner managers can see opportunities, cases, and shipments | Partner Community | External OWD.Create partner roles. Create a sharing set for a partner company and partner team. |
| The internal actor creates opportunities they manage and wants to share with an external partner | Partner Community | External OWD = private.On-demand can use manual sharing of opportunity. |
| Shipment data for a select customer must not be visible except for sr. leadership | Partner Community | Create a record type.Change profiles to limit/remove access to shipment object. Add permission set for sr. leadership. |
| Partner managers in the United States to manage all users in their partner account | Partner Community | Enable Partner Super User access; assign to individual users; add the "Portal Super User" permission to a permission set. |
| Global internal user can create and freeze users | System admin | Manage user "permission" or set up as delegated admin. |
| Seasonally allow a partner to support cases of any customer | Partner Community | External OWD.Create partner roles. Create a sharing set for a partner company and partner team. |

(*continued*)

***Table 5-14.*** (*continued*)

| Requirement | Environment Settings | Solution(s) |
|---|---|---|
| User should be able to share opportunity in the sibling role for JUST ONE WEEK | Internal user | Criteria-based sharing ruleusing time-based trigger. |
| Sr. user wants to be able to collaborate with individual customers | Community | Chatter. |
| A senior user wants to collaborate with an external partner, individual, or business customer | Internal user | Private groups and Chatter. |
| The price book should be visible to the customer via the community. Limit other views of price book | Community | OWD = No access.Sharing rule. |
| Restrict access to cases created internally to internal users. No access to the customer portal | Community | Remove external OWD to price books. |
| Support wants to share a case with sales agents, but not sales management | Internal | Sharing using private group.Remove hierarchy check. |
| Sales user allowed to delete opportunities they own if less than $100,000. | Internal | Validation rule on an opportunity. |
| Sr. leader wants access to CASES for customer with the sum of OPPORTUNITIES greater than $100,000. | Internal | Criteria-based sharing rulewith opportunity roll-up value. |

**Note**    The solutions are notional, as the full details of the scenarios are unknown.

# Chapter Summary

In this chapter, we learned

- The three pillars Salesforce uses to stay ahead of the ongoing cyberthreats, including nail the basics, engineering, and business agility

- The security attributes Salesforce employs to safeguard data access, sharing, and visibility

- The building blocks used to create a scalable and efficient security model, including an under-the-covers look at the system-level share tables and group maintenance tables used to manage sharing grants

- How Salesforce uses ever-widening sharing features to expand access to business data from permission sets to territories

- The impact of licenses and internal and external users on sharing within the Salesforce instance

- That Salesforce provides both application-level and infrastructure-level security features

- The eight options available to encrypt and secure your data

- The features available with Salesforce Shield

- The security available for Salesforce communities

- How to use groups to streamline access and visibility

- The types of implicit sharing grants created automatically by Salesforce

- How to use external OWD, external role hierarchy, sharing sets, and share groups to extend sharing to external users

- How to use the different sharing options to make good design decisions

# CHAPTER 6

# Salesforce Integration Architecture

Salesforce integration includes several disciplines to provide comprehensive and scalable technical solutions that meet end-to-end integration requirements and best practices. You must understand the capabilities, patterns, concepts, and tools available and used within the Salesforce platform.

The chapter reviews four primary integration architecture areas: **integration strategy**, **options, design patterns**, and **appropriate use**.

In this chapter, we cover

1. The key considerations used when designing the integration strategy for cloud-to-cloud, cloud-to-on-premise, and multi–Salesforce org integration scenarios.

2. When to use Canvas apps vs. integrating with Heroku apps vs. integrating using Salesforce Connect vs. integrating using a middleware vs. integration using external services

3. The various integration patterns and justification of their use as part of the overall integration architecture

4. Which integration to use when and how to justify the appropriate integration strategy and integration patterns

© Dipanker Jyoti and James A. Hutcherson 2021
D. Jyoti and J. A. Hutcherson, *Salesforce Architect's Handbook*, https://doi.org/10.1007/978-1-4842-6631-1_6

# Integration Strategies

During the system design phase and throughout the system expansion, an architect needs to review, evaluate, and select the most appropriate systems integration strategy. It is more than just knowing the API protocols and patterns. It recognizes both how integration design is accomplished and how the integrations are performed.

Integration architecture must align with the existing IT environment, the business objectives, and the solution capabilities to maximize the business outcomes. Integration architecture should not follow industry frameworks for the sake of consistency. Instead, the architecture should "mix and match" the optimal integration choices to meet the business requirements. The overall business value of the integration choice must be considered. The integration architecture should support the various use cases required to support the current and future requirements.

Figure 6-1 may initially appear overwhelming, as it shows the many integration features available within Salesforce. Refer back to this figure as you read the following sections to see how they interact with the environment.

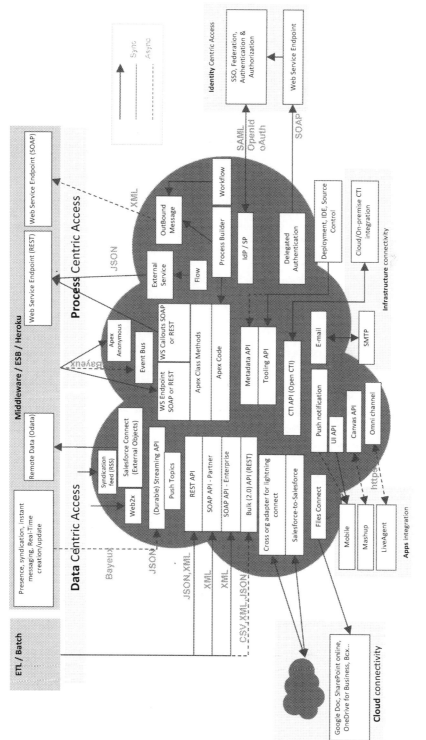

**Figure 6-1.** *Mix and Match Integration in Salesforce*

# Integration Architecture Use Case

An integration architecture should support many different approaches, such as cloud-to-cloud (i.e., Salesforce t -Salesforce), cloud-to-on-premise (i.e., Salesforce to ERP), on-premise-to-on-premise (i.e., ERP to on-premise EDW), and special integration (i.e., middleware or tools). Let us look at each integration design in more detail.

**Point-to-point integration** uses some sort of process or code to allow data sharing between two different systems. The developed process simplifies the data transformation and the method of transferring the data:

- Each system is connected to or integrated with every other system with direct integration points.

- It is easy to implement for a few systems.

- It becomes more challenging to scale as the number of systems increases.

**Hub-and-spoke integration** uses one connection point with a central "hub," which arbitrates requests, decoupling senders and receivers of data:

- Each system is linked to a centralized hub.

- All data transfer is performed through the hub.

- It is easy to design and implement a hub-and-spoke design.

- Each hub architecture is proprietary.

- The hub presents a single point of failure.

- It is limited in that it does not support large transaction volumes.

**Enterprise Service Bus (ESB)** is a service-oriented methodology to connect numerous applications, data sources, and API to orchestrate the integration and interconnection of systems. There are several different ESB systems on the market. Salesforce uses MuleSoft as its ESB system:

- The bus uses a distributed services architecture.

- Employs distributed adapters.

- Highly scalable.

- Significantly higher cost than a few point-to-point integrations.

Figure 6-2 presents an example of various design requirements.

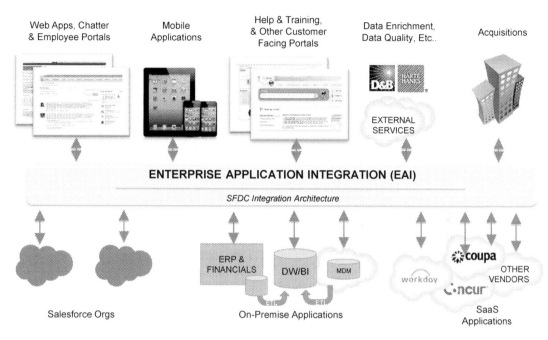

***Figure 6-2.*** *Scalable Architecture*

Figure 6-2 shows how an architect must synchronize our salesforce.com orgs, on-premise application, and cloud-based business applications with a focus on the integration needs:

- **Internal Web Applications**: The ability to publish data services for internal consumption (e.g., internal web apps, internal mobile apps, etc.)

- **Internal Mobile Applications**: Ability to provide data services to internal mobile applications

- **Customer-Facing Web Applications**: Ability to provide data services to customer-facing web applications such as help and training, web store, and other portals

- **Data Enrichment and Quality**: Ability to interface with external services for data enrichment and data quality

- **Acquisitions**: Ability to quickly integrate data from systems across organizations, such as different divisions, branches, and companies

Table 6-1 presents a few integration use cases that are common in the enterprise.

***Table 6-1.*** *Common Integration Use Cases*

| Use Case | Description |
|---|---|
| Salesforce to DMZ | A Salesforce message is relayed to a DMZ (demilitarized zone) service endpoint that could be a firewall, services gateway appliance, or reverse proxy. The architecture must support DMZ layer access to authenticate with internal resources such as whitelisted IPs, two-way SSL, and basic HTTP. |
| DMZ to on-premise | An Enterprise Service Bus (ESB) can handle any orchestration, transformation, and mediation services required by the On-Premise System. The ESB relays the external message through the DMZ to the trusted on-premise system. |
| Salesforce to SOA web services | An Enterprise Service Bus (ESB) can push a message to an SOA infrastructure such as enterprise data and business services. Many organizations provide SOA web services to reduce time and costs and promote reuse of standard integrations into legacy systems. |
| Salesforce to on-premise database | On-premise database access allows Salesforce to read data from enterprise database systems in real time or near real time. Often this data is available from an enterprise data warehouse (EDW) or an operational data store. This use case supports external objects in Salesforce. |
| On-premise to Salesforce | Often organizations do not have ESB middleware to handle orchestration, transformation, and mediation services to and from systems. Instead, they rely on point-to-point integration from the on-premise application to Salesforce. For this type of Salesforce web service call-in integration, the authentication flow must be addressed. |

*(continued)*

***Table 6-1.*** (*continued*)

| Use Case | Description |
| --- | --- |
| Batch data | Batch data integrations are often the fastest way to get data in and out of Salesforce. An ETL (extract, transform, and load) solution will support batch data integrations. ETL moves large data volumes using Bulk API in Salesforce. Commercial tools are also available to support this use case. |
| Data backup and archive | This use case is often overlooked. The architect's responsibility is to provide a backup solution for your Salesforce data into a replicated or archive copy. It is vital to create a solution that uses Change Data Capture rather than continually backing up the entire data volume. |
| Data migration to Salesforce | An ETL solution can move data in and out of your data environment. The ETL tool can stage data imported into Salesforce (such as accounts, contacts, and opportunities) from the EDW. The preceding batch processing pattern can be considered. |
| Multi-org | Organizations that have multiple Salesforce orgs will often require integration between the various Salesforce orgs. Salesforce offers a ***Salesforce to Salesforce*** tool to support this use case. Alternatively, one Salesforce org integrates with another org using REST web service integration. This use case often requires the synchronization of data across the various Salesforce environments. A hub-and-spoke design may also be an excellent way to provide read-only access across your environment. |
| Salesforce–o external web services | A point-to-point integration use case is easily supported within Salesforce. That said, the more that Salesforce is used as a hub of integration activity, the more time is required to spend building, maintaining, and troubleshooting. It is not best practice to use Apex as your primary integration technology. Instead, these types of use case requirements should be accomplished with middleware, if possible. |
| Integration as a service | Integration as a service offers cloud-to-cloud integration. While not technically an ESB, Integration as a service provides solutions tailored explicitly for Salesforce and other popular SaaS vendors. Integration as a service can reduce the time to build and deploy an integration instead of using on-premise ESB solutions. The cloud service bus can handle service transformation, routing, mediation, and error handling for other cloud-based endpoints. |

# Integration Levels

The integration levels specify how tightly coupled the integrated systems are between the user interface, application logic, and data. The user interface presents information from an external system in the Salesforce applications. Solutions using mashups and Canvas applications are tightly coupled to the user interface. The application logic leverages interfaces, such as APIs, to interact with external data and business processes. REST- and SOAP-based API solutions are examples. The data integration level manages the extraction, transformation, and loading of data between data stores.

The connection between the MVC Salesforce model and the types of integrations is shown in Figure 6-3. The view uses Visualforce pages, web controls, sites, and Canvas apps to support user interface integration. The controller uses Visualforce controllers, Lightning Aura and LWC, Apex, and web service APIs to support business logic integration. The model uses OData and metadata and web service APIs to access data.

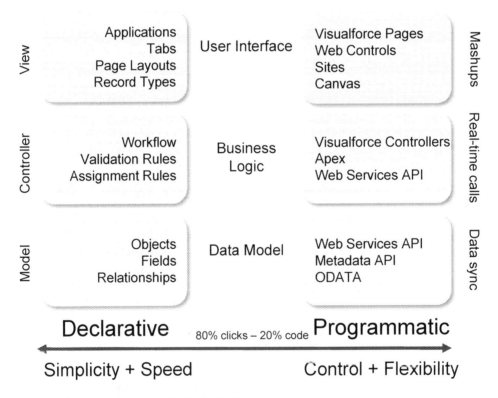

***Figure 6-3.*** *Integration Levels in Salesforce*

The Salesforce architecture is designed to support integration using both declarative and programmatic services. The declarative framework can support most integration processes with powerful tools such as platform events, flows, workflows, Process Builder, and external services. Figure 6-3 identifies available features to support all three MVC layers with both declarative and programmatic options.

# Integration Layer

Salesforce has a rich set of integration APIs across all different integration layers. These layers span across the environment, including security, user interface, application logic, data, and infrastructure. Table 6-2 aligns each layer to the various Salesforce capabilities.

***Table 6-2.*** *Salesforce Integration Capabilities*

| Integration Layer | Layer Example | Salesforce Capability |
|---|---|---|
| Security | Authentication mechanisms | Support for SAML 1.0 and 2.0. Support for OpenID Connect (based on OAuth 2.0). Support for SCIM. |
| User interface | Screens exposed to the end users | To view/interact with data that resides outside of the cloud, you can leverage browser integration through mashup with own UI, mashups with custom UI, contextual links, tabs, and Canvas (internal users only). Other available OOB tools also include Lightning for Outlook and Lightning for Gmail. |
| Application layer | Business logic before, after, or during data display | It uses inbound and outbound callouts. Both REST and SOAP web services can be custom developed using Apex. Some applications installed via AppExchange could also be considered part of this category. |

*(continued)*

***Table 6-2.*** (*continued*)

| Integration Layer | Layer Example | Salesforce Capability |
|---|---|---|
| Data | Data model includes batch and real time | Salesforce has native out-of-the-box available APIs: REST API, SOAP API (enterprise and partner), Bulk API, Streaming API. Salesforce also supports CDC and platform events. A Pub/Sub (publish and subscribe) event subscription and publication service based on the Bayeux Protocol and CometD and OData V2.0 and V4.0 are also supported. Data replication is supported through Salesforce to Salesforce, Heroku Connect, and MuleSoft, plus a wide range of third-party middleware (such as Informatica, Jitterbit, etc.). |
| Infrastructure | Omni-channel connectivity | Supporting channels such as email and CTI using Open CTI. |

**Note**   Any developed point-to-point connection, however, would still need to build mechanisms for exception handling, retry, and so on.

# API Protocol Types

As discussed in Chapter 2, integrations refer to the connections made between external systems and Salesforce. Salesforce takes an API-first approach to building all its features on the Salesforce platform. With this approach, virtually every feature and the underlying data within Salesforce can be accessed directly by another system or application without using a Graphical User Interface (GUI). This approach allows us to connect all the non-Salesforce systems with Salesforce and vice versa, using one of Salesforce's many APIs. Among the most common API protocols supported by Salesforce are

- REST API

- SOAP API

- Bulk API

- Streaming API

These four APIs together form the basis for Data APIs that allow you to manage data changes in Salesforce and other systems. There are other APIs that are available from Salesforce, which we will discuss later in this chapter. These four API types are the essential APIs that most architects will need to be intimately familiar with, so let's discuss this a bit further to identify the appropriate integration between Salesforce and any other systems listed in the system landscape.

**REST API** is a lightweight but robust web service based on RESTful principles. Salesforce exposes all of its functionalities and data in either XML or JSON format using REST API over a secure HTTP-based web transport protocol. REST API supports the ability to create, read, update, and delete records. It also allows support search or query of any data in Salesforce from an external system. You can retrieve object metadata and access information about governor limits about your Salesforce instance from an external application. Due to its lightweight writing style and simple request and response framework, it's the best choice to build and integrate mobile apps and websites.

**SOAP API** is a formal and tightly written web service protocol based on an industry standard protocol. It is a powerful web service that exposes Salesforce data only via a tightly typed Web Services Description Language (WSDL) file that strictly defines all the parameters for accessing data using this API. The WSDL file is in the format of an XML file; and, as such, SOAP API only supports XML file formats. Almost all the Salesforce functionalities available via SOAP are also available via REST API. Still, most architects use SOAP API due to the formal and consistent writing style and the mandatory use of a WSDL file as the formal contract between Salesforce and the external systems. It allows uniformity and structure to the interactions between Salesforce and the external systems.

There are two WSDL types, Enterprise and Partner:

- **Enterprise WSDL**: Intended primarily for customers:

  - The Enterprise WSDL is strongly typed and easy to use.

  - The Enterprise WSDL is tied to Salesforce's specific configuration.

  - The Enterprise WSDL changes are made to an organization's Salesforce configuration.

- **Partner WSDL**: Intended primarily for partners:

  - The Partner WSDL is loosely typed and more challenging to use.

  - The Partner WSDL can be used to communicate with any configuration of Salesforce.

  - The Partner WSDL is static and does not change if modifications are made to an organization's Salesforce configuration.

Due to this reason, SOAP API is excellent for use with system-to-system integrations, which don't change dynamically and need to remain durable for their lifecycle.

**Bulk API** is a specialized API built based on the same principles as REST API. It is primarily intended for loading and searching large volumes of data within a single transaction. Large volumes of data can mean 50,000 records or more. Bulk API services are asynchronous, meaning you can submit a request, continue with your work, and receive the Bulk API results later whenever they are ready. This approach frees up Salesforce and the end user from merely waiting on the results of processing large volumes of data. Instead, Bulk API runs in the background while the end user works on other items within Salesforce. Salesforce currently has two versions of Bulk API, Bulk API 1.0 and Bulk API 2.0. Both versions do the same thing in handling large volumes of data, but my recommendation is to use Bulk API 2.0 because it is much easier to use in writing the integration code. Bulk API is mainly used to perform tasks involving large volumes of data, such as during initial data migration from a legacy application into Salesforce.

**Streaming API** is a specialized API that operates based on the recently popular industry standard publish and subscribe (Pub/Sub) messaging model. In the Pub/Sub model, notifications are set up to look for data changes. When changes in the data set occur, a notification message is sent to all the notification subscribers. A notification set up to listen for data changes is known as a "topic." Subscribers of the Pub/Sub messaging service can be any system or application that subscribes to any number of topics created within Salesforce using Streaming API. The notifying message can contain the details of the data changes or any other message relevant to the systems that subscribed to that topic. Streaming API is also asynchronous. It significantly reduces the number of API requests needed between Salesforce and other systems by eliminating the need for constant polling between multiple systems to identify data changes. Streaming API is excellent for integrations where systems need to interact with each other only when a data change occurs in one system. It is also an excellent integration option for building and managing decoupled applications that need to work synchronously and efficiently with other systems, without constantly polling system changes.

At this point, it is vital to emphasize that all integrations require authentication to access Salesforce. The SOAP API authentication works a bit differently from all the other APIs. SOAP API uses a "login()" method in its first integration call to establish a secure session with the other system before exposing or extracting any data. We will discuss the various authentication methods in Chapter 7. During the FUSIAOLA analysis, it is essential to identify which systems need to integrate and which integration technique is most appropriate for the integrations. Often this exercise leads to a well-evaluated justification of investing in integration tools such as an Enterprise Service Bus (ESB) or whether an Extract-Load-Transform (ETL) tool is appropriate or not.

# Middleware

Middleware is deployed to reduce the effort required to integrate different systems. It is a layer created for communications between two systems. This layer makes it possible for two systems to communicate without a direct connection. Middleware plays a critical role in a distributed environment.

Middleware comes in many forms, including APIs, enterprise application integration, point-to-point, data integration (ETL), message-oriented middleware (MOM), content centric (Pub-Sub), object request brokers (ORBs), and the Enterprise Service Bus (ESB). Next, we will discuss a few popular middleware tools in Salesforce.

## Point-to-Point

In a point-to-point integration model, a unique connector component is implemented for each pair of applications or systems that must communicate. This connector handles all data transformation, integration, and any other messaging-related services that must take place between only the specific pair of components it is designed to integrate. This connector would typically handle challenging tasks such as

- Queueing mechanisms

- Retry mechanisms

- Exception handling

- Handling different batch sizes

- Providing a secure way to link cloud-based solutions with on-premise or private cloud solutions

Point-to-point integrations work well with simple scenarios when there is a minimal set of connected systems. But with complex scenarios where there are several connected systems and there's potential to add more in the future, the number of point-to-point connections required to create a comprehensive integration architecture increases exponentially – and with that, the cost of development and maintenance.

Each of these point-to-point connectors must be separately developed and maintained or, in some cases, even purchased at a high cost from a vendor, across system version changes, scalability changes, underlying data model changes, and more.

Custom-developed connectors are, by nature, less reliable and more expensive to maintain. This development requires the availability of a dedicated development team.

## ETL: Extract, Transform, and Load

ETL middleware tools support the process of extracting, transforming, and loading large volumes of data to and from your Salesforce environment. The ETL process, shown in Figure 6-4, refers to the process that involves

- Extracting data from an originating source. Often, data will come from relational and non-relational databases. The middleware uses source adapters to extract data from legacy applications and database files.

- Transforming the extracted data to fit the operational needs of the target system. The process of transformation uses rules, lookup tables, and other sources to create the target data.

- Loading the transformed data to the target system using target adapters. The loaded data can be applications, databases, data stores, marts, and warehouses.

**ETL Process from Source data to Target data**

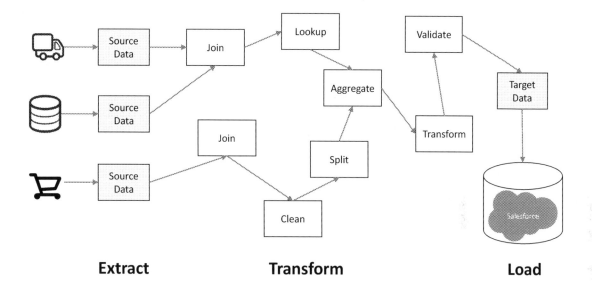

| Extract | Transform | Load |
|---------|-----------|------|

***Figure 6-4.*** *Extract, Transform, and Load Process*

ETL is used for batched, scheduled, and ad hoc data operations. The transformation should reduce the manipulation of data on the target system. The source and target adaptors are generally proprietary to the associated system. Chapter 4 has additional information.

# ESB: Enterprise Service Bus

An Enterprise Service Bus provides the means to move work among different systems without the given systems being aware of the enterprise bus. Each app is connected to the bus using various protocols and sends or receives information by subscribing to the ESB's messaging system. It is a unified way to send and receive information and data.

The integration architecture allows communications via the bus and the connected systems. The bus can support virtually all of the API protocols and many other proprietary systems. The bus uses a service-oriented design with three main heterogeneous components: the service consumers, an enterprise bus, and the service providers. Figure 6-5 shows how the service consumer and service provider interact with the ESB.

**Figure 6-5.** *ESB Components*

The ESB can employ one of many design architectures:

- **Message-Oriented Middleware (MOM)**: Can communicate across multiple nodes using messages and event-driven processes. The connected system is not aware of the middleware, as it uses industry standard protocols such as a SOAP-based WSDL.

- **Integration Broker**: Is used as a centralized hub that connects all message traffic. It uses standard MOM connectivity as well as newer web services.

- **Application Services**: Middleware that uses application creation support such as Java EE to support customized integration endpoints.

- **Business Process Management System**: It supports orchestration, transformation, and automation processes to extend the traditional ESB design.

An ESB can support multiple protocols, including HTTP REST, SOAP, and FTP, to receive and process messages. By converting traffic into a standard protocol, the ESB can receive, process, and produce messages to be used by a service consumer.

ESB is not suitable for large data volumes and should not be used as a substitute for ETL solutions. Its design manages messages from many different systems and processes than for the consumer. Large data payloads will bog down the typical ESB transaction and impact overall performance.

# Integration Choices

When should an architect use a given middleware solution? Salesforce offers options such as Canvas apps, Heroku apps, Salesforce Connect, and Files Connect. Which options is best? The selection of the best integration is dependent on a given use case, including the time available, the costs associated with the integration, and the cost, or

ROI, required to maintain integrations. The answer is not always immediately apparent. Often, the choice requires a balance between the time, cost, and quality required. This balancing process is called the triple constraint. Let's look at a few use cases in Table 6-3.

***Table 6-3.*** *Middleware Options with Uses Cases*

| Middleware Option | Use Cases | Considerations |
|---|---|---|
| Canvas app and mashup integration | Integrate third-party application in Salesforce. | - Used with custom web app.<br>- App rationalization to consolidate many apps using Salesforce App Launcher.<br>- External app should be web based and support custom development for integration. |
| Heroku app integration | Enhanced branding for web apps, improved mobile/IOT services with API service, and data manipulation. | - Must maintain users outside of Salesforce.<br>- Good use case for data backup and archival solutions. |
| Salesforce Connect | Integrate to external database tables with full CRUD access using SOAP, REST, or OData and external data searching. | - Limited to 100 external objects.<br>- No more than four joins per table.<br>- 2,000 rows visible. |
| Apex integration | Point-to-point integration with external systems, such as payment gateway services. | - Salesforce governor limits. |
| Files Connect | Integration to external cloud-based file storage systems, such as Google, Box, and Office 365. | - Lacks sorting within Salesforce.<br>- Low daily API limits. |

**Note**    Each middleware solution requires authentication and authorization to initiate services.

# Overview of Integration Patterns

Before we look at the different integration patterns available within Salesforce, we need to establish a baseline for reviewing and evaluating their fit for a given use case. This pattern baseline will include the following components: approach, timing, source-target and direction, calling mechanism, idempotent design considerations, error handling and recovery, security consideration, and state management and considerations.

## Approach

An integration pattern has three primary approach categories: data integration, process integration, and virtual integration. Each approach pattern focuses on several areas, such as the size of the data, how it handles exceptions and failures, the type of system used, and the degree to which the solution is transactional.

**Data integration** is used to synchronize data between two or more systems. It can be described as combining data from different sources into one cohesive view. Data integration is the most common type of integration between disparate data sources. The outcome of data integration should be trusted data that is meaningful and valuable to the business process.

**Process integration** combines business processes from two or more systems to complete a given process task. Process integration is more complicated as it needs to orchestrate the processes from a central trigger point or choreograph the processes across several business process systems. This approach requires extensive design efforts, including testing and exception handling to manage the vast number of possible outcomes. Process integration requires more robust systems and extended transaction timing to complete the integration.

**Virtual integration** is used to search, report, and update data in one or more external systems. The integration provides the target system access to real-time data using remote calls to the source system or systems. Because the integration is virtual, the data does not need to be replicated. This type of integration requires real-time access and retrieval of data from the source system.

# Timing

The integration process requires that the systems communicate with each other. How this communication happens is called timing. It can happen synchronously, asynchronously, or some combination of the two.

**Synchronous communication** is when one system sends a request to another system and must wait for the receiving system to respond. An example of this is when the requesting transaction system looks for a credit card approval to complete a sale. The requesting system must wait until it receives an answer to proceed with the transaction. Synchronous timing is generally expected in real time.

**Asynchronous communication** occurs when one system sends a request to another system and does not wait for the receiving system to respond. An example of this is when the requesting order system sends a transaction to the ERP system for processing. The requesting system does not need to wait for an answer to close the transaction. Asynchronous timing does not require real-time communications.

Why is this important? As an architect, your design will dictate the required timing. The integration pattern must support the timing without undue stress on the underlying systems.

# Source, Target, and Direction

Integration can vary depending on the point of reference. It is crucial to understand how the systems interact with each other in terms of the source, target, and direction of data and information flow. Each integration must have a source or sending system and a target or receiving system. The direction is the indication of how data flows. It is vital to know the direction for each interaction. Direction can be more than a pointer. Integration can be unidirectional (one-way), bidirectional (two-way), omni-directional (broadcast or one-to-many), correlation (many-to-one, if TRUE), or aggregation (many-to-one).

# Calling Mechanism

Integration is an active process that only occurs when it is requested. The calling mechanism is the specific actions that can be used to start the integration process flow. Salesforce has several ways to initiate integrations, including triggers, controllers, workflows, processes, flows, platform events, and batch processes. Each integration pattern can have one or more calling mechanisms. Table 6-4 provides descriptions for many different calling mechanisms.

***Table 6-4.*** *Calling Mechanisms in Salesforce*

| Mechanism | Description |
| --- | --- |
| Apex callouts | Call external SOAP, REST, and other web services from Apex. |
| Bulk API | Extract and load large volumes of data in and out of Salesforce. |
| Canvas | Canvas integrates third-party applications in Salesforce using tools and JavaScript APIs to expose an application as a Canvas app. Canvas presents existing applications within Salesforce. |
| Chatter REST API | Chatter REST API presents Chatter feeds, users, groups, and followers in external applications. |
| Email | Integrate by sending and receiving emails using InboundEmailHandler. |
| External objects | Virtual integration where Salesforce Connect is used to fetch data from an external system. |
| Metadata API | An integration mechanism that manipulates the metadata model, not the actual data stored in the system. |
| Middleware | Any integration application, tool, or system that facilitates the interaction between two or more disparate systems. |
| Outbound messages | It is used to send SOAP messages over HTTP to a receiving endpoint. Outbound messages are triggered by a specific workflow or platform event. |
| Platform event | Using an event-driven architecture (EDA) framework to process events, platform events are a special entity that manages how events from the creators are consumed. |
| Push notifications | Form of outbound message to send push messages to external devices and systems. |
| RESTful API | It uses a robust, lightweight RESTful web service. Salesforce exposes all of its functionalities and data in either XML or JSON format using REST API over a secure HTTP-based web transport protocol. REST API supports the ability to create, read, update, and delete records. |

(*continued*)

***Table 6-4.*** (*continued*)

| Mechanism | Description |
|---|---|
| SOAP-based API | It uses a tightly written web service. It exposes Salesforce data only via a Web Services Description Language (WSDL) file that defines all the parameters for accessing data. |
| Streaming API | Specialized API that operates based on the recently popular industry standard publish and subscribe (Pub/Sub) messaging model, supported via PushTopics. |
| Tooling API | Provides "fine-grained" access to Salesforce metadata using REST or SOAP. |

# Error Handling and Recovery

Integration patterns react to errors and perform rollbacks in different ways. The approach used to manage error handling and recovery is critical in selecting and managing a given integration pattern.

# Idempotent Design Considerations

To create an idempotent integration method, you must produce the same result whether you run the method once or multiple times. This process means that the expected result is generated even if the source sends the same information multiple times, even as an error. An integration method is idempotent if it manages the outcome and tests to eliminate the same transaction running multiple times, or the results are duplicated in error. The most common method of creating an idempotent receiver is to search for and track duplicates based on unique message identifiers sent by the consumer. Where possible, it is recommended that the remote system manage the error handling and the idempotent design. Not all patterns require idempotent methods.

# Security Consideration

As with any system connection, the relevant security protocols must be maintained with integration patterns. These protocols often include reverse proxy servers, encryption, and Specialized WS-* Protocol Support. Salesforce does not support these protocols directly. Refer to the external systems if these are needed in your environment. Salesforce recommends two-way SSL and appropriate firewall mechanisms to maintain the confidentiality, integrity, and availability of integration requests.

## State Management

The use of primary and unique foreign keys allows different systems to maintain the state of data synchronization. The integration pattern manages the master system or which system is storing the unique key. If Salesforce is the master, the remote system must store the Salesforce ID, and if the remote system is the master, Salesforce must store the unique remote ID.

## Integration Patterns

Table 6-5 lists the integration patterns supported by Salesforce.

***Table 6-5.*** *List of Six Integration Patterns Used in Salesforce*

| Pattern | Description |
|---|---|
| Request and Reply | As a requesting system, Salesforce invokes a remote system call for data and waits for the integration process to complete. |
| Fire and Forget | As a requesting system, Salesforce invokes a remote system call for data, is acknowledged by the remote system, and does not wait to complete the integration process. |
| Batch Data Synchronization | Either Salesforce or a remote system invokes a batch data call or published event to synchronize data in either direction using a third-party ETL solution or Salesforce Change Data Capture. |
| Remote Call-In | As a target system, Salesforce receives a remote system call to create, retrieve, update, or delete data by a remote system. |
| UI Update Based on Data Changes | As a requesting system, Salesforce listens for a PushTopic (CometD protocol) and updates the user interface (UI) to represent the received change. |
| Data Virtualization | As a requesting system, Salesforce establishes a virtual connection using Salesforce Connect to create an external object to access real-time data. |

# Integration Patterns, Uses Cases, and Justification

Table 6-6 shows the various integration patterns available and the justification for their use as part of the overall integration architecture.

***Table 6-6.*** *Choosing the ideal integration pattern*

| Source/Target | Type | Timing | Optimal Pattern |
|---|---|---|---|
| SF ➤ Remote | Process | Sync | Request and Reply |
| SF ➤ Remote | Process | Async | Fire and Forget |
| SF ➤ Remote | Data | Sync | Request and Reply |
| SF ➤ Remote | Data | Async | UI Update with CDC |
| SF ➤ Remote | Virtual | Sync | Data Virtualization |
| Remote ➤ SF | Process | Sync | Remote Call-In |
| Remote ➤ SF | Process | Async | Remote Call-In |
| Remote ➤ SF | Data | Sync | Remote Call-In |
| Remote ➤ SF | Data | Async | Batch Data Sync |
| Pub ➤ Sub | Process | Async | Fire and Forget with platform events |

*Legend: SF = Salesforce, Remote = Remote system, CDC = Change Data Capture, UI = User interface*

# Selecting the Appropriate Integration Strategy and Integration Pattern

This section of the chapter will help you understand when to select and use a given strategy and pattern for your integration requirements. As with many options in Salesforce, it is possible to have more than one choice. Tables 6-7 through 6-12 will present the options uniformly to help find and select the correct strategy and pattern and help justify your choice. The tables will include the following:

- **Pattern**: The integration pattern name

- **Direction**: The source and target with the direction of the integration flow

- **Considerations**: The reasons and forces that can lead to the pattern

- **Idempotent**: The mitigation approach for the idempotent requirement

- **Solutions**: The calling mechanism, fit, and considerations for each

- **Calling Mechanism**: The type(s) of mechanisms used to start the integration pattern

- **Error Handling and Recovery**: How error handling can be managed with recovery options if they occur

- **Integration Flow**: A visual swim lane of the integration process

- **Additional Factors of Note**: Different factors for the pattern to consider, such as time limits, size of data volumes, security, and endpoints available

# Request and Reply

The Request and Reply integration pattern is used to support synchronous communication where message is sent to an external system and the sender is expecting a return of information. Table 6-7 shows a uniform review of the pattern to identify its requirements.

***Table 6-7.*** *Request and Reply Integration Pattern*

| | |
|---|---|
| **Pattern** | Request and Reply integration to an external system. |
| **Description** | As a requesting system, Salesforce invokes a remote system call for data and waits for the integration process to complete. |
| **Direction** | Salesforce ➤ Remote system ➤ Salesforce waiting for a response |
| **Consideration** | 1. What is the remote system? |
| | 2. What is the size of the data payload? What is the return size? |
| | 3. Does the result need to be processed upon receipt? |
| | 4. Does the integration call occur after an event or DML? |
| | 5. Does the remote system have throughput issues or peak times that can cause delays in its response? |
| | 6. Is the response consistent? Does it need to be transformed to be useful? |

*(continued)*

***Table 6-7.*** (*continued*)

| Idempotent and state management | Idempotent is required, as the reply is associated with a given request. The result will be tied to a specific state. The state can be stored in Salesforce as a unique remote ID or in the remote system using the Salesforce ID. The process must limit the response to change the results if it fails and is retried or multiple responses are received. | | |
|---|---|---|---|
| **Solutions** | **Calling Mechanism** | **Fit** | **Consideration** |
| | Use external REST API call | Best | • Can invoke declaratively.<br>• Best used when host supports REST and Open API 2.0.<br>• The response has a similar field to Salesforce objects.<br>• Can be invoked from flow.<br>• Transaction size will not exceed sync limits. |
| | Lightning component or Visualforce page initiates SOAP or REST callout | Best | • Support WSDL consumption.<br>• Supports REST methods.<br>• User-initiated actions execute a call. |
| | Custom Visualforce page or button initiates sync Apex HTTP call | Best | • Supports REST methods.<br>• Can support SOAP.<br>• Uses Apex class to make a call. |
| | Use trigger on data change to perform sync SOAP or REST call | Suboptimal | • A trigger can perform automation, but all calls made in trigger must execute asynchronously.<br>• Solution not recommended. |
| | Use Batch Apex job to perform sync SOAP or REST call | Suboptimal | • A batch can perform automation, but has limits on the number of calls .<br>• Solution not recommended. |

(*continued*)

***Table 6-7.*** (*continued*)

| | |
|---|---|
| **Error handling and recovery** | • Apex must include handling the error and preventing the DML execution until the remote response is received to support the required idempotent. A class should support the ability to retry the request. |
| **Integration flow** | **Request and Reply**: Synchronous, small data volumes, error handling, orchestration via middleware |

| | |
|---|---|
| **Additional factors** | • Calling remote systems to require secure Apex SOAP or REST calls using one-way or two-way SSL, consider using Crypto class methods, and support firewall mechanisms.<br>• Requires low data volume.<br>• Response from remote must be timely. |

# Fire and Forget

The Fire and Forget integration pattern is used to support asynchronous communication where message is sent to an external system and the sender is **not** expecting a return of information. Table 6-8 shows a uniform review of the pattern to identify its requirements.

***Table 6-8.*** *Fire and Forget Integration Pattern*

| | |
|---|---|
| **Pattern** | Fire and Forget integration to an external system. |
| **Description** | As a requesting system, Salesforce invokes a remote system call for data, is acknowledged by the remote system, and does not wait to complete the integration process. An acknowledgment from the remote system is expected. |
| **Direction** | Salesforce ➤ Remote system (optional response in another process) |

(*continued*)

***Table 6-8.*** (*continued*)

| Consideration | 1. Does the remote system need to reply? |
| --- | --- |
| | 2. The remote system confirms receipt. |
| | 3. Can Salesforce continue the process without results? |
| | 4. If an update can process asynchronously, the remote system sends information later with another process. |
| **Idempotent and state management** | Salesforce does not require idempotent. Is the remote procedure idempotent? If so, the remote system must manage the state by storing the Salesforce ID if required. The remote system must manage the impact of multiple requests occurring for the same transaction. |

| Solutions | Calling Mechanism | Fit | Consideration |
| --- | --- | --- | --- |
| | Use process-driven platform events | Best | • The declarative solution recommended using a remote request is made from an insert or update event. <br> • Uses Pub/Sub/CometD. |
| | Use custom action such as a component, trigger, Apex calls, or VF | Good | • Uses a trigger on insert or update to invoke remote request. <br> • Uses Pub/Sub. |
| | Use workflow-driven outbound messages | Good | • Uses a declarative solution using workflow outbound messages. <br> • The process will retry until an acknowledgment is received. |
| | Use outbound message with callback with a session ID | Good | • Mitigate out-of-sequence idempotent. <br> • Can request or provide more information. |
| | Lightning component or Visualforce page or trigger initiates callout or batch | Suboptimal | • The process is not waiting for a response. |

(*continued*)

***Table 6-8.***  (*continued*)

| | |
|---|---|
| **Error handling and recovery** | As Salesforce is not waiting for the resulting processing, the primary error handling is relegated to the remote system. The recovery is more complex, requiring the remote system to determine if a retry is required and then make a callback to Salesforce. Salesforce does need to handle acknowledgment errors such as timeouts and service availability. |
| **Integration flow** | **Fire and Forget**: Asynchronous, small data volumes, error handling, trigger-initiated process, orchestration via middleware |

| | |
|---|---|
| **Additional factors** | • Response time is not critical.<br>• Data volume should be low because of Salesforce governor limits. |

# Batch Data Sync

The Batch Data Sync integration pattern is a common pattern used to support data migration in and out of a receiving system. Table 6-9 shows a uniform review of the pattern to identify its requirements.

***Table 6-9.***  *Batch Data Sync Integration Pattern*

| | |
|---|---|
| **Pattern** | Batch Data Synchronization to import data into Salesforce or export data out of Salesforce. |
| **Description** | Either Salesforce or a remote system invokes a batch data call or published event to synchronize data in either direction using a third-party ETL solution or Salesforce Change Data Capture. |
| **Direction** | Salesforce ➤ Remote system or<br>Remote system ➤ Salesforce |
| **Consideration** | 1. Where should the data be stored? Is Salesforce the primary source?<br>2. Can the data update as a result of a change in either Salesforce or the remote system?<br>3. Is the remote system using Salesforce data for business-critical reports or analytics?<br>4. Are data changes occurring on a schedule? |

(*continued*)

***Table 6-9.*** (*continued*)

| Idempotent and state management | Idempotent is not a concern. State is managed by using foreign keys between the two systems. If specific transaction management is required, use a Remote Call-In pattern instead. | | |
|---|---|---|---|

| Solutions | **Calling Mechanism** | **Fit** | **Consideration** |
|---|---|---|---|
| | Extract Salesforce data using Change Data Capture (CDC) | Best | • CDC publishes changes which can be processed in near real time.<br>• Requires integration with a remote system for updates and events. |
| | Extract Salesforce data using ETL tools such as DataLoader.io or Informatica | Good | • Uses third-party ETL tools to run CDC.<br>• CDC responds to change in Salesforce data and calls Salesforce Bulk API. |
| | Load data in Salesforce using ETL tools | Best | • Uses third-party ETL tools to run CDC.<br>• CDC responds to change and calls Salesforce Bulk API. |
| | Remote call-in from the external system to extract data | Suboptimal | • Custom integration on the remote side.<br>• Requires significant traffic between systems.<br>• More error handling and recovery is needed within Salesforce. |
| | A remote process from Salesforce to extract or load data to a remote system | Suboptimal | • Requires significant traffic between systems.<br>• More error handling and recovery is needed within Salesforce. |

| Error handling and recovery | Error handling and recovery must be handled by the remote system, as the process is asynchronous. | | |
|---|---|---|---|

(*continued*)

***Table 6-9.*** (*continued*)

| Integration flow | **Inbound Batch Synchronization**: Data integration, asynchronous, one-time migration of data **to** SFDC, near real-time Change Data Capture (CDC) using ETL |
|---|---|

| | **Outbound Batch Synchronization**: Data integration, asynchronous, one-time migration of data **from** SFDC, near real-time Change Data Capture (CDC) using ETL |
|---|---|

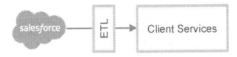

| Additional factors | • The timing of the process is not critical. However, as both systems' performance can be impacted, care should be taken when the process is initiated. |
|---|---|

# Remote Call-In

The Remote Call-In integration pattern is used to support synchronous communication where a message is sent from an external system to the receiving system. Table 6-10 shows a uniform review of the pattern to identify its requirements.

***Table 6-10.*** *Remote Call-In Integration Pattern*

| Pattern | Remote call-in to Salesforce from an external system. |
|---|---|
| Description | As a target system, Salesforce receives a remote system call to create, retrieve, update, or delete data by a remote system. |
| Direction | Remote System ➤ Salesforce |
| Consideration | 1. Which integration pattern will the remote system use?<br>2. Is the call to one object or several objects? Are the objects related?<br>3. Is the response size small or large?<br>4. Can the remote system support SOAP? |

*(continued)*

***Table 6-10.*** (*continued*)

| | |
|---|---|
| **Idempotent and state management** | Idempotent consideration is required. The result will often be tied to a specific process or record. The process must limit the response to change the results if it fails and is retried or multiple responses are received. The concern is related to duplication. |

| **Solutions** | **Calling Mechanism** | **Fit** | **Consideration** |
|---|---|---|---|
| | Calling Salesforce using SOAP API | Best | • Defined using WSDL.<br>• Secure with required authorization and authentication.<br>• All-or-nothing commits.<br>• Support for bulk and PE-based transactions. |
| | Calling Salesforce using REST API | Best | • Uses a straightforward, lightweight integration.<br>• Synchronous process.<br>• Secure with required authorization and authentication.<br>• All-or-nothing commits.<br>• Support for bulk and PE-based transactions. |
| | Calling Salesforce using Apex web service | Suboptimal | • A complex Apex application must be managed in Salesforce.<br>• Requires process logic to commit data.<br>• Does not support PE. |
| | Calling Salesforce using Apex REST services | Suboptimal | • A complex Apex application must be managed in Salesforce.<br>• If it must be used, it is better than SOAP API, as multiple updates can be supported and the WSDL is not required by the remote.<br>• Does not support PE. |
| | Using Bulk API | Best for bulk data | • External tools and systems can perform bulk actions using REST-based API designed for large data sets. |

(*continued*)

***Table 6-10.*** (*continued*)

| | |
|---|---|
| **Error handling and recovery** | • The remote system manages all error handling and recovery. |
| **Integration flow** | **Remote Call-In**: Synchronous call-in from hosted systems to invoke Salesforce services.<br><br> |
| **Additional actors** | • OAuth flows must be used to support the remote call-in.<br>• Transaction time is critical for this pattern, as timeouts can occur. |

# UI Update

The UI Update integration pattern is used to update the receiving system UI based on changes in the sending system. Table 6-11 shows a uniform review of the pattern to identify its requirements.

***Table 6-11.*** *UI Update Integration Pattern*

| | |
|---|---|
| **Pattern** | User interface (UI) update based on data change. |
| **Description** | As a requesting system, Salesforce listens for a PushTopic (CometD protocol) and updates the user interface (UI) to represent the received change. |
| **Direction** | Salesforce ➤ Salesforce with UI update or Salesforce ➤ Remote system ➤ Salesforce with UI update |
| **Consideration** | 1. Does the update need to be seen by the user as changes are made without a refresh?<br>2. Where is the updated data stored? |
| **Idempotent and state management** | Error handling and recovery must be handled by the remote system, as the process is asynchronous. |

(*continued*)

***Table 6-11.*** (*continued*)

| Solutions | Calling Mechanism | Fit | Consideration |
|---|---|---|---|
| | Calling Salesforce using Streaming API and presenting using component or VF page | Good | • Uses a PushTopic, VF/LC, and static JS library.<br>• Provides updates without refresh.<br>• Delivery and order of execution are not guaranteed. |
| | Use platform events to publish an update and another PE to subscribe to listen for updates | Best | • Fully declarative approach.<br>• Provides updates without refresh.<br>• Delivery and order of execution are not guaranteed.. |
| | Create a custom polling mechanism | Suboptimal | • Highly custom solution requiring custom polling and feedback loop. |
| **Error handling and recovery** | Delivery and order of execution are not guaranteed. As such, consideration should be made to confirm the impact of error and how to recover. | | |
| **Integration flow** | **UI Update – Salesforce Streaming API:** Used to provide the UI layer with asynchronous updates to the Salesforce data elements.<br><br> | | |
| **Additional factors** | • Uses internal security to support org-level requirements.<br>• User browser can impact the result of update and UI display. | | |

# Data Virtualization

The Data Virtualization integration pattern is used to support synchronous communication where a message is sent from an external system to the receiving system and presented as a virtual object. Table 6-12 shows a uniform review of the pattern to identify its requirements.

***Table 6-12.*** *Data Virtualization Integration Pattern*

| | | | |
|---|---|---|---|
| **Pattern** | Data virtualization to support external objects in Salesforce. | | |
| **Description** | As a requesting system, Salesforce establishes a virtual connection using Salesforce Connect to create an external object to access real-time data. | | |
| **Direction** | Salesforce ➤ Remote system ➤ Salesforce with virtualization | | |
| **Consideration** | 1. Where should the data be stored? Inside Salesforce or in a remote environment?<br>2. Will the data need to be displayed in real time?<br>3. What is the volume of data required?<br>4. Will a declarative or programmatic approach be needed? | | |
| **Idempotent and state management** | Idempotent is not required, as data resides on the external system. The external record ID is used in Salesforce to manage the state. | | |
| **Solutions** | **Calling Mechanism** | **Fit** | **Consideration** |
| | Using Salesforce Connect to access external object(s) | Best | • Fee-based option from Salesforce supports OData, cross-org, and custom adaptors.<br>• Provides an external object within Salesforce by mapping Salesforce external objects to data tables in external systems. |
| | Use Reply and Request pattern to access external data | Suboptimal | • A complex Apex application must be managed in Salesforce.<br>• Requires process logic to commit data.<br>• Does not support PE. |
| **Error handling and recovery** | Standard system error handling processes apply to Salesforce Connect. Custom solutions will require additional code to support error handling and recovery. Salesforce Connect Validator can be used to test connections. | | |

*(continued)*

***Table 6-12.*** (*continued*)

| Integration flow | **Data Virtualization – External Object:** Used to provide real-time visibility into data in external systems, allowing users to view, search, and modify data that is stored outside their Salesforce environment. |
|---|---|
| |  |
| Additional factors | • Uses internal security to support org-level requirements.<br>• Requires low data volume.<br>• Response from remote must be timely.<br>• Intricate external designs will need to be supported by the remote solution. |

# Other Integration External Service Options

Salesforce provides many prebuilt or ISV-supported solutions to reduce integration requirements. As of early 2021, Salesforce promoted solutions for Google Cloud, Slack, QuickBooks, MailChimp, LinkedIn, DocuSign, Jira, HelloSign, Code Science, ActiveCampaign, and Dropbox.

**Note**   See `www.salesforce.com/solutions/small-business-solutions/integrations/#!page=1` for the latest options.

Salesforce also provides native integration tools to accelerate integration. One example is Files Connect. Files Connect can be used to share files between Google Drive or SharePoint and Salesforce.

Salesforce provides integration for industry-leading email systems, including Outlook and Gmail. This integration is a declarative process that provides a wizard and the instructions needed to support one-way or bidirectional integration.

Salesforce enables third-party data companies to offer data services to provide, update, groom, and augment your Salesforce data. The providers provide declarative data integration rules to access and update data in your instance. Companies such as Dun & Bradstreet or ESRI can enhance geospatial and organizational data quickly.

---

**Note**    The declarative options listed here are using point-to-point integration.

---

## Variety of Integration Options Available

If you remember early in the chapter where Figure 6-1 seemed overwhelming, Figure 6-6 should help to summarize the available options that can be used within the Salesforce environment. As an architect, you will need to understand each option and select and implement those that support the business and technical requirements.

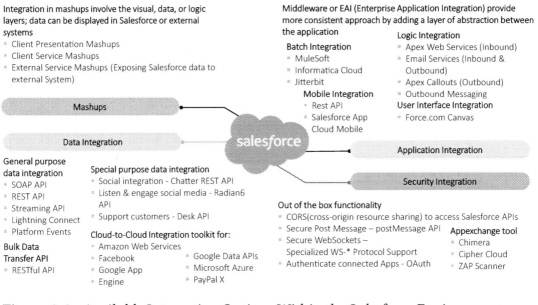

*Figure 6-6.* *Available Integration Options Within the Salesforce Environment*

# Chapter Summary

In this chapter, we learned about

- The key considerations used when creating an integration strategy

- The three different integration architectures: point-to-point, hub-and-spoke, and Enterprise Service Bus

- Several standard integration use cases used in the enterprise

- The three levels in integration: user interface, business logic, and data model

- The integration layers that should be considered

- The four most used integration protocols in Salesforce integration

- How middleware is used to support connections between systems

- The factors that should be considered when selecting an integration pattern

- The various integration patterns and how to justify their use as part of the overall integration architecture

- When to use other middleware approaches such as Canvas apps, integrating with Heroku apps, integrating using Salesforce Connect, and integrating using middleware

- Which integration to use when and how to justify the appropriate integration strategy and integration patterns

# CHAPTER 7

# Salesforce Identity and Access Management Architecture

Let's dive deeper into the domain of identity and access management. As you know, cloud technology has enabled enterprise business applications and business transactions to be more ubiquitous and accessible by anyone, anywhere, with just a web browser and an Internet connection. This level of convenience comes with a multitude of security considerations for designing and managing cloud-based solutions. The potential threats vary from hacked user accounts and data breaches to malicious attacks that can bring down the entire system. If a breach occurs in a cloud-based system, the recoverability of the system is not the only concern. The risk of damaged reputation and loss of customer trust can be far more devastating than just recovery for business. An identity and access management breach often requires a complete overhaul of the system because most identity and access management breaches are deep-rooted. Identity and access management also becomes complicated over time because of the ever-growing size of the user base and the diverse user needs. Identity and access management is the most critical security aspect of every system and designed for the full life of the system, which can last as long as a decade.

Identity and access management streamlines and automates the critical aspects of managing users, system identities, and access rights to one or many systems in the enterprise. The different elements of protection offered by identity and access management (IAM) solutions are a vital starting point in building a robust information security framework for your company.

© Dipanker Jyoti and James A. Hutcherson 2021
D. Jyoti and J. A. Hutcherson, *Salesforce Architect's Handbook*, https://doi.org/10.1007/978-1-4842-6631-1_7

When we ask people to describe identity and access management, we hear phrases like "SSO," "SAML," "OAuth," "username/password," "user provisioning," and so on. Identity management is not just one of these terms; it is all of them. Identity and access Management is a lifecycle of security measures that span across the life of a user's use of a system.

In this chapter, we cover

- The nine stages of an identity and access management lifecycle

- An overview of key concepts including provisioning, access, authentication, authorization, session management, single sign-on (SSO), logouts and redirects, deprovisioning, and user account management

- The options available in Salesforce for designing identity and access management for each stage of the identity and access management lifecycle

# Stages of an Identity and Access Management Lifecycle

To introduce the fundamental concepts of identity and access management, I (James) would like to start by sharing a story of my travel experience.

I visited Barcelona, Spain, for vacation, and my journey started with me finding a fantastic multi-carrier round-trip flight deal on `www.expedia.com` from Washington, DC, to Barcelona, Spain. Figure 7-1 shows the various stages of my flight experience.

**Figure 7-1.** *Experience on Flight from Washington, DC, to Barcelona, Spain*

My flight experience was as follows:

1. **Booking and Flight Registration**: I found a multi-carrier flight deal on Expedia. I registered as a new user and then completed my booking by entering personal details from my passport. I received a confirmation number from the airline, which also included a link to complete check-in before the date of my flight.

2. **Check-In and Boarding Pass**: On the day of my flight, I arrived at the airport and checked in at a United Airlines kiosk to get my boarding pass. The boarding pass had all of my booking details. Additionally, the pass included other information such as my TSA pre-check, [1] the terminal, and the gate from which my flight was departing. It also had my seat assignment and my boarding group details.

---

[1] *TSA pre✓ is an expedited security screening program offered by the Transportation Security Administration in the United States.*

3.  **Passing Security**: When I arrived at the designated terminal, I noticed that I had the option to either pass through the TSA security that was shorter and fast-moving or the general security, which was longer and slower. I chose the TSA security line. When I reached the security officer, she asked for photo identification and a valid boarding pass. She acknowledged my identity based on the information already stored in the TSA database and allowed me to enter the terminal.

4.  **Locating Departure Gate**: After passing security, I checked my boarding pass to find the assigned gate for my flight. When I arrived at the gate printed on my boarding pass, the gate official announced that the gate assignment had changed, and I had a newly assigned gate. They also assured me I would not need to pass through security again to move to my new loading gate since all gates and terminals for the airport are accessible from inside the security checkpoint seamlessly.

5.  **In-Flight Experience**: I arrived at the new gate of departure and boarded the flight. Once the flight boarded, the flight agent shut the plane doors before the plane could leave the terminal. Based on the seat assignment on my boarding pass, the flight attendants already knew my meal preferences. They offered in-flight experience specific to my favorites and in the context of my seat class.

6.  **Connecting Flights with Different Airlines**: My flight landed at the first stopover, which was at Heathrow Airport in London. I switched airlines from United to British Airways in a separate terminal for my next flight. When I arrived at the British Airways gate, I was required no additional security check.

7.  **Exit Terminal with No Reentry Allowed**: I landed at BCN airport in Barcelona, Spain, and as I exited the customs, I saw the sign "No reentry allowed." I acknowledged that I had everything I needed from the terminal facilities, and I exited the terminal.

8. **Made Changes to My Return Trip**: I was enjoying Barcelona, and hence I decided to stay longer than I planned. To change my return flight, I went online on Expedia and made changes to my return date and chose new flights. Expedia confirmed my changes and the date and time of my return flight. They also provided me with new boarding passes.

9. **Access to My Past Flights Removed**: After returning from my trip, when I tried to log in to view my past flights online, I could not access my recent flight information. The website displayed a message stating that I did not have access to my past trips, and if I needed any additional information, I should call their customer service for further help.

I know you are wondering, what does this have to do with identity and access management? Before I clarify that, let me discuss the nine stages of an identity and access management lifecycle that need to be considered for every Salesforce solution. Figure 7-2 outlines the nine stages that we talk about in more detail.

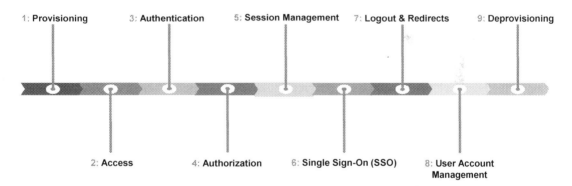

***Figure 7-2.*** *Lifecycle of Identity and Access Management (IAM)*

1. **Provisioning**: The process of setting up a user in Salesforce, including collecting and storing personal and system registration details about the user or an external system. In my flight experience story, the provisioning is similar to the experience of booking my flight on Expedia, where I self-registered my user account and provided personal details to register myself also with the airline's database that operates the trip interests.

227

2. **Access**: The setup defines a user's access or systems privilege to specific resources in Salesforce such as objects, records, fields, and UI pages. An admin must define and set up access before a user is authenticated or authorized into Salesforce. Salesforce strictly enforces the assignment of a user profile and a license type to each user, which is the minimum access configuration needed for every user. We can provide additional access in Salesforce via permission sets, role hierarchy, group memberships, queues, teams, and a large variety of configurable sharing rules. Access can be changed before, during, and after the user authorization. In the flight example, my boarding pass had all the details, such as the terminal, gate, and seat details of the flight.

3. **Authentication**: Refers to the process of verifying the identity of the user or a remote system requesting access to Salesforce. The authentication process verifies a set of identification credentials stored within Salesforce or an external identity store to confirm that the user or remote system is authentic. This process is similar to my experience at the airport security gate, where the TSA security officer asked me to identify myself by requesting a photo identification and a valid boarding pass. I used the TSA pre line, which is like using a high-assurance authentication method in Salesforce. I passed through security without requiring additional security steps such as removing my laptop out of my bag or removing my shoes, belt, and watch when passing through security. The security officer also verified that I was in the correct airport and at the right terminal for my flight.

4. **Authorization**: The validation of the user's access rights/privileges to resources in Salesforce, such as objects, records, fields, and UI pages, at the time of access. When conducting authorization, Salesforce checks, at minimum, the license type, user profile, permission sets (if any), and role hierarchy (if any) assigned to the user. The flight and terminal details in my boarding pass allowed the security officials to validate that I was requesting entry into the correct terminal at the right date and time, as listed on my boarding pass.

5.  **Session Management**: The duration of a seamless user or system experience during their active use of Salesforce. After authentication and authorization into Salesforce, a user may navigate across multiple screens, access various data, and conduct a variety of transactions, without requiring Salesforce to reauthenticate and reauthorize the user after every single user activity. Session management is similar to getting access to service for the duration of that flight described in the flight example. Sessions for each user are uniquely managed based on a session token, which contains specific details about the user's sessions. In the flight experience, a session token is like the unique seat number assigned to my flight. My seat number on the flight was used by the flight attendant to identify my meal preferences and for tracking my overall flight experience.

6.  **Single Sign-On (SSO)**: The method of centralizing user authentication processes via the use of a single identity-providing system known as the "identity provider" (IPD). The IDP enables the users to authenticate with multiple systems by logging in once. In my flight example, I arrived at Terminal 3 of Heathrow Airport in London via United Airlines, and my next connecting flight departing Heathrow Airport was with British Airways from Terminal 3, Gate D17. I walked over to the designated gate of my next flight, without requiring to go through security again. Even though I was flying with a different airline for my next flight, I was able to bypass all security requirements at the airport and seamlessly board my next flight with British Airways. Here, the booking service acted as the identity provider and registered my details with both airlines, airports, and terminals to ensure that my transition from one flight to another was part of a seamless, unified experience.

7. **Logouts and Redirects**: The termination of a user's current active session securely as per the user's intent to end their current session or due to the deprovisioning of the user while in an active session of Salesforce. The termination of the user's active session navigates the user to an external alternative site. The post-logout navigation of the user can be customized to redirect the user to a custom web address or be set to default Salesforce redirect experience. In my flight example, I arrived in Barcelona and picked up my bags. I noticed a sign at the exit that said "No reentry after this point." As I exited the secure part of the airport, I entered the public access area of the airport, without a need for a boarding pass or ticket.

8. **User Account Management**: The process of supporting user access to a secure environment. User management may require login recovery and password resets, freezing a user's account temporarily, or deactivating a user. Often, login recovery refers to unlocking a user account for failed authentication or authorization attempts. It may also require changing user-assigned login hours and IP restrictions. In my flight experience, this is like the flight changes I made to my return flight, which changed my access and authorization from the initially scheduled flight.

9. **Deprovisioning**: The deactivation of user access in the Salesforce instance. In Salesforce, users cannot be deleted or removed. They can only be deactivated. Deactivating a user disables the user's access to the Salesforce instance. It also releases the Salesforce license previously assigned for use by other users or new users added to the Salesforce environment. In my flight example, the airline removed access to my previous trips. The access to the data was deprovisioned.

By now, I hope you have drawn similarities between my fight experience and the nine stages of an identity and access management lifecycle. In Figure 7-3, I have mapped the nine stages of identity and access management to my recent flight experience.

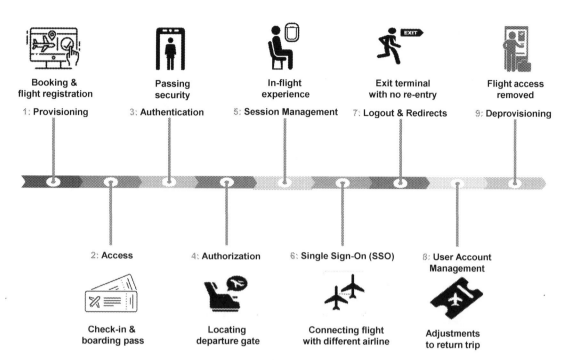

***Figure 7-3.*** *Mapping the Identity and Access Management Stages to the Flight Experience*

Now that we have covered the nine stages of identity and access management at a high level, let's dig deeper into each one. Let's understand the considerations that an architect should have when architecting an ideal identity and access management solution in Salesforce.

# Architecting Identity and Access Management in Salesforce

Identity is a loaded term in the technology industry. To some it means verification of users; to others it is just a security parameter. But identity and access management is not a singular concept; it is a lifecycle that covers every aspect of access to a system for the entirety of the system's life. At the basic level, identity and access management ensures that the user or remote system accessing the system is authentic, has access only to system resources they are entitled to, and respects all security parameters set within the system.

# Provisioning

Provisioning refers to the process used to set up users in Salesforce for access. An architect must plan and include an ideal approach for user provisioning since user provisioning can quickly become an expensive administrative overhead for most companies. Also, when many users need provisioning or in a company with an ever-growing population of Salesforce users, the ideal setup for user provisioning makes all the difference.

At the time of this writing, Salesforce offers nine methods of provisioning, outlined in Table 7-1.

***Table 7-1.*** *Provisioning Methods in Salesforce*

| User Provisioning Method | How Does It Work? |
|---|---|
| **Internal Users** | |
| Manual provisioning | The administrator is creating users manually. |
| API provisioning | Users are provisioned individually from an external system or application through integration via the SOAP API[2] or REST API on the user object. |
| Programmatic provisioning | Users provisioned programmatically using Apex code. |
| JIT provisioning with SAML | Users provisioned using the just-in-time (JIT) provisioning method, along with a SAML assertion to create users immediately when they first attempt to log into Salesforce. Advanced user account creation is not required. This method is dependent on the implementation of single sign-on. |
| Mass user provisioning | Users can be created in bulk either using Bulk API from another system or application or via CSV file uploaded using Salesforce Data Loader. |

*(continued)*

---

[2]SOAP API Developer Guide, https://developer.salesforce.com/docs/atlas.en-us.api.meta/api/sforce_api_objects_userprovisioningrequest.htm.

***Table 7-1.*** (*continued*)

| User Provisioning Method | How Does It Work? |
|---|---|
| Identity Connect with AD | This method uses the Salesforce Identity Connect feature, which integrates Microsoft Active Directory (AD) with Salesforce. In this method, the user information is maintained in Microsoft Active Directory (AD), and any changes to users are reflected in Salesforce. |
| **External Users (via Salesforce Community Cloud)** | |
| Manual setup | Users set up as contacts can be provisioned access to Community Cloud by internal users or Community Plus super users or Partner super users. |
| Self-registration | Users can self-register when first visiting the site. |
| Social sign-on provisioning | Users can sign in using social site credentials, such as LinkedIn, Facebook, Twitter, Google. These services implement the OpenID Connect or OAuth 2.0 framework. |

# Access

Access refers to the itemized list of all things that a provisioned user can do in Salesforce as per the capacity of their security rights. The "capacity" of access refers to the fine-grained detail of whether they get read-only access, read-write access, read-write-transfer access, or modify all access to a specific object, record, or field in Salesforce. Access determines the user's access to objects, records, and fields.

Salesforce defines access for a user based on the following security settings:

1. Salesforce user license

2. User profile

3. Role hierarchy

4. Permission sets

5. Sharing rules

6. Queue membership

7. Group membership

8.  Team membership

9.  Territory hierarchy

10.  Implicit sharing

11.  Apex sharing

12.  Manual sharing

13.  Account-based data sharing rules

14.  External account hierarchy

15.  Sharing sets

16.  Share group

Visibility and sharing is the label given to "access" in the Salesforce ecosystem. We discussed visibility and sharing in greater depth in Chapter 5.

# Authentication

Authentication in Salesforce uses two distinct steps, identification and authentication as part of a single process. The identification step requires a provisioned user to prove who they are to Salesforce by providing a set of identifiable credentials that can only be produced by the actual user. Salesforce verifies the user-provided credentials, which, in the simplest of scenarios, include a unique user ID and a user-created password. Salesforce matches the user-provided credentials against the user's credentials stored in Salesforce. Once the user's identity is verified, Salesforce conducts the second step of authenticating the user by performing the following checks:

- **Domain Access**: Checking for the Salesforce instance(s) to which the user has access and verifying if the Salesforce instance being requested by the user is one that the user can access.

- **IP Restrictions**: Checking for any user IP range restrictions. Salesforce denies access if the user is accessing from an IP range outside the IP range set for the user or the IP is not part of a whitelisted IP address for the organization.

- **Login Hours**: Checking for any login hour restrictions that have been set by the administrator, applicable to the user. If the user is accessing Salesforce outside of the login hours set up for the user, then the user's access to Salesforce is denied.

- **Two-Factor Authentication (2FA)**: Checking if the user is required to authenticate themselves via an additional, alternate form of authentication. As an example, a Salesforce-generated dynamic code is sent to the user's mobile device, or a one-time password (OTP) is sent to the user's email or mobile device.

If the requirements of the authentication step are not satisfied by the user, then the user authentication fails, and the user is not provided access into Salesforce.

Salesforce leverages the three most common industry standard authentication frameworks for user authentication management. The three frameworks used are

1. **Username/Password Framework**

   This is the most common and most straightforward framework, where users enter their unique user ID and a self-created secret password on the Salesforce login page. This method of authentication is considered the least secure form of authentication compared to other frameworks because the user's credentials can be easily compromised and the breach can remain unnoticed until significant damage occurs in the user's account. An approach to secure this method of authentication is to enable multifactor authentication along with this method of authentication as it mandates the user to verify themselves using an alternate source such as a user's mobile device or email address, which can only be accessed by the real user.

2. **The Security Assertion Markup Language (SAML) 2.0 Framework**

   Security Assertion Markup Language (SAML) is an XML-based framework for exchanging user authentication information between two or more systems that have established a trust relationship with each other. In SAML, the system that provides the user's identity is known as the "identity provider," and the system that leverages the authentication function of the identity provider to offer the user access to its services and resources is known as the "service provider." In SAML, the service provider delegates its user authentication function entirely to the identity provider. The SAML identity provider conducts the user's authentication and returns the results of the user's authentication attempt in an XML-based message called a SAML assertion to the service provider. The SAML assertion contains details about who the user is and how the identity provider authenticated the user.

In most cases, an identity provider can be an identity broker such as Microsoft Active Directory (AD) or Okta, and the service provider is Salesforce. But in other cases, when user details are only stored and managed in Salesforce, the real source of the user's identity, Salesforce, can act as the identity provider for other systems that serve as the service provider.

3. **OpenID Connect Framework for Authentication**

The OpenID Connect framework enables Salesforce to leverage the user's authentication stored in an external system referred to as the "OpenID authentication provider" in this context. The OpenID Connect framework combines user authentication with OAuth-based authorization *(more on OAuth-based authorization later in this chapter)*. The OpenID framework assumes that Salesforce can rely on the authentication method established in the OpenID authentication provider such as a user's Amazon, Twitter, Google, PayPal, or Janrain account or the user's identity stored in Microsoft Active Directory Federation Services (ADFS). A registration handler needs to be set up in Salesforce to match the user info requested from the OpenID provider.

Based on the principles of the three authentications as mentioned in the frameworks, there are seven approaches to authenticating users into Salesforce, that is, four methods to authenticate internal users and three ways to authenticate external users via the use of Salesforce Community Cloud. See Table 7-2.

***Table 7-2.*** *Methods to Authenticate Users into Salesforce*

| # | Authentication Method | How Does It Work? | Framework Used |
|---|---|---|---|
| **Internal Users** | | | |
| 1 | Salesforce username/ password | Users are authenticated using their unique username and password entered on the standard or custom login page of Salesforce. | Username/ password |
| 2 | Multi-org Salesforce authentication | SSO can be set up between multiple instances of Salesforce existing in the company via simple out-of-the-box configuration. | SAML 2.0 |
| 3 | Federated authentication | In this method, Salesforce receives a SAML assertion via an HTTP POST request from an identity management system or an external system with identity management capabilities. The SAML assertion contains a unique identifier and a validity duration and is digitally signed by the external system. | SAML 2.0 |
| 4 | Delegated authentication | An internal web service authenticates users based on information stored and provided by an external system. The external system provides a Salesforce username, password, and source IP to Salesforce to authenticate the user into Salesforce. | Web service |
| **External Users (via Salesforce Community Cloud)** | | | |
| 5 | Salesforce username/ password | Users are authenticated using their unique username and password entered on the standard or custom Salesforce Community Cloud login page. | Username/ password |
| 6 | Social sign-on access | Users can sign in using social site credentials. Supported sites include LinkedIn, Facebook, Twitter, Google, Janrain, Salesforce, and any service that implements the OpenID Connect protocol or OAuth 2.0 protocol. | OpenID Connect |
| 7 | Customer Identity and Access Management (CIAM) | Authentication provided by an external tool such as Okta acting as a CIAM directory that hosts all customer identity information and authenticates access into Salesforce using SAML SSO for external users. | SAML 2.0 |

# Authorization

Authorization refers to verifying access rights/privileges to resources in Salesforce. When conducting authorization, Salesforce checks the license type, user profile, permission sets, and role hierarchy (if any) assigned to the user based on which the user's access to the requested resources in Salesforce will be determined. Many people believe that access and authorization are synonymous. They are not.

Access is an itemized list of everything that a user can do in Salesforce, whereas authorization is validating the defined access at the time of entry into Salesforce. Access differs from authorization in the same way as placing a food order for pickup at a restaurant differs from the act of picking up the food from the restaurant when it is ready. What you pick up is what you ordered, but they are not the same thing. Access is the definition of what a user can do, whereas authorization is the execution of what the user can do in Salesforce. Just as you cannot pick up anything from the restaurant unless you first place an order, user authorization cannot work unless you first define the user's access in Salesforce. A user's access needs to be defined and completed before a user is authorized into Salesforce. Luckily, Salesforce does not allow a new user to be set up or saved successfully without at least assigning a user profile and a Salesforce license. Every user must have at least a user profile and a Salesforce license assigned to them; requiring these two access configuration items at the time of user creation ensures that no user is created without at least some basic access rights being defined.

Going along with the analogy of the food order, if you arrive at the restaurant and you want to order more or make a few changes to the current order, with the understanding that the restaurant is still okay with making changes, you can make real-time modifications to the order while you are at the restaurant. It would be a terrible experience if the restaurant asked you to leave the restaurant immediately, call them again to modify the order, and come back to the restaurant only after the changes have been made. Similarly, If the user is already authorized in Salesforce and the user's access is modified, the user's experience will be instantly and seamlessly altered by the system to match the user's new access configuration.

It is essential to cover another aspect of authorization, which relates to authorizing an external system to gain access to Salesforce on behalf of a specific user. Let's take a scenario such as when a user of an external ERP system conducts a transaction in the ERP system. The ERP transaction then needs to update a field in Salesforce on behalf of the same user, as long as the user has the permissions to update the field. In such cases, the external system's authorization into Salesforce on behalf of a specific user needs to follow a system authorization framework.

System authorizations in Salesforce can be managed using two industry standard authorization frameworks. The two frameworks are

- OpenID Connect framework

- OAuth 2.0 framework

## OpenID Connect Framework for Authorization

As discussed earlier, the OpenID Connect framework combines the functions of user authentication through delegated authentication via an OpenID authentication provider (also known as identity provider) with the authorization functions leveraging the OAuth 2.0 framework. Hence, the OpenID Connect framework addresses both the authentication and authorization for the user or system accessing Salesforce.

The OpenID framework assumes that Salesforce can rely on the authentication method established between the user and the OpenID authentication provider, such as the user's Google account or Amazon account or Twitter account. Since Salesforce relies on the OpenID authentication provider for authentication, Salesforce in this context is referred to as the relying party.

To support the authentication method using the OpenID framework, Salesforce (relying party) receives an ID token and a UserInfo endpoint from the "identity provider" to convey the authenticity of the user. There needs to be a registration handler set up in Salesforce (the relying party) to match the UserInfo received from the "identity provider" with the personal details of the user stored in Salesforce, such as the user's email address or phone number.

Once the authentication process is completed between Salesforce (relying party) and the identity provider, Salesforce follows any of the OAuth 2.0 flows mentioned in the next section.

## OAuth 2.0

The OAuth 2.0 authorization framework allows a system to gain access into Salesforce on behalf of a specific user, without sharing the user's identity or login credentials with the external applications. When an external system accesses Salesforce on behalf of a particular user, Salesforce grants access based on the scope of that user's access in Salesforce.

To do so, the external system requesting access to Salesforce needs first to establish a trust relationship between itself and Salesforce. It is important to note that the process of authorizing an external system to access Salesforce on behalf of an authenticated user is a complex multi-sequence process requiring extensive back-and-forth API-based exchanges between Salesforce and the external system requesting authorization. This multi-sequence process of authorizing an external system into Salesforce is known as an "OAuth flow."

It is important to note that OAuth does not conduct user authentication for the user since it cannot see a user's identity or user credentials at all. It only manages the authorization functions needed on behalf of the user. It relies entirely on Salesforce confirming authentication on its own or via an OpenID authentication provider by using the OpenID Connect framework.

At the time of this writing, Salesforce supports 13 authorization flows, which are outlined in Table 7-3. For detailed flow diagrams with common scenarios of the commonly used authorization flows, refer to Appendix A.

***Table 7-3.*** *Authorization Flows*

| # | OAuth 2.0 Authorization Flow | Description | When to Use |
|---|---|---|---|
| 1 | Web Server Flow | This flow is used when a server-side application is a trusted service and can protect the client secret. The User-Agent is redirected to an authorization server that was previously configured with the client secret. The flow relies on the trusted connection where the access token does not go through a browser. | Machine-to-machine authorization where the apps are hosted on a secure server, such as Single-page apps Native mobile apps This is the most common flow. |
| 2 | User-Agent Flow | This flow does not use an authorization code; rather, the resource owner submits credentials directly to the client, and the access token is the client. The flow does not use a redirect, nor does it exchange credentials directly. | Established trust between the resource owner and the client application, such as Desktop or mobile integration app |

*(continued)*

***Table 7-3.*** (*continued*)

| # | OAuth 2.0 Authorization Flow | Description | When to Use |
|---|---|---|---|
| 3 | JWT Bearer Flow | This flow allows an authorized server to access a given systems' data without logging in each time. It uses a certificate to sign the JSON Web Token (JWT) request and doesn't require explicit user interaction. This flow is stateless; no tokens are used. | Created for server-to-server API integration, such as In-house applications LDAP solutions |
| 4 | Device Flow | Often devices have a limited ability to accept input or display information and can support user direct input. This flow redirects the User-Agent to a specific URL to request and confirm access. | Primarily used with IoT devices such as Smart TVs Appliances Bluetooth devices Command-line apps |
| 5 | Asset Token Flow | An asset token similar to an open-standard JWT token is used in this flow. Once authorized, an OAuth access token and an actor token are exchanged for an asset token. | Primarily used to combine issuing and registering asset tokens for efficient token exchange and automatic linking of devices to Salesforce (`https://help.salesforce.com/articleView?id=sso_delauthentication.htm&type=5asset`) data, such as scanners, RFID, and so on. |

(*continued*)

***Table 7-3.*** (*continued*)

| # | OAuth 2.0 Authorization Flow | Description | When to Use |
|---|---|---|---|
| 6 | Username and Password Flow | This flow requires the user to authorize a client. It is supported for connected apps, and both the username and password are passed to the application. This flow should be avoided, as its credentials are not secure. The resource owner and the client must have a high degree of trust. If you do have to use this flow, then utilize the named credentials feature to store and service your username/password through the API. | Primarily used when a client legacy application does not support another option such as Custom application created by client Internal application without ability to store access token or credentials |
| 7 | OAuth 2.0 Refresh Token Flow | This flow supports other flows such as the Web Server and User-Agent flows to renew their access tokens. Once the client is authorized for access, it uses a refresh token to get a new access token. This flow reduces the need to repeat the full authorization flow continually. | Renews the session with a new session ID for Web Server and User-Agent flows, without requiring reauthorization. |
| 8 | Canvas App User Flow – Signed Request | This flow supports a feature in Salesforce called Canvas, which is used to integrate third-party applications with Salesforce. The signed request is the default. | It is used to provide access to an app using admin access or user self-authority. |
| 9 | Canvas App User Flow – OAuth 2.0 | This flow is the default authorization method for Canvas apps. The signed request authorization flow is dependent on the Canvas app's Permitted Users field whether it is set to "Admin approved users are pre-authorized" or "All users may self-authorize." | It uses either Web Server OAuth Authentication Flow or User-Agent OAuth Authentication Flow. |

(*continued*)

***Table 7-3.*** (*continued*)

| # | OAuth 2.0 Authorization Flow | Description | When to Use |
|---|---|---|---|
| 10 | SAML Assertion Flow | This flow is used to access a web service API using a SAML assertion. In this flow, an app can use an existing SAML authentication. This flow can be used without the need for a connected app. | This flow extends an existing Web SSO connection to authenticate a requested API. |
| 11 | SAML Bearer Assertion Flow | An app can reuse an existing authorization. A signed SAML 2.0 assertion can be used to renew with a digital signature applied to the SAML assertion. | Renews the assertion with a new session ID for SAML Assertion Flow. |
| 12 | SAML Single Sign-On for Canvas Apps Flow | Whether you use a signed request or OAuth authorization, you can use SAML-based single sign-on (SSO) to provide your authentication flow. | Leverages Salesforce as an ID provider or SP. SAML SSO can provide automatic authentication into your Canvas app via SAML. |
| 13 | Social Sign-On with Social Agent Authorization | This flow facilitates Salesforce identity to use standard OpenID public authentication, such as Facebook, LinkedIn, Twitter, Google. These provider connections are created in Salesforce and used to allow access to known and unknown users. | Social sign-on can also be used to create and update users by presenting the user identity information to Salesforce. |

# Authorization Scopes

As of the time of writing this, ten different scopes can be created in Salesforce. Table 7-4 outlines the different scope types in Salesforce.

***Table 7-4.***  *Authorization Flows using OAuth 2.0*

| # | Scope Type | Description |
|---|---|---|
| 1 | api | Provides access to the current user's account via API. |
| 2 | chatter_api | Provides access to only Chatter REST API. |
| 3 | custom_permissions | Provides access to custom permissions associated with a connected app. |
| 4 | full | Provides full access to all data accessible by the logged-in user. |
| 5 | id | Provides access to identity, such as profile, email, address, or phone. |
| 6 | openid | Provides access to OpenID identifier. |
| 7 | refresh_token | Provides refresh token to be returned. |
| 8 | visualforce | Provides access to Visualforce pages. |
| 9 | web | Provides use of access_token on the Web. |
| 10 | Custom Scope | Custom Scope as defined by an admin or developer. |

# Session Management

A user's interaction with Salesforce for a duration of time is a session. After authentication and upon being authorized with the allowed scope of access, a user session is established. A session contains the details about the user, session type, and duration of the session among other session details,[3] all of which are stored in the user's browser as session cookies. Hence, a session is similar to the in-flight experience in my travel experience. Everything needed for the duration of my flight was stored and provided as part of my in-flight experience. The session secures and limits the user's exposure and prevents unauthorized and unintended use of the system by any user other than the user authenticated and authorized to use the system during a specific time. Salesforce uses TLS (Transport Layer Security) and requires secure connections (HTTPS) for all communication by default.

Each session in Salesforce maintains a "session state" that contains information about the user and the authentication level used by the user to authenticate themselves into Salesforce. There are two types of security level for authentication that impact

---

[3]https://help.salesforce.com/articleView?id=security_user_session_info.htm&type=5.

session security. They are standard-assurance and high-assurance authentication levels. High-assurance authentication requires users to authenticate into Salesforce using a two-factor authentication.

# Two-Factor Authentication

This form of authentication requires a two-step verification process which requires not only a username and password but also an additional confidential set of information that only the real user possesses. Two-factor authentication can also be set up to be required when a user meets specific criteria, such as attempting to view reports or accessing a connected app. When a user accesses Salesforce from outside a trusted IP range or uses a browser or app that Salesforce does not recognize, the user is challenged to verify their identity.

There are five different ways to set up two-factor authentication in Salesforce:

1. Push notification or location-based notification automated with the Salesforce Authenticator mobile app connected to the user's account

2. U2F security key registered on the user account

3. Code generated by a mobile authenticator app such as the Google Authenticator app

4. Code sent via SMS to mobile phone

5. Code sent via email to the user's email address

After the verification is successful, the user does not have to verify identity again from that browser or app because the browser or the app retains the session ID that authenticates the entire session for the user for the duration of that session.

The only situations when a verified user needs to reverify is when the user

- Manually clears browser cookies and instructs the browser to delete cookies

- Browses in private or incognito mode and then opens new browsers or browser tabs to access the same pages

- Removes "**Don't ask again**" on the identity verification page and times out as per the configured session timeout

An administrator can restrict access to certain types of resources in Salesforce based on the level of authentication used by the user to authenticate into Salesforce. The administrator can define access policies requiring a high-assurance authentication to access specific sensitive data or sensitive operations in Salesforce. If a user authenticated into Salesforce using a standard assurance, they would be blocked from accessing the sensitive data or sensitive operations that require a high-assurance authentication. In such cases, the users will have to log out and log back in using a high-assurance authentication such as the use of two-factor authentication. The users that have already authenticated using a high-assurance authentication are provided seamless access to all data, including sensitive data and sensitive operations without any reauthentication and authorization requirements. Although no other user can access a user's active session other than the user itself, an administrator of Salesforce can view the type of session that the user is engaged in.

As of the time of writing this, there are 23 different session types that can be created in Salesforce. Table 7-5 outlines the different session types in Salesforce.

***Table 7-5.*** *Session Types in Salesforce*

| # | Session Type | Description |
|---|---|---|
| 1 | API | Created when accessing an org through the API. |
| 2 | APIOnlyUser | Created to enable a password reset in the user interface for API-only users. |
| 3 | Aura | Created for access to Lightning Experience functionality. |
| 4 | ChatterNetworks | Created when using Chatter Networks or Chatter Communities. |
| 5 | ChatterNetworksAPIOnly | Created when using the Chatter Networks or Chatter Communities API. |
| 6 | ChatterNetworksAPIOnlyOAuth | Created when approving OAuth access by a Chatter Communities user. |
| 7 | Content | Created when serving user-uploaded content. |
| 8 | DataDownloadOnly | A session that can only be used to download data. |
| 9 | LightningContainerComponent | Created for use with Lightning container components. |

(*continued*)

***Table 7-5.*** (*continued*)

| # | Session Type | Description |
|---|---|---|
| 10 | LivePreview | Created to use the live preview functionality in Experience Builder. |
| 11 | Node | Created for NodeJS access. |
| 12 | OAuthApprovalUI | A session that allows access only to the OAuth approval page. |
| 13 | OAuth2 | Created using OAuth flows. For example, if you use OAuth authentication for a connected app, this type of session is created. |
| 14 | SamlOAuthApprovalUi | Created when approving OAuth access during a SAML flow. |
| 15 | SiteStudio | Created when using the Experience Builder user interface. |
| 16 | SitePreview | Initiated when an internal Canvas app is invoked. |
| 17 | STREAMING_API | Created for use by Streaming API. |
| 18 | SubstituteUser | Created when one user logs in as another user. For example, if an administrator logs in as another user, a SubstituteUser session is created. |
| 19 | UI | Created for access to the Salesforce Classic UI. Represents the core session for a login to the user interface. |
| 20 | UnspecifiedType | Created by an unknown source. |
| 21 | UserSite | Initiated when a Canvas application is invoked. |
| 22 | Visualforce | Created to access Visualforce pages. |
| 23 | WDC_API | A session using Work.com API. |

When users have authenticated into Salesforce via single sign-on, they can have multiple sessions active at the same time.

The length of time a user is allowed to remain active before reauthentication is known as a session duration. An administrator can set up a session timeout duration that automatically ends a user's session due to inactivity for the admin's chosen session timeout duration. The default session timeout in Salesforce is two hours of inactivity. When the session timeout is reached, the user is prompted with a message on the screen that asks the user if they want to log out or continue working. If the user does not respond to this message, then they are automatically logged out in a few minutes from the message being displayed.

A common misconception with many Salesforce users is that they believe that closing the web browser window or tab, which has the active session of Salesforce, will automatically log them out. This is not true. An active Salesforce session remains active even when all web browser windows or tabs are closed. It remains active until either a session timeout is reached due to user inactivity or until the user logs out, whichever is earlier.

# Single Sign-On

Single sign-on is the approach by which a single user credential, maintained and stored in a single centralized identity management system, is used to authenticate and authorize the user's access into multiple systems.

Single sign-on works using the Security Assertion Markup Language (SAML) 2.0 framework to allow the identity management system, referred to in this context as the "identity provider," to remotely authenticate users requesting services existing in another system, referred to in this context as the "service provider." When authenticating in this manner, the user is seamlessly given access to multiple service providers without being required to individually log into any of "service providers."

There are two key authentication flows for SSO using SAML 2.0 that an architect needs to design for:

1. Identity provider (IDP)–initiated SAML SSO flow

2. Service provider (SP)–initiated SAML SSO flow

It is important to note that both the SAML-based SSO flows are needed for an SSO approach to work, and it's not a matter of choosing one over the other since the two flows cover the two possible scenarios by which a user is authenticated and authorized into the system using SSO.

## Identity Provider (IDP)–Initiated SAML SSO Flow

In identity provider (IDP)–initiated SAML SSO flow, the user begins their user experience by first logging into the identity provider and then requesting access to the service provider after successfully authenticating itself with the identity provider.

Figure 7-4 illustrates the sequence of activities that occur between the user, the identity provider *(assumed to be Microsoft Active Directory in this illustration)*, and the service provider *(assumed to be Salesforce in this illustration)*.

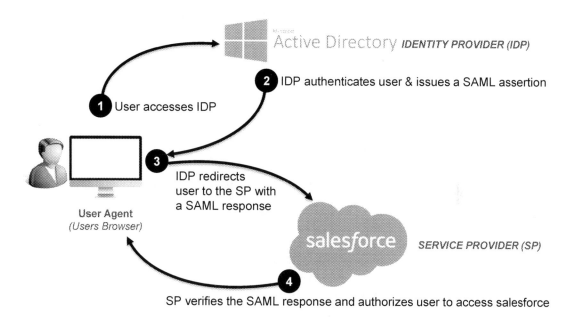

*Figure 7-4. Identity Provider (IDP)–Initiated SAML SSO Flow*

## Service Provider (SP)–Initiated SAML SSO Flow

In service provider (SP)–initiated SAML SSO flow, the user begins their user experience by directly attempting to access the service provider. In this case, the service provider routes the user to the identity provider to complete authenticating themselves with the identity provider. The identity provider redirects the user back to the requested Salesforce page that the user was trying to access in the first place by completing a sequence of authorization steps to gain access into the service provider. The service provider–initiated flow is an extension of the identity provider–initiated flow, and hence the latter is a prerequisite for the former.

Figure 7-5 illustrates the sequence of activities that occur between the user, the identity provider *(assumed to be Microsoft Active Directory in this illustration)*, and the service provider *(assumed to be Salesforce in this illustration)*.

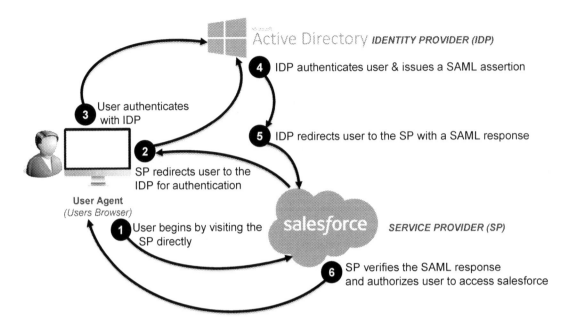

***Figure 7-5.*** *Service Provider (SP)–Initiated SAML SSO Flow*

There are four methods of setting up SSO in Salesforce, that is, three methods to set up SSO for internal users and one method to set up SSO for external users who log in via Salesforce Community Cloud, as shown in Table 7-6.

***Table 7-6.*** *Single Sign-On (SSO) Methods Available in Salesforce*

| # SSO Methods | How Does It Work? | Framework Used |
|---|---|---|
| **Internal Users** | | |
| 1 SSO with multiple orgs | SSO can be set up between multiple instances of Salesforce existing in the company via simple out-of-the-box configuration. | SAML 2.0 |
| 2 SSO with Microsoft Active Directory (AD) | Salesforce is integrated with Microsoft Active Directory (AD) using Identity Connect or Microsoft Active Directory Federation Services (ADFS). | OpenID Connect |

(*continued*)

***Table 7-6.*** (*continued*)

| # | SSO Methods | How Does It Work? | Framework Used |
|---|---|---|---|
| 3 | Federated authentication | In this method, Salesforce receives a SAML assertion via an HTTP POST request from an identity management system or an external system with identity management capabilities. The SAML assertion contains a unique identifier and a validity duration and is digitally signed by the external system. | SAML 2.0 |
| **External Users (via Salesforce Community Cloud)** | | | |
| 4 | Social sign-on access | Users can sign in using social site credentials. Supported sites include LinkedIn, Facebook, Twitter, Google, Janrain, Salesforce, and any service that implements the OpenID Connect protocol or OAuth 2.0 protocol. | OpenID Connect |

# Logouts and Redirects

Logout refers to the termination of an active, authenticated session. Once the user is logged out, the user will need to reauthenticate with Salesforce to regain access into Salesforce. Users can also be logged out in one of two ways:

1. **User-Initiated Logout**

   In this type of logout, the user has initiated the logout by clicking a logout function in Salesforce, or the identity provider initiated it in the case of single sign-on.

2. **System-Initiated Logout**

   System-initiated logout can occur when the system automatically logs the user out of an active session or when a session timeout is being reached due to user inactivity and no user response is received on the session timeout screen message prompting the user to continue working or log out.

# Single Logout (SLO)

Salesforce also offers a "Single Logout" feature, which can be seen as an antonym feature to single sign-on for login. When SLO is enabled, logging out of a single session of Salesforce automatically logs users out from all other sessions of Salesforce and any connected apps that were used in any of the sessions. To use SLO, the identity provider, service provider, and relying parties must be all configured to use single sign-on (SSO).

Single Logout can be set up in the following four scenarios for Salesforce:

1. When Salesforce is the service provider (SP) in a SAML 2.0–based single sign-on (SSO) setup.

   In this scenario, Salesforce is set up as the service provider connected to an external SAML-based identity provider. The identity provider uses SAML to log users into Salesforce; and when they log out of the identity provider or the Salesforce session, the users are logged out of both, Salesforce and the identity provider.

2. When Salesforce is the identity provider (IDP) in a SAML 2.0–based single sign-on (SSO) setup.

   In this scenario, Salesforce is set up as the identity provider connected to an external SAML-based service provider. Salesforce uses SAML to log users into the service provider through a connected app. When users log out of the service provider or the Salesforce session, the users are logged out of both, Salesforce and the service provider.

3. When Salesforce is the relying party in an OpenID Connect setup.

   In this scenario, the users authenticate themselves using an OpenID authentication provider such as Google or Amazon to log into Salesforce as the relying party. In this case, when the users log out of the Salesforce session or the OpenID authentication provider session, they are automatically logged out of both, Salesforce and the OpenID authentication provider.

4.  When Salesforce is the OpenID authentication provider in an
    OpenID Connect setup.

    In this scenario, the users authenticate themselves using
    Salesforce as the OpenID authentication provider to log into
    a Salesforce-connected app that acts as the relying party. In
    this case, when the users log out of the Salesforce session
    or the connected app that acts as the relying party, they are
    automatically logged out of both, Salesforce and the relying party.

Logout is considered a part of the user's active user experience in Salesforce, and the
user experience is not concluded until the user is gracefully redirected out of Salesforce to
a web page, outside the authenticated area of Salesforce. By default, Salesforce redirects
the users back to the login page of Salesforce. However, administrators can choose to
redirect the users to a different location, such as the company's website, by specifying a
redirect URL in Setup ➤ Session Settings ➤ Logout Page Settings ➤ Logout URL.

# User Account Management

User account management refers to the process of supporting ongoing changes required
to a user's scope of access in the Salesforce instance. It also includes designing for self-
recovering user accounts via guided forgotten username/password flows on the login
page. There may be user lockout policies based on the number of failed login attempts,
requiring an administrator to unlock the user's account after cautious review of the
user's login activities.

User account management is a key aspect of every Salesforce administrator's role,
and there are several online resources and books available on the topic of Salesforce
administration, so we will refrain from covering Salesforce administration related to user
account management in this book.

# Deprovisioning

User deprovisioning in Salesforce refers to the process of deactivating a user's access to
the Salesforce instance. In Salesforce, users cannot be deleted or removed completely;
they can only be deactivated. Deactivating a user disables the user's access to the
Salesforce instance and releases the Salesforce license previously assigned for use by
other users or new users added to the Salesforce environment. If a user is deactivated

while the user is in an active session in Salesforce, then an immediate system-initiated logout is executed by Salesforce, and the user's session ends instantly. In this scenario, the user realizes the session termination when they attempt to take any actions in their active session or when they attempt to navigate to another page in Salesforce. Any data not committed by the user is automatically removed as a result of the session being terminated.

# Chapter Summary

In this chapter, we covered the following:

- The nine stages of an identity and access management lifecycle: provisioning, access, authentication, authorization, session management, single sign-on (SSO), logouts and redirects, user account management, and deprovisioning.

- Provisioning refers to the process of setting up a user in Salesforce, which includes collecting and storing personal and system registration details about the user or an external system. There are nine methods of provisioning within Salesforce as of this writing.

- Access refers to the process of defining a user's access or system's privilege to specific resources within Salesforce such as objects, records, fields, and UI pages.

- A user's access needs to be defined and set up prior to a user being authenticated or authorized into Salesforce. Access can be changed before, during, and after the user has been authorized in Salesforce.

- Access configuration in Salesforce is often referred to as "visibility and sharing" in the Salesforce ecosystem.

- Authentication refers to verifying the identity of the user or an external system, by requesting them to provide a set of identifying credentials as part of their request for access to the correct instance of Salesforce and then validating those credentials against the credentials stored in Salesforce as part of user provisioning.

- Authentication into Salesforce can be managed using one of three industry standard frameworks, which are the username/password framework, SAML 2.0 framework, and OpenID Connect framework. There are seven methods of authentication into Salesforce using any of the three authentication frameworks as of this writing.

- Authorization refers to validating the user's access rights/privileges to resources in Salesforce such as objects, records, fields, and UI pages. We also discussed that access is different from authorization, as access refers to the setup of user privileges, whereas authorization is the execution of the defined user privileges at the time of user's entry into Salesforce.

- Authorization into Salesforce can be managed using one of two industry standard frameworks, which are the OpenID Connect framework and OAuth 2.0 framework. There are 13 authorization flows for configuring authorizations using the OAuth 2.0 framework as of this writing.

- Every authorization request utilizes one or more authorization scopes to determine the scope of access being granted to the user or an external system on behalf of a user. There are nine authorization scope types in Salesforce, as of this writing.

- Session management refers to the duration of a seamless user or system experience during their active use of Salesforce. After authentication and authorization into Salesforce, a user may navigate across multiple screens, access various data, and conduct a variety of transactions, without requiring Salesforce to reauthenticate and reauthorize the user after every single user activity. There are 23 different session types that can be established within Salesforce as of this writing.

- Single sign-on (SSO) refers to the method of centralizing user authentication processes via the use of a single identity-providing system known as the "identity provider" that enables users to authenticate with multiple systems in your company by logging in only once.

- Single sign-on for Salesforce can be managed using one of two industry standard frameworks, which are the OpenID Connect framework and SAML 2.0 framework.

- There are two key authentication flows using single sign-on; they are identity provider (IDP)–initiated SAML SSO flow and service provider (SP) –initiated SAML SSO flow.

- Using either the OpenID Connect framework or the SAML 2.0 framework for SSO, there are four different methods to set up SSO in Salesforce, as of this writing.

- Logouts and redirects refer to the process of terminating the user's current active session securely as per the user's intent to end their current session or due to the user being deprovisioned while the user is in an active session of Salesforce. The termination of the user's active session navigates the user to an alternative site outside the user's authorized access to Salesforce, which is known as a "redirect." There are two main types of logout; they are user-initiated logout and system-initiated logout.

- Salesforce provides a feature known as "Single Logout" (SLO) which can be enabled if SSO is enabled for the Salesforce org. This feature logs a user out of all active Salesforce sessions when the user logs out of any single active session of Salesforce.

- User account management refers to the process of supporting ongoing changes required to a user's access, supporting login recovery and password resets, or freezing a user's account temporarily or deactivating a user completely. Login recovery often refers to unlocking locked user accounts for failed authentication or authorization attempts.

- Deprovisioning refers to the process of deactivating a user's access to the Salesforce instance. In Salesforce, users cannot be deleted or removed completely. They can only be deactivated.

# CHAPTER 8

# Salesforce Mobile Architecture

Our mobile devices have become the most critical tools in our lives. Today's business success relies on providing customers, employees, and stakeholders with real-time information wherever they are working, playing, or living. As architects, we need to design our systems around the way our stakeholders consume that information and how they want that information. The users are virtually connected to information 24 hours a day, so our designs must include mobile access and availability.

In this chapter, we will cover

- The importance of the mobile architecture as it relates to the overall Salesforce design

- The high-level concepts needed to select the correct mobile strategy

- How to manage enterprise mobile applications

- Understanding the design approaches using Mobile SDK, Salesforce app, and custom mobile development

- The extension of mobile application with the use of wearables and connected devices

## Why Mobile Architecture Is Important

A mobile application is more than an application on a phone. It is an end-to-end solution that includes system design, security umbrella, data management, and application usability and accessibility. The design must anticipate how the information is viewed, consumed, and worked. Mobile data must be highly secure and be available whenever and wherever the user needs it, connected or disconnected. Additionally, a mobile device

257

© Dipanker Jyoti and James A. Hutcherson 2021
D. Jyoti and J. A. Hutcherson, *Salesforce Architect's Handbook*, https://doi.org/10.1007/978-1-4842-6631-1_8

is primarily used for micro-activities such as reading a text, taking a picture, and looking at a map. As such, the interface must be streamlined, intuitive, and easy to use.

This chapter will provide a deep dive into the concepts, considerations and trade-offs, security implications, development approaches, device management, and available Salesforce architecture and approaches.

## It's a Lifecycle

Mobile architecture is more than a device and application selection. Good mobile architecture should consider and include the full lifecycle of information, where and how it is used. Figure 8-1 shows the fundamental considerations for mobile data management elements and device management.

***Figure 8-1.*** *Mobile Data and Device Considerations*

Mobile Device Management is related to the direct management of the physical device. It includes access, security, and data management. The major areas required to manage a mobile device are as follows:

- **Identity Management**: How does the device know the user's identity?

- **Application Process**: How does the application use the device?

- **Policy Enforcement**: How does the device enforce data and application rules?

- **Data Logs and Auditing**: How are activity logs created and tracked?

- **Encryption**: Does the device encrypt data at rest or transmission?

- **Mobile Security**: How is the device secured and protected?

- **Data Sovereignty**: How is the nationality of the data managed on the device?

- **Identity Federation and User Access**: How does the device link the data to the device user?

Mobile data management is related to how the device is used. It includes what data is acquired, managed, and destroyed. The major areas required to manage mobile data are listed as follows:

- **Collection**: How is the device used to capture data?

- **Access**: How does the user gain access to data on the device?

- **Usage**: How is the data used by the device?

- **Storage**: How is data stored?

- **Transfer**: How is data moved to and from the device?

- **Deletion**: How is the data removed from the device?

# Leverage Devices

Mobile devices are not just a communications device for voice and text-based communication. Today's mobile devices are robust. They combine virtually all the specialized hardware and software used in business applications. Current mobile features include

- Cellular and Wi-Fi access

- Voice and SMS/text

- Voice recording

- Photography

- Image recognition

- Language translation

- Geolocation and mapping

- Native applications and web applications

- Search engine

- Touchscreen and facial and fingerprint identification

- Voice searching

- Commerce, stores, and payment

- Email, contact, calendar, and to-do/reminders

- IoT such as heart monitor and external device access

- Music, TV, games, books

- Social interaction

An excellent mobile architecture will use as many native device features as possible.

# Virtual and Mobile Security

Managing mobile devices is challenging. Often, these devices are personally owned and managed by individuals with varying degrees of expertise and security. The balance between access and security is daunting. Your mobile architecture needs to consider what, when, where, why, and how data is being accessed, used, shared, and destroyed and by whom. Your design must address each of these areas.

# Connects the World

How often have you filled out a form or written an email only to find out that you were "offline" and the work you performed was lost? Mobile users demand applications and systems that can anticipate such network outages and transparently handle them without the user even knowing this issue exists. A well-designed mobile architecture can move back and forth seamlessly between the connected and disconnected world.

# Important Mobile Concepts

On the surface, mobile design and mobile application development may seem straightforward. However, as you look at the many constraints surrounding mobile devices, you will quickly notice the complexity involved in building the best architecture. Let's examine nine common technical constraints that should be considered in mobile design and development.

# Modern Mobile Applications

Application development for mobile devices uses one of three major types: web application, native application, and hybrid application. Each approach offers different value attributes and should be selected to match the specific expected and ultimate use case. It is important to understand each development approach and select the one aligned to your specific needs. Making the correct choice is often making a trade-off decision between two critical features. Later in the chapter, we will provide the major options, advantages, and disadvantages of each of the following development approaches:

**Web Application**: A software program that is accessible via a web browser and runs on a web server. The application runs on a back-end server and is presented on a mobile device. The mobile device always requires online connectivity to work.

**Native Application**: A software program that is developed and installed on a specific mobile device using proprietary development software such as iOS and Android. The application is stored on the device and can work offline without access to a network.

**Hybrid Application**: A software program that uses both native and web applications as a framework to support applications on multiple platforms. The business application is written in a hybrid framework environment and pushed to the respective proprietary mobile environments. The application is stored on the device and may work without access to a network.

---

**Note**    The study and practice of mobile development is extensive and beyond the scope of this book. However, it is important to understand how making the right design choice requires an architect to evaluate many different factors including mobile user experience, access to device features, speed to market (single platform or cross-platform), development costs, application performance, required development skills, and application deployment.

---

# User Experience

A key component of mobile application design is the user interface and the user experience. The interface should be easy to use and provide an effective and enjoyable user experience. The UX should consider four main attributes:

1. Information architecture, or the integration of the application and the environment it is sharing such as the browser and its inherent navigation.

2. Interaction design, or how the user interacts with the application.

3. Usability, or how the user obtains the information or the way it functions.

4. Visual design, or the visual impact the application has on the users.

All the attributes call on the whole person as a user. It is not just the visual aspect of the design. Consider the whole human experience of not only what the user is doing but also how they feel about doing the activity (i.e., the user experience, a.k.a. UX).

The three types of development call on very different attributes with pros and cons that must be considered in the mobile architecture decision. Native applications inherit the device persona directly for the UX features built into the operating environment of the device. In contrast, a hybrid application inherits the UX features from the framework used in the hybrid development environment. This concept allows a developer to create an application that runs on different device types, such as Apple and Android devices. A web application uses the UX features created and presented from the cloud and takes on UX features from the browser and the application framework.

Native applications allow users to use devices that inherit UX such as screen manipulation (swipe, pinch, expand). In contrast, a hybrid application can use these UX features, but they are emulated or applied in the framework, losing some of the device behavior in favor of speed to market.

## Access to Device Features

Our mobile devices are more than a cellular phone. Our smartphone devices include features that range from an advanced camera and video system to navigation system, native and cloud-based storage, CRM, game system, voice recorder, web browser, financial tools and e-wallet, news platform, password repository, electronic tape measure, TV and music, and personal health monitor. All these features fit in the user's hand. The users expect for the applications they use to have access to the features they use every day. The decisions you make regarding access to features can impact the usability of the application.

As you consider the designed uses and outcome associated with your application, make sure to include the different ways the application will be used. Think about how the application can take advantage of the device(s). As an example, if your business application requires the user to log meetings, routes, and destinations, having direct access to the native navigation feature could significantly improve the user experience. Which features are available to your potential development options? Of course, native development offers the full range of features, but at the cost of knowing the device your stakeholders will use. Often, you will need to develop for several different mobile platforms, thus increasing the costs and the time required to deliver a solution.

## Speed to Market

Operating at the "speed of business" is not just a cliché; it is the reality of the market. Consumers and businesses demand mobile solutions. Often the business pressures will dictate that a mobile solution be delivered quickly to the users. Businesses have many different pressures, and social and economic conditions are constantly changing. As an architect, you need to consider more than the features gained or lost. You must also look at the social and economic impact of the choices.

If speed to market is a primary consideration, web applications or hybrid applications offer the best solutions. Building native applications on multiple platforms takes longer to produce. Conversely, hybrid frameworks offer a solution. The frameworks

CHAPTER 8    SALESFORCE MOBILE ARCHITECTURE

reduce the time to produce applications by supporting a subset of features that can be delivered across many mobile platforms. Another option is to use a prebuilt application that can use existing SaaS-based solutions quickly on a mobile device. One such solution is called "Salesforce app." This proprietary framework can significantly decrease the time and effort to release an application to the market while providing most of the features used on a desktop version of the application. Salesforce app will be discussed later in this chapter.

Another consideration is the velocity of applications that are needed. You will also need to weigh the pros and cons of the design framework as it relates to the number of applications you are building, the number of users you are supporting, and the financial budget the project can support.

# Development Costs

Mobile application development requires an investment in people, time, skills, creativity, and deployment. This reality has been a business dilemma from the start. As the applications we use in the office migrate to the applications we use everywhere, the struggle to support impacts your company's bottom line. You will need to be aware of how these decisions are made, the real and perceived values of the mobile solutions, and most importantly the ways to mitigate the cost while maximizing the usability and efficiency of the application.

Choosing the right development model is part technical, part business realities, and part finesse. Your architecture solution must consider all three competing needs. Consider asking yourself the following questions:

1. How will my solution be used?

2. Will device features improve or distract from the goals of the application?

3. Will the application bring additional revenue or reduce cost to the business?

4. Is the business requesting features that are already available on mobile devices?

5. Does my development platform support the business requirements?

6.  What is the velocity of business requirements, and can my team meet the demand?

7.  Does the usability improve the brand of the business?

8.  Will I need to hire or train developers to support the mobile development framework?

9.  Does my selected framework provide most or all the features our users want and desire?

10. Do I have the budget to provide the applications using the selected approach?

Each of these questions will help you better understand the recommendations and choices you make. It is not a one-size-fits-all approach. Each new business requirement and application will need to be evaluated independently and collectively.

The development cost is often the great equalizer. The best solution may be suboptimal from a technical perspective. It may also be suboptimal from a cost perspective. In the end, as the architect, you need to be aware of the realities of the economics of the decision.

# Application Performance

Users expect high-performing mobile applications. However, the device speed and the responsiveness of the connection are not the only consideration. Your design needs to evaluate the several performance factors including device and connectivity speed; business processes and efficiency; device usage in terms of memory, battery, and data plan requirements; and general stability. It is important for you to consider the following performance factors within your design.

---

**Note**   Consider creating mobile microservices as you create applications, so that Salesforce apps that are rendered on mobile devices have minimal attributes for queries and displaying data. This approach can improve the overall performance. A human-centered design approach can identify the various microservices used or needed in a given application.

---

**Application Errors, Bugs, and Updates**: Nothing is more impactful to the performance of a mobile application than the disruption of an application that crashes, locks up, or is continually loading updates and patches. As with any application development process, mobile application development should start with a clear design for capturing and handling exceptions and errors. Additionally, the design should include a recovery path for both exceptions related to connectivity and application process failures. Your architecture should provide the required exception and error handling approach so that your development team includes test-driven development principles to improve the application performance.

Updates and patches are a natural and accepted part of mobile applications. Virtually all mobile device platforms include an update process for providing enhancements and bug fixes. More about this in a few paragraphs.

**Startup Time and Task Load Times**: A critical consideration of performance for users is how quickly the application starts and how easily and efficiently the application supports the required tasks. A mobile device is "always on" and as such, the applications are also expected to be "always on." Many factors can impact the startup time of an application including the authentication and authorization process to access the underlying data and systems, the amount of local device memory used, and the amount of data needed to present the application to the user. All factors need your clear consideration and design documentation to minimize the requirements through design rather than sacrificing security and application features. It is a balancing act that can be managed.

**Information Capture Process and Times**: How many times have you been required by an application to enter repetitive information such as your name, email, phone, and address information? What about private information such as credit card numbers, expiration dates, and security codes? How can your mobile design take advantage of device features like auto-populate and wallet features? Does your design maintain the security of the information?

How often have you been required to type large amounts of information in the application using a very small, error-prone keyboard? I guess you might have a notice on your mobile email application to "forgive typos and auto-correction errors" in your messages. A good mobile architecture looks at each information capture requirement and offers a design approach to improve the user experience and reduce errors and bad data.

**Server-Side Response Time to Support the Application**: While writing this book, we often used tools like Google Drive and Google Sheets. Additionally, we used add-on features such as online dictionaries and thesauruses. The applications are server-side applications that require both connection and access to use them. The performance and access to these applications can significantly impact application performance. The design should look at response times, load time, and offline functionality.

**Memory Usage Required by the Application**: The mobile devices are getting more powerful and support larger internal storage. However, the device hardware has a lot of demand from the device OS and other "always on" applications. The application memory and online storage requirements should be limited to only what is needed. Again, it is a balancing act between competing requirements, and you need to design to reduce overhead whenever possible. The difference between native and hybrid applications can often come down to the overhead needed to support the application.

**Battery Drain and Power Consumption Requirements of the Application**: Every user dislikes seeing the battery icon blink "low." The more device resources your application uses, such as memory, processing, and GPS features, the more impact it has on battery life. Popular applications such as GPS and video applications are notorious at draining your device's battery. The trade-off decision may not be directly available. However, if your application design allows the user to change default settings, you will allow the user to decide which performance features are important to them. An example is the ability to notify users of updates and changes that require the application to stay in active memory and consume power. The option would be to allow the user to decide if they want the notices all the time or just when they have the application open. This capability is available in native applications and to a limited extent in hybrid applications. This feature is not available for web applications.

**Data Plan Usage**: The new 5G data delivery networks tout an increase of data at reduced cost. However, that increase in data has a lot of competition for device applications. Better pictures and 4K videos require more data and data throughput, and many business applications are also requiring significant data bundles to provide the best user experiences. The architectural design must estimate and evaluate the size of the data requirements and the throughput of the cellular and Wi-Fi networks.

**Page, Image, and Video Size, Compression, and Load Times**: I recall, not so long ago, that I would turn off the image load on my mobile device to speed up how quickly the application would load or calculate an outcome. That luxury is virtually gone. Users expect to have high-quality images and videos within applications. They also expect speed. Most mobile architects and developers use tools to test the speed of page loads to optimize. The design considerations that impact load times are listed in the following. You should review and optimize the following application design elements:

- HTTP requests.

- Minify (reduce white space and formatting) and combine files.

- Use asynchronous loading for CSS and JavaScript.

- Defer or reorder the loading of JavaScript until after the content is loaded.

- Minimize the TTFB (time to first byte). The initial request includes the DNS lookup, server processing, and the response.

- Reduce server response time by evaluating and selecting the best hosting service.

- Compression of loaded content.

- Optimize the scripts and files used in front-end web services and understand the impact of the content delivery network (CDN).

- Use browser caching where possible.

---

**Note**   Salesforce limits your ability to change many parts of this list. However, it is important to understand what impact it has on load times.

---

# Security (Device and API) Considerations

Application and data security is of vital importance for today's mobile applications. Security threats appear in data theft, user surveillance, user impersonation, financial wrongdoing, and botnet activities and attacks. Your design must safeguard the security of the user, the data and information, and the organization. Ensuring this security will also impact application performance. Several key security measures do not directly impact performance including requiring longer mobile pin length and setting up two-factor authentication (2FA) to improve user authentication and data security. Adding these features along with native mobile features such as biometric authentication will also increase security without performance degradation. Developing an enterprise standard can also improve security without a performance hit. We covered different security architectures in Chapter 5.

# Development Skills

Mobile application developers require analytic, communications, creativity, problem-solving, and programming skills. A developer also needs to understand UX design described earlier in the chapter. Because the mobile world does not run on a single standard, they need cross-platform and/or hybrid platform development expertise. Virtually all mobile applications interact with back-end computing; the developer needs to understand server and network security, database management, hardware interaction, and memory management and allocation.

The specific development skills include the following:

- Programming languages such as C#, Java, Objective-C, Swift, and Salesforce Apex/VF, Lightning Aura, and LWC

- Web development languages such as Angular, React, HTML5, CSS, and JavaScript

- Mobile SDK

- Mobile platform Application Programming Interfaces (API) such as Apple iOS and Android

- Cross-platform mobile frameworks like Ionic, React Native, Flutter, Xamarin, and Node.js.

Regardless of the development model, you and your development team will need to invest in hiring and training on mobile development to make the most of your architectural design.

# Deployment

As will be discussed in Chapter 9, the development lifecycle includes the deployment and release of applications following a DevOps framework. Mobile application deployment must include the following aspects:

- **Environment**: As it is nearly impossible to know the individual environment, the mobile release process must consider the most likely scenarios. This can complicate the release process.

- **Risk and Impact**: The complication listed in the preceding text also increases the risks associated with application development.

- **Schedule**: Providing a clear release schedule will reduce the risk and alert the users of changes.

- **Pilot**: Using testing pilots also reduces the risk but allows a small set of users to smoke test and provide feedback on the application and release features.

- **Measure**: The key to successful releases is establishing clear measurements of success and tracking the outcomes.

- **Rollback**: All release plans must include a rollback plan to revert the application to an earlier version. This plan should allow some or all users to revert to a previous release.

# Pulling It All Together

The considerations described are all impacted by the device, development approach, and architectural design choices. Table 8-1 provides a summary of considerations for each of the factors across the application architectures.

***Table 8-1.*** *Summary of the Factors Against the Design Approach*

| Factors | Native | Hybrid | Web App |
|---|---|---|---|
| User experience | Uses the device features such as look and feel and behaviors | Uses an emulated approach with framework features | Provides application features but often does not take advantage of the device usability |
| Access to device features | Full access to device features | Limited access to device features | Limited access to device features |
| Speed to market * | Slow (duplicative) | Medium | Quickest option |
| Development costs | Higher (duplicative) | Lower | Lowest |
| Application performance | Faster | Slower | Slowest (dependent on connectivity) |
| Application errors, bugs, and updates | Applications hang or quit | Applications hang or quit | Extended wait or hang |

*(continued)*

***Table 8-1.*** (*continued*)

| Factors | Native | Hybrid | Web App |
|---|---|---|---|
| Startup time and task load times | Faster | Slower | Slowest (dependent on connectivity) |
| Information capture processing times | Faster | Slower (limited) | Slowest (dependent on connectivity) |
| Service-side response time | Slow (connectivity dependent) | Slow (connectivity dependent) | Faster (already server side) |
| Memory usage | High | Very high (added application) | Low |
| Battery drain and power consumption | Application dependent | Normally higher | High, due to connection requirement |
| Data plan usage | Lower | Lower | Highest |
| Page, image, and video load times | Fastest – fewer loads | Fast – fewer loads | Slowest, due to download speeds |
| Development skills | Objective-C, Java | HTML5, CSS, Frameworks, and JavaScript | HTML5, CSS, JavaScript |
| Deployment | Device store | Device store | Web |

*Salesforce app can reduce the time to market significantly while providing most of the features used on a desktop version of the application.*

# Using and Accessing Mobile Features

Today's mobile device is rich in features and capabilities. Users expect to have access to these features while they are using an application. The following story outlines the mobile usage of a business application user, and Figure 8-2 illustrates their needs.

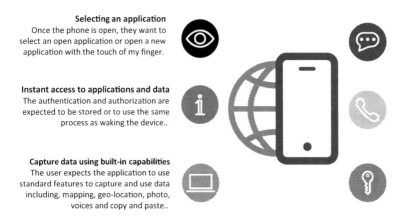

**Selecting an application**
Once the phone is open, they want to select an open application or open a new application with the touch of my finger.

**Instant access to applications and data**
The authentication and authorization are expected to be stored or to use the same process as waking the device..

**Capture data using built-in capabilities**
The user expects the application to use standard features to capture and use data including, mapping, geo-location, photo, voices and copy and paste..

**Sending notices via email and SMS**
While using a device, the user expects to application to fully integrate with built-in communications to email and text other internal and external users.

**Enterprise communications**
Additionally, the user wants to me about to connect with available enterprise functions such as conference calls, web meetings, screen sharing.

**Switching applications**
Users move rapidly between applications thousands of times every day. They expect the device and applications to recall the connections and placemark where they were.

***Figure 8-2.*** *Example of a Typical Mobile Usage*

Mobile users want to pick up a device and authenticate and authorize using the standard features of the device such as facial recognition, fingerprint identification, or access pin. Any one of these features will confirm their identity and access through stored authorization tokens on the device.

To fully support these requirements, the application framework must consider the following functional requirements.

# Instant Access to Applications and Data

Authentication and authorization are expected to be stored or to use the same process as waking the device.

Accessing a mobile device has been expedited with facial recognition and fingerprint identification built into the mobile device functionality. Today's applications are expected to support these easy-to-use features. The architecture design must consider the support of the device authentication features. User adoption and general use drastically drop if the application requires users to enter a username and password each time the application is used.

# Application Access (Authentication and Authorization)

In the preceding story, a user expects to have instant access to the application and its data. The architecture design must facilitate the features and security of the application and associated data. This starts with the authentication and authorization options discussed in Chapter 7. Most frameworks and designs use a User-Agent Flow.

In this flow, the users can authorize a desktop or mobile application to access data using a User-Agent for authentication. At the application side, many apps use a scripting language, such as JavaScript. This flow uses the OAuth 2.0 implicit grant type. The instant access is managed with the refresh_token scope and interconnected with the device access authorization (facial, fingerprint, and code-based access) to request a refresh token if the session has expired. See Chapter 7 for more information.

## Application Use

As the preceding story continues, the application needs the ability to access device features such as voice dictation, capturing phones, and sending SMS and emails. The application framework will dictate which device features are available and the robustness and speed of operation. Native applications have an advantage over hybrid and web-based applications, as all the device features are available to the developer. Hybrid and web applications support only a subset of features. Speed to market and reduced cost in the management of multiple applications are a couple of factors that must be considered in a mobile architecture design.

## Mobile Security

Like laptop and desktop computers, mobile devices (smartphones and tablets) are frequently used to access and store both personal and organizational information. However, because of their portability, mobile devices are more susceptible to loss and theft. The following safeguards can be used to reduce the risk of someone accessing personal and organizational data when your mobile device is lost or stolen:

- **Physical Security**: Establish a policy for devices that use and/or access organizational data to maintain physical possession.

- **Locking Device**: Enhance locking codes from four digits to six digits or require facial or fingerprint options to improve security.

- **Access to Data and Systems**: Limit or lock application form saving, copying, and screen photo'ing data with device SDK features.

- **High Assurance**: Use high-assurance 2FA token generators to support BYOD access.

- **VPN**: Use VPN access and server-side applications from mobile devices.

- **Remote Lock and Data Wipe**: Use enterprise tools or vendor access to lock or delete data on a missing or stolen device.

- **Training**: Provide ongoing training to educate and remind employees about the dangers and risks associated with using a mobile device.

# Managing an Enterprise Mobile Environment

Managing access and security of mobile devices is a critical consideration. Mobile users routinely access content and applications that expose them to security threats. These threats can extend well beyond the users' devices. As an example, Timehop, a mobile application, allowed hackers to access and compromise more than 21 million names, emails, and phone numbers. The attack took advantage of social engineering, the use of phishing, and other social means to access data and exploited the access to extract private data. The mobile user did not know the application stored the data. Besides social engineering, hackers can gain access to your device or the data saving in the applications used on the device.

Solutions have been created to protect an enterprise against many of these threats, most notably Mobile Application Management (MAM), Mobile Device Management (MDM), Enterprise Mobility Management (EMM), Mobile Content Management MCM), and Unified Endpoint Management (UEM). Let's go through each one.

## Enterprise Tools

As an architect, you are responsible for determining which approach is best for the environment you are managing. Which approach (MDM, MAM, EMM, UEM, or MCM) is right for your environment? Let's start with a brief definition of terms.

**Mobile Device Management (MDM)** monitors, manages, and secures mobile devices that are deployed across different cellular carriers. The process installs an application on the device to give access to and control of the device.

**Mobile Application Management (MAM)** controls the functionality of individual applications. This allows a company to control how an application works on the device and the data it uses. MAM is deployed using either preconfigured applications or application extensions. This approach is used when a company does not want to or cannot control the mobile device. It should be noted that the MAM approach requires added development effort to support the preconfigured applications or extension.

**Enterprise Mobility Management (EMM)** is used to manage the use of mobile devices within an organization. EMM deals with both the business and technology issues of using mobile devices in routine business operations. It is common that both MDM and MAM approaches are included in EMM solutions.

**Unified Endpoint Management (UEM)** provides enterprise management of endpoints, including mobile devices, printers, laptops, and desktops, IoT devices from a single management platform. The UEM approach includes EMM and MDM as it relates to mobile devices.

**Mobile Content Management (MCM)** supports and controls content access from mobile devices. It uses either a secure container or a content push. In both cases, the device and application are secondary. The content is encrypted and password protected for added security.

Table 8-2 will help you understand the differences between each approach.

**Table 8-2.** *Advantages and Disadvantages of Mobile Management Solutions*

| Approach | Focus | Advantage(s) | Disadvantage(s) |
|---|---|---|---|
| Mobile Device Management (MDM) | Remote control of devices. | Supports remote lock and wipe. | Does not track the specific data used. Limited control of the device. |
| Mobile Application Management (MAM) | Applications and their related data. | Controls the data. Can segregate company data from personal data. Support of bring-your-own-device (BYOD). | User privacy concerns. Cost of application development. |
| Enterprise Mobility Management (EMM) | Combines MDM and MAM. | Best of both MDM and MAM. | Increased complexity and costs. |
| Unified Endpoint Management (UEM) | Network and management of corporate endpoints. | Full control of the information and data at the network and endpoint level. | Costly and management intense. |
| Mobile Content Management (MCM) | Content presented and used on the device. | Corporate content is protected without consideration of the user's device. | Only pertains to the content. Applications and devices are not considered. |

# Salesforce Mobile App Features

Salesforce introduced a new mobile application and **retired** support of its mobile web experience and the Salesforce1 product with the Summer '20 product release. This release was a significant change in the overall mobile strategy. Salesforce stated the reason for the retirement was to focus on an enhanced Salesforce mobile app. Salesforce mobile app is a new name and an upgrade of the original mobile application called Salesforce1. Additionally, Salesforce is also providing a new application specifically designed for the iPad. So what does all this change mean for you as the enterprise architect? I will outline the major changes as follows:

**Mobile UI Navigation Changes**: One of the first things you will notice is that the mobile UI navigation now follows the desktop flow. This change will allow your users to have a more seamless experience. Users can move back and forth between the desktop and mobile Salesforce applications. This includes the tabs, apps, and menu items.

**Mobile Page Layout and Lightning Support**: A major enhancement is the ability to use Lightning record pages on your mobile applications. This will reduce the time to market and provides a seamless experience for your users. At the time of the writing of the book, the features were limited, but the direction for the future is clear. A few limitations are as follows:

- Editing does not support double-click activation.

- Buttons added for mobile will also show up on the desktop.

- Managing record types is different.

Adding mobile support for Lightning record pages is as easy as selecting the option for both desktop and mobile during the creation or editing of the Lightning page. The developer can select the form factor in the development UI. If the mobile experience needs to be different, the new development UI allows you to also create desktop-only and mobile-only Lightning page layouts.

With the new Salesforce app, users will also see all the tabs configured and assigned on the Lightning page. This changes the page layout for the details but provides a seamless experience.

**Desktop Features such as Path and list Views Are Available**: Because of the addition of Lightning pages, features such as path and list view management are now available on mobile devices. The path feature is a graphical display of a picklist field to present a progression, status, or stage. This allows the user to quickly see what is changing or where a record is at.

Mobile users traditionally needed to use the desktop to manage the selected list view. The mobile user would see the list view that was last selected or pinned on the desktop. This feature was created prior to the release of Salesforce app but is maintained with the new environment.

**Voice Commands**: Salesforce app is fully integrated with Apple, Google, and Alexa technologies. The app will let you execute a voice command on one of the devices, and the application will react to the command on your mobile device. This provides continuity for your users.

It is important for you to review and understand the **features gained and lost** with the changes to Salesforce's mobile development and strategic direction. Most of the changes are favorable but can cause user adoption and change management concerns. Make sure to prepare the environment and the users for a series of mobile features from Salesforce soon.

## Application Design Considerations

Application design starts with both the user interface (UI) and the user experience (UX). The concepts are two different sides of any front-end design. UI allows you to use the application, and UX is the way you feel about using the application. It is important to address both aspects of design in your final solution. Figure 8-3 identifies a few items to consider that will impact both the UI and the UX of your application.

***Figure 8-3.*** *Interaction Between UI and UX*

**Responsiveness**: Be conscious of load times and the response time for a given action. Users are not patient. They want immediate information and outcomes.

**Simplicity**: It is important to know the difference between simple and minimal. Users are looking for feature-rich applications, but they want to be able to intuitively understand how to use the features.

**Iteration and Consistency**: Users want new features, but normally want a consistent look and feel. It is critical to use an iterative process of prototyping, testing, analyzing, and refining your mobile application. This design approach will keep the users satisfied while adding the features they want. The best approach is to create a long-term design plan and establish clear UI/UX guidelines.

**Device Pages and Scrolling**: Excessive scrolling will annoy users. The design should not use long scrolling through content. Create Salesforce navigation that directs the user to the specific content they want.

**Current User Expectations**: Effective UX and UI means staying current on design and use trends to create a user-friendly and elegant design.

**Interface Limitations**: Recognize the limitations of the device. Asking a user to complete a long form or to type more than a few words can impact usability and adoption. Additionally, make sure that your application works according to how the user uses the device. As an example, I like to keep my iPad in landscape mode and my iPhone in portrait mode. Applications that do not adapt to my style are quickly deleted.

**Notify Users**: Applications sometimes take time to load screens and data. Take advantage of lazy loading to speed up the user interaction. A user may not want to wait for an application to load. Without feedback on the status, the user may also think the application is broken and close the application. It is important to notify the user about the status of the loading and the completion and acceptance of actions. Notifying the user at each application step will reduce confusion and frustration.

---

**Lazy loading or infinity loading** is a technique of adding a resource reference or placeholder to the page (image, video, etc.) that loads instantly. The final resource is cached by the browser and replaces the placeholder when the area of the page is viewed. Lazy loading allows the page to load quickly so that the user can see content almost instantaneously. As they scroll or move around the page, the larger and slower loaded content is retrieved from cache. One downside of lazy loading is that it can impact your SEO ranking because the lazy-loaded content will be missing or ignored.

---

In Salesforce, the developer can use an Apex class, Lightning component, JavaScript controller, or JavaScript helper to implement lazy loading. In each case, the code segments support the caching of resources after the initial page is loaded.

# Salesforce Mobile Development

As previously mentioned, mobile devices have profoundly changed how we work and play. Similarly, Salesforce mobile development has evolved to meet this changing need. This section will review the available resources and tools that should be considered in developing mobile applications in Salesforce. This section will provide an overview of the tools, rather than a step-by-step guide. To find a detailed set of tools, education, and documentation, please review the Mobile Development Center at `https://developer.salesforce.com/developer-centers/mobile/`.

**Mobile Development Center**: The Salesforce development center is a robust mobile development center to support a mobile development team. The major elements of the development center include (1) Discovery, (2) Start Building, (3) Read the Docs, (4) Get Tools, 5) Dive Deeper, and 6) Developer Forums.

Salesforce offers two ways to create and deploy mobile applications. The first is the **Salesforce Mobile SDK**. Mobile SDK gives developers the tools to build mobile applications with customized user experiences. Mobile SDK helps you create custom applications. These applications can be delivered via the Apple App Store or Google Play Store. Applications can be developed using either native or web technologies. Mobile SDK provides a significant array of resources and tools to build reliability and security applications.

The second way to develop Salesforce mobile applications is to use the **Salesforce app**; it is the fastest way for Salesforce administrators and developers to deliver mobile applications. It uses point and click tools for administrators and the Lightning web development platform for advanced developers. This book does not cover the details for development of Salesforce app solutions.

Again, this chapter will not provide specific details or training on the use of any of the specific development environments. Rather, the chapter is designed to help an architect to identify the differences to make the best architecture approach decision for their environment.

# New Salesforce App

Salesforce app is a powerful mobile application development environment, but it does not include all the features and functionality available in Salesforce Lightning Desktop. Table 8-3 identifies features that are not supported by Salesforce app.

*Table 8-3.* *Limitations of Salesforce App*

| Lightning Functionality | Not Available on Salesforce App (Mobile) |
| --- | --- |
| Data access and views | Lightning apps. |
| | Console. |
| | Advanced currency. |
| | Division or territory management fields. |
| | Combo boxes. |
| | Picklist behavior. |
| | Phone number display. |
| | Rich text content is inconsistent and varies on devices. |
| | User field display. |
| | List view creation and editing, multi-select, mass actions. |
| | and auto-updating. |
| | Record view; sections are not collapsible. |
| | Related list behavior. |
| | Notes and attachments. |

(continued)

***Table 8-3.*** (*continued*)

| Lightning Functionality | Not Available on Salesforce App (Mobile) |
|---|---|
| Sales features | Account field automatically added. |
| | Social accounts. |
| | Manage external account. |
| | Account hierarchy. |
| | Merge accounts |
| | Edit notes and attachments. |
| | Edit or delete person accounts. |
| | Account contact role. |
| | Account and opportunity teams – team member access. |
| | Campaign management. |
| | Contacts (multiple and social). |
| | Contracts. |
| | Einstein. |
| | Forecasts are read-only. |
| | Leads (social leads and lead conversion). |
| | News limitations. |
| | Opportunity limitations. |
| | Order limitations. |
| | Quote limitations. |
| Productivity features | Salesforce Today is available on mobile but not on the Web or desktop. |
| | Task limitations. |
| | Event calendar limitations. |
| | Notes limitations. |
| | Email limitations. |
| | Dialer not available. |
| | Skype not available. |
| | Work.com limitations (does not apply to newly added Emergency Response Management (ERM) features to Work.com). |
| Data quality and enhancement | Duplicate management limitations. |
| | Data.com limitations. |

(*continued*)

***Table 8-3.*** (*continued*)

| Lightning Functionality | Not Available on Salesforce App (Mobile) |
|---|---|
| Customer service features | Case and case feed limitations. |
| | Entitlements and milestones – milestone and tracker not shown. |
| | Field Service Lightning limitations. |
| | Knowledge limitations. |
| | Social Customer Service limitations. |
| | Work order and linked articles view only, linked articles not available. |
| Reports and dashboards | Report limitations. |
| | Dashboard limitations. |
| | Chart limitations. |
| Salesforce files | Chatter MUST be enabled. |
| | File type limitations. |
| | Content Library limitations, that is, private libraries not available. |
| Chatter | Feed limitations. |
| | Topic limitations. |
| | Chatter Questions limitations. |
| | Groups limitations. |
| | People and Profiles limitations. |
| | Messenger is not available. |
| Salesforce communities | Community management and workspace. |
| | Web-based app template. |
| | Site.com branding. |
| | Other community limitations. |
| Navigation and actions | Navigation supported in portrait orientation. |
| | Utility bar. |
| | Save and new action button. |
| | URL passing parameter. |
| | Email action limitations. |

(*continued*)

***Table 8-3.*** (*continued*)

| Lightning Functionality | Not Available on Salesforce App (Mobile) |
|---|---|
| Search | Search behavior difference. |
| | Pinned searches. |
| | Search results limitations. |
| | Lookup search limitations. |
| Entering data | Creating limitations varies by object. |
| | Editing limitations varies by object |
| Approvals | Cannot unlock. |
| | Approval in Chatter limitations. |
| | Layout and list view difference. |
| Offline access | Can cache data for recent records for FIVE most recently used objects. |
| | Can update while offline for quick actions, record type, lookups and picklists, notes, events, and tasks. |
| | Communities NOT supported. |
| Salesforce customization | Custom home pages. |
| | Custom action and button limitations. |
| | Custom help. |
| | > 100 Lightning components. |
| | Pull request. |
| | Web tabs and S-controls. |

The new Salesforce app allows the architect to use Lightning app development to also support mobile development. Conversely, Mobile SDK provides the architect with functions and hooks to create native applications that are not related to the Lightning app builder environment. The primary difference between the Salesforce app and Salesforce Mobile SDK development is shown in Table 8-4.

*Table 8-4.* *Comparison Between Salesforce App and Salesforce Mobile SDK Capabilities*

| Functional Capability | Salesforce App | Mobile SDK |
|---|---|---|
| Interface | Predefined. | Fully customizable. |
| Salesforce org access | Full org access. | REST API, Visualforce, remoting, jQuery, and Ajax. |
| User experiences | Integrated with Salesforce UX using either declarative or programmatic development. | Custom UX and brand. |
| Custom functionality | Lightning component, Visualforce, Canvas pages. | Full range of development options. |
| Security | Integrated in Salesforce app. | Custom security wrapper. |
| Features, notification, and actions | Action bar and inherent Salesforce. | Push notification and custom actions. Significant offline functionality. |
| Distribution | The Salesforce app is distributed on Apple App Store or Google Play. Windows mobile is not supported. Custom mobile apps and managed in Salesforce. | Must be compiled and distributed on Apple App Store or Google Play. |
| Salesforce update support | Included with Salesforce app and Salesforce org updates. | Additional maintenance required. |

# Development Environment Differences

**Native apps** (Apple Native iOS and Google Native Android) have superior usability, features, and experience because you are developing in the device language. This approach allows the developer to maximize features such as device graphics, animations, built-in components, and direct access to device-specific features.

To develop native applications, you will need to know the device environment and the tools used to build, test, and deploy custom code. This will require more experienced developers. However, this gives the developer a higher level of freedom to create unique applications.

The **major benefits** of native app development include the following:

- Access to all device components and features

- Speed and performance of the application

- Advanced offline features

- Recognizable and consistent look and feel for users

- Device aspect ratio for images easier to support

- Better device security

The **major disadvantages** of native app development include the following:

- Application is tied to a specific device type.

- Expensive development costs.

- Longer development times.

- Frequent updates required.

- Fee to delivery services such as the iOS App Store can be high.

**React Native** is a hybrid app framework invented by Facebook. React Native uses JavaScript code and converts it into a native application for both iOS and Android devices. The hybrid framework uses native UI development blocks connected using JavaScript and React.

This approach saves development time, effort, and costs, as it is possible to reuse the code, add functionality, and use extensive libraries. Using the Salesforce Mobile SDK, React supports native features such as Salesforce SmartStore, Mobile Sync, REST API, and Salesforce login and authentication.

The **major benefits** of React Native app development include the following:

- Lower cost of development

- Supports both iOS and Android development

- Improved speed over other hybrid environments

- Speed and performance of the application

- Code reuse and large development community to draw from

- Modular architecture

- Use of live or hot reloading

The **major disadvantages** of React Native app development include the following:

- Limited version updates

- Troubleshooting and bug fixes more difficult

- Reliance on Facebook

- Can still require native development to access advanced features

- Limited security robustness

- Limited memory management

- No support for decimals which limits computation capabilities

**Cordova-based hybrid apps** are built with a standard web development approach using a device-specific wrapper or container. This container provides access to native platform features such as gestures, GPS, voice, and camera features. Hybrid apps can be faster to develop, like web apps, while taking advantage of robust native features. The Salesforce Mobile SDK offers features such as Mobile Sync to access and cache the data for offline use. This feature also supports cached data offline and syncing with Salesforce servers once the connection is restored.

The **major benefits** of hybrid app development include following:

- Development speed to market

- Ease of development using standard web development

- Flexible UI/UX because of native framework

- Reduced costs

- Compile once, run everywhere approach

The **major disadvantages** of hybrid app development include following:

- Slower performance compared to native.

- Nonstandard user interface.

- Updates and bug fixes lag environments.

- Reliant on the hybrid interface and integrations.

- Limited device features compared to native.

Figure 8-4 shows the interactions between web development, the framework, and the mobile device using Adobe Cordova.

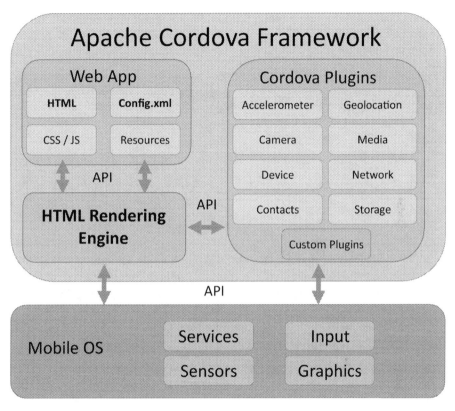

***Figure 8-4.*** *Framework of Design Environment Used with Adobe Cordova*

**HTML5 and JavaScript mobile apps** are web pages that are designed to work on a mobile device. Web apps are device independent and will support most mobile browsers. Web apps are a "write once, run anywhere" approach and are easy to develop and support on a wide range of devices. They are deployed with a simple URL address to the application.

The major benefits of HTML5 app development include the following:

- Development speed to market.

- Reduced cost of development compared to native apps.

- Ease of development using standard web development.

- Easier to maintain, as the application is centralized.

- Deployment of the application is easier.

The major disadvantages of HTML5 app development include the following:

- Online accessibility required, not offline solution.

- Limited by user browser; does not support all browser types.

- Applications run slower, as they use server-side resources and are limited by available network speeds.

- Very limited access to device features.

- Lacks device native look and feel.

- Unfriendly security features - identity authentication is managed by cookies and the web server.

- No secure offline storage.

# Salesforce Mobile SDK Development

Mobile SDK includes support for the following development requirements:

- **Native Apple iOS, Native Google Android, HTML5, Hybrid, and React Native Development**: Uses support for both native mobile operating systems, web development, Cordova-based hybrid framework, and React Native. The Salesforce Mobile SDK supports development in the following environments: Apple Native iOS, Google Native Android, React Native, Cordova-based hybrid, and HTML5 and JavaScript.

- **Mobile Services**: Uses services such as push notifications, geolocation, analytics, collaboration tools, and business logic in Salesforce.

- **Offline Management with SmartStore Encrypted Database**: Uses an AES-256 encrypted database to store and retrieve data locally. Supports secure key storage in iOS and Android.

- **Mobile Sync**: Uses a simple API for synchronizing data between your offline database and the server side on Salesforce.

- **Push Notification**: Uses Salesforce-connected apps and SDK to develop and test push notifications.

- **Salesforce Communities**: Uses the access to Salesforce communities to build applications quickly.

- **Enterprise Identity and Security**: Uses the Salesforce-connected app policy. It uses SAML and advanced authentication flows. Supports OAuth 2.0 User-Agent Flow, SSO, and OpenID tokens for access to external services.

- **API for File Management**: Uses REST API open source libraries to manage uploading and downloading files, using encryption and caching for both iOS and Android.

The Salesforce Mobile SDK supports development in the following environments: Apple Native iOS, Google Native Android, React Native, Cordova-based hybrid, and HTML5 and JavaScript.

- **Native apps** use a given mobile device operating system, either iOS or Android.

- **React Native apps** use the Facebook framework to run JavaScript apps as native code.

- **Hybrid apps** use a Cordova-based framework to combine HTML5 web app development with the native platform using a hybrid container.

- **HTML5 apps** use standard HTML5, JavaScript, and CSS to support a mobile web browser.

# Salesforce Supports IoT, Wearables, and Other Connected Devices

Internet of Things, or IoT, is the connection of devices or instruments to the Internet so that users can examine the collected data or access standalone controls. IoT is changing how we interact with our cars, homes, and medical and business systems.

The Internet opens access to millions of systems and endpoints previously relegated to private systems or direct connects. The personal and business possibilities are endless. In my personal life, I use IoT in many ways, such as

- Controlling my thermostat in three different locations

- Watching my front door for packages and visitors

- Confirming my doors are locked and even allowing visitors access when I am away from home

- Tracking my steps taken each day

- Monitoring my heart rate with my watch and iPhone

- Automatically mapping my biking path

- Tracking driving habits to reduce my insurance bill

- Even helping my wife find a location from hundreds of miles away

IoT has established its presence in all parts of the enterprise business environments, including banking, farming, finance, manufacturing, and healthcare. The applications are virtually endless.

# Understand IoT Architecture Patterns

Understanding the concepts, benefits, and risks associated with different IoT platform solutions will help you select the best option to deploy. Let's start with the device. The device can be connected directly or indirectly to the Internet. In fact, most devices were in place before the advent of IoT as an architecture, so it is important to review and understand how the device is currently collecting information. Your design needs to account for how the device information will get to a connected system.

There are many types of IoT solutions that support remote monitoring and rules generation. They are segregated into four major types:

- **End-to-End**: Manage all aspects of IoT connection and use

- **Cloud**: PaaS environment to manage devices.

- **Data**: Use device data to support analytics.

- **Connectivity**: Connect devices to support use.

# Connecting Salesforce with IoT Devices

As described in Chapter 7, the connection between an IoT device and Salesforce will require a connected application using OAuth 2.0 Device Authorization Grant that supports browser-less and input-constrained devices. This flow requires that an architect creates a connected application before starting the authorization request. The authorization steps are as follows:

1. The device requests a code from the IDP.

2. The IDP sends back a URL and authorization code to the device.

3. The device sends the code and URL to the user via a browser on a separate device.

4. The user logs in and gives consent to the IDP.

5. The device polls the IDP waiting for a response, once step 4 is complete.

6. The IDP returns the token response to the device.

7. The device uses the token to authenticate with the IDP.

8. Connection is complete.

# Implementing IoT on Salesforce

Salesforce has made significant investments in the IoT ecosystem. Salesforce recommends implementing IoT using a clear plan including planning, connecting, transforming, building, and deploying. Before you start, you will need to enable Salesforce IoT in your instance. It is included in the Developer Edition and an add-on for Enterprise, Performance, and Unlimited editions at an extra cost. If enabled, the high-level steps needed to implement Salesforce IoT are as follows:

- **Plan Phase**: Will identify the events and triggers that will be used, and you create the actions needed to react to the events. This requires understanding the customer and what will provide the best outcomes.

- **Connect Phase**: Will select how data sources will connect to the device data required from the plan phase.

- **Transform Phase**: Will determine how to convert the device information into actionable data that can be consumed in the Salesforce IoT environment.

- **Build Phase**: Will create the new orchestration rule in Salesforce IoT. Orchestration is a declarative process used in Salesforce to manage the events.

- **Deploy Phase**: Will activate the orchestration rules and test the outcomes. Once confirmed, the IoT solution is ready for use.

# Chapter Summary

In this chapter, we covered

- A review of the important aspects of end-to-end mobile architecture including the device and data management considerations

- The nine constraints surrounding mobile architecture: mobile applications, user experiences, device access, speed to market, development costs, application performance, security concerns, development skills, and application deployment

- How to mitigate security threats using enterprise solutions such as Mobile Device Management (MDM), Mobile Application Management (MAM), Enterprise Mobility Management (EMM), Unified Endpoint Management (UEM), and Mobile Content Management MCM)

- An overview of Salesforce mobile architecture design considerations, trade-offs, and risks including a review of the differences between user experience (UX) and user interface (UI)

- A comparison of developing mobile applications using Salesforce app and Salesforce Mobile SDK including a deep dive into the available resources included in the Salesforce Mobile SDK

- The importance of the Internet of things (IoT) as it relates to mobile architecture and deployment

# CHAPTER 9

# Salesforce Development and Deployment Lifecycle

When you rate a restaurant in Yelp, do you rate based on just the food or the environment, presentation, and service?

Say you went to a fancy restaurant for brunch and ordered Eggs Benedict. To your surprise, the server brings you two uncooked runny eggs in a pan, a cup of hollandaise sauce, two slices of frozen English muffins with some tomatoes, and spinach on it. In reality, it has all the ingredients described in the menu, but we bet your Yelp review for that restaurant is not going to be superhigh. It's worse if you liked what you were served and the restaurant cannot make it the same way the next time around.

Building a product once is not the same as building, integrating, and delivering the product incrementally and consistently every time without interruptions to regular use. DevOps is a practice that solves for the latter.

DevOps is not an architectural design of any one system. It's a practice designed by an architect and established by an enterprise to manage the end-to-end practice of developing an application, testing it, releasing it for operational use, and repeating the process through continuous integration and continuous delivery of new components and newer versions of the application, with no disruption to the current operational use of the solution.

In this chapter, we will cover

- Six archetypes of standard DevOps

- Choosing the ideal delivery methodology

- Roles, responsibility, and team structure needed for a Salesforce project delivery

- Environment management and source code control strategies

© Dipanker Jyoti and James A. Hutcherson 2021
D. Jyoti and J. A. Hutcherson, *Salesforce Architect's Handbook*, https://doi.org/10.1007/978-1-4842-6631-1_9

- Testing strategies and decisions for manual vs. test automation strategies

- Establishment of Center of Excellence, governance, and monitoring for Salesforce project delivery

# DevOps

DevOps is a colloquial term that stands for "Development and Operations." In our research, we have not seen a single standard definition for DevOps, but have observed unanimous agreement on what typical DevOps consists of. Unanimously, DevOps refers to establishing the six archetypes as part of the continuous development and delivery model.

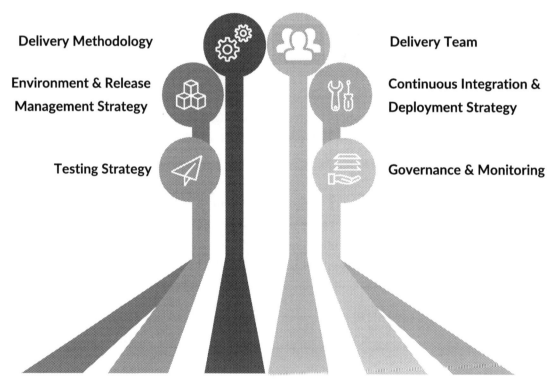

***Figure 9-1.***  *Six Archetypes of DevOps*

As indicated in Figure 9-1, the six archetypes to establish an efficient DevOps process are

- Delivery methodology

- Delivery team

- Environment and release management strategy

- Continuous integration and deployment strategy

- Testing strategy

- Governance and monitoring

Using the six archetypes, an architect can control how your product would be developed, assembled, and delivered iteratively and consistently for operational use in any environment, including production. As your solution evolves with newer versions and features, your DevOps design will need to account for the continuous integration of these features with existing versions of your product in every environment. A great example of an efficient DevOps practice in play is Salesforce as the company itself. Salesforce releases hundreds of new features in three major releases each year to millions of its customers globally without any disruption to their regular use of Salesforce.

DevOps is a new and maturing practice compared to traditional approaches to the development and delivery of software. Before we can discuss the why's and how-to's of DevOps, let's quickly take a look at some of the traditional approaches to building software without DevOps.

# Traditional Software Development Approach

To make this enjoyable, we will demonstrate the traditional software development approach by illustrating the design, development, and delivery of a custom made-to-order car in Figure 9-2.

1 - What the business users imagined

2 - What was captured as business requirements

3 - What was architected as the solution design

4 - What was being developed

5 - What was tested prior to delivery

6 - What was delivered as the final solution

***Figure 9-2.*** *Traditional Development Practice Illustrated via a Custom Made-to-Order Car Example*

Here's what happens in a traditional software development approach, as illustrated in Figure 9-2:

- **Step 1**: A product sales engineer sells a vision to the business users about their product capabilities. The business users, of course, hang on to the best version of the described product as their desired solution.

- **Step 2**: The business analysts on the team capture the business requirements from the business users and interpret them based on the scope and collective descriptions of the functionality desired. Since all of this is captured on paper, there is no way for business analysts to align with the business users' vision.

- **Step 3**: The architect reviews the captured business requirements and aligns them with the security requirements indicated by the company's IT team and other technical stakeholders. Once again, since nothing is built so far, the architect's design adds a level of sophistication and complexity, which was probably never brought up by business users nor captured in the business requirements.

- **Step 4**: Multiple developers and admins get assigned to building various business requirements and attempt at aligning the business requirements with the architect's solution design to develop their component as per their understanding. Because multiple developers build multiple features in a silo, it's hard to administer the various parts and the components made by the different developers until the product is built. This is the first time an actual product is visible to the project team. Still, it is often too late to modify or refactor anything because all allocated development time has already been spent. There is not enough time to realign with anyone else's vision of the final product.

- **Step 5**: It would be great if the product developed by the developers in their development environment can be integrated with other developers seamlessly, but this is never the case. To deploy the code from a development sandbox to an integration or test sandbox, there is a significant amount of back and forth and coordination with other developers. Eventually, when the developed product is deployed and tested, the testers soon realize that the product isn't working as developed, so they are only able to approve a scaled-down version of the developed product that is ready for final delivery.

- **Step 6**: At this point, the tested product needs to be deployed to the final environment for customer use. The architects and the developers fail to reconcile the conflicts between their work and preexisting functionalities in the production environment. Even after an extended timeline and an overexceeded budget, when the final product is delivered to the business users, it is an understatement to say that it is significantly different than what they imagined as the ideal solution.

It's easy to dismiss the example as a joke, but you will be surprised how real this scenario is in the software industry. It is also easy to think that DevOps is a nice-to-have and not a must-have, but companies and professionals who believe this are often caught by surprise when they cannot make even small upgrades to their current system due to lack of DevOps. With Salesforce specifically, the only time when DevOps is a nice-to-have is when your use of Salesforce is minimal and limited to out-of-the-box Salesforce functionalities (i.e., no customizations).

An efficient DevOps practice reduces the manual overhead needed to test, integrate, and deploy, resulting in a reduced time to deliver a testable, viable product. The complexities of capturing business requirements, designing a solution, and building, integrating, testing, and deploying it in a production environment without any feedback loop to monitor, course-correct, and realign with the business users throughout the entire process are the key problem that an efficient DevOps practice intends to solve. An ideal DevOps practice creates a factory-like assembly line for all steps involved, from requirements capturing to delivery, such that the product features can be broken into smaller chunk sizes to capture each stakeholder's feedback during the functional design and development phase before it's too little or too late.

An efficient DevOps process offers many benefits; here are at least the four most commonly known benefits:

1. Time to market for both the initial version of the product and incremental versions

2. Accelerated customer and team feedback inclusion

3. Continuous improvement and continuous delivery with focus on improved efficiency, effectiveness, quality, and frequency

4. Delivery consistency through the establishment of an assembly line approach to delivery

It's important to note that setting up an efficient DevOps practice is not cheap and takes some time and investment, at least initially. An efficient DevOps practice is less erroneous when it is automated and has a limited human intervention. An efficient DevOps practice requires investment in software tools such as

- Application lifecycle management tools

- Continuous improvement/continuous deployment (CD) tools

- Static code analysis tools

- Automated testing tools

Once an efficient DevOps pipeline is set up, the initial investments are often recovered within the first few releases managed through the channel.

So now, how do we begin with setting up DevOps?

# Delivery Methodology

The first step in establishing a DevOps practice is an implementation methodology that needs to be selected and followed. An implementation methodology refers to the orchestration required among the team members to collect business requirements, conduct analysis, transform analysis into a solution design, build the solution per the solution design, test the solution, deploy the solution in the right technical environment for business use, and finally maintain the solution for its intended lifetime.

The three most common methodologies used across the software industry are

- Waterfall methodology

- Agile methodology

- Hybrid methodology

We will not cover many details on the how-to's for any specific methodology in this book, as several books do better justice in explaining these methodologies. However, we will go over the basics of each and the selection criteria for choosing one over the other. One such book to refer to on this topic is *A Guide to the Project Management Body of Knowledge.*[1]

Figure 9-3 provides a quick overview and a side-by-side comparison of the waterfall methodology vs. the Agile methodology.

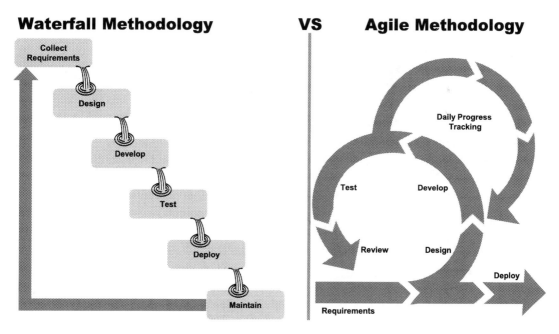

***Figure 9-3.*** *Waterfall Methodology vs. Agile Methodology*

---

[1]*A Guide to the Project Management Body of Knowledge* (PMBOK® Guide) Sixth Edition, published by the Project Management Institute.

# Waterfall Methodology

The waterfall methodology follows a sequential, nonoverlapping method of execution starting from requirements gathering, analysis, development testing, and deployment such that you do not start the next stage until the previous phase is completed thoroughly, hence the name waterfall. The waterfall method is the most common and traditional methodology used in the software industry. Even though it has significant disadvantages compared to the more modern Agile practices, there are, however, some significant advantages to using this methodology, such as the following:

1. Simple and easy to manage approach with all activities and outcomes clearly defined at the start.

2. Dependencies and complexities of a large project can be determined sooner since the full scope and requirements of the solution are being defined within the initial stage.

3. Resource staffing can be staggered and spread across stages since the entire team is not required from the start.

4. The cost of development needs to be determined at the beginning of the project, with the option to cancel the project after the initial analysis and design stage.

5. Stakeholder availability is limited, and providing feedback iteratively is not reasonable.

6. Best for projects with a fixed budget and schedule, expecting a predictable, single full-featured release of the final solution.

7. High priority is given to formal documentation and formal sign-offs.

# Agile Methodology

In an Agile methodology, a self-organized, cross-functional team is assembled for a project duration known as the "scrum." The scrum is broken into two to three weeklong intervals known as "sprints." Each sprint consists of a full cycle of requirements gathering, design, development, testing, and review of the features built with the project stakeholders and sponsors. Usually, live demos of the features being built during each sprint are conducted to capture instant feedback from all stakeholders and participants. The feedback, along with the desired features, is then planned for future sprints by maintaining and prioritizing a backlog of requirements. Daily, the team provides a quick update on their earlier day's activities, current day's plans, and any impediments blocking them from continuing with their projects. These daily updates allow other team members to identify dependencies on other team members' activities as well as assist in addressing the impediments faced by other team members. The Agile methodology was developed as a methodology in the early 2000s to address the limitations and challenges of the waterfall methodology, such as the lack of a feedback loop, lack of instant visibility into project progress, impediments and dependencies, and inability to easily accommodate changes or course-correct the solution based on stakeholder feedback.

Some key advantages of the Agile methodology over the waterfall methodology are as follows:

1. The Agile methodology follows an incremental approach to software development, whereas the waterfall method follows a sequential approach.

2. The Agile methodology prioritizes flexibility, whereas the waterfall method prioritizes completeness.

3. High stakeholder participation is required compared to the waterfall method.

4. Best for simple, less complex projects with no/low-complexity integrations.

5. Rapid development with a feedback loop with flexibility in budget and schedule

6. Quicker time to market due to an incremental and iterative development approach

7. Low priority given to formal documentation and formal sign-offs

# Hybrid Methodology

Although Agile has gained high popularity within the software industry in modern days, in reality, most companies tend to implement a custom-tailored hybrid approach. The hybrid methodology is the best of both worlds, in which companies leverage the sequential waterfall approach to manage certain stages, such as requirements gathering and certain types of testing and deployment. In contrast, design and development are managed using an iterative Agile approach.

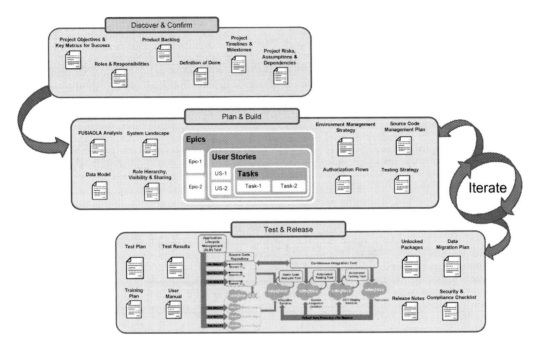

***Figure 9-4.*** *Sample Hybrid Methodology*

In Figure 9-4, we have recommended a hybrid method that incorporates all the artifacts and approaches suggested in this book. The sample hybrid methodology, presented in Figure 9-4, proposes distributing the project activities in three key phases:

1. Discover and confirm phase (waterfall methodology)

2. Plan and build (Agile methodology)

3. Test and release (Agile methodology)

The hybrid methodology illustrated in Figure 9-4 proposes that the requirements gathering and analysis be conducted within a fixed period using the waterfall method, termed here as the "discover and confirm" phase. Following the one-time discover and confirm phase, an iterative series of plan and build phases are initiated to transform the backlog of requirements captured during the discover and confirm phase into fully functional solutions. The iterative series of plan and build phases is paired with a less frequent, iterative series of testing and release activities to match the product delivery and time to market expectations.

The most significant advantage of the hybrid methodology over its previous two predecessors is that it provides flexibility along with coverage and completeness. It can be calibrated and designed to address fixed-budget and fixed-schedule issues, accommodate most stakeholder participation levels, iterate development with feedback loops, and adjust resource allocations.

Our recommendation would be to tailor a hybrid methodology that suits your project needs best by dialing up or down the benefits of waterfall methodology vs. Agile methods.

Now that you have figured out the ideal methodology that works for you and identified the scope of work to be accomplished, it's time to gather the right team members and professionals.

# Salesforce Delivery Team

There is quite a bit of confusion within the Salesforce community about the Salesforce roles and responsibilities for corresponding Salesforce professionals. People often ask, "Does the business analyst role in Salesforce mean the same as a Salesforce admin role?" or "What's the difference between a Salesforce technical architect and a Salesforce solution architect?"

To address these and many other questions, Table 9-1 presents the distinct Salesforce professional titles and their corresponding roles and responsibilities.

***Table 9-1.*** *Salesforce Roles and Responsibilities*

| Salesforce Title | Roles and Responsibilities |
|---|---|
| Salesforce technical architect | <ul><li>Communicate enterprise-level design overviews to executives and technical team.</li><li>Assess, identify, and plan for technical opportunities and technical threats to formulate enterprise architecture strategies.</li><li>Provide oversight on technical solutions and design considerations for application features being developed by the project team members.</li><li>Implement, govern, and monitor best practices to ensure technical feasibility, scalability, and maintainability of solutions being developed.</li><li>Ensure the soundness of the application-level architecture and system-level architecture of the solution being developed.</li><li>Provide Salesforce-specific technical oversight and strategic guidance.</li><li>Provide expert guidance on the Salesforce licensing model for the overall solution delivered.</li><li>Establish coding standards and baseline quality standards.</li><li>Ensure security architecture of all technical components.</li><li>Manage and mature the Center of Excellence (COE) for the enterprise.</li></ul> |
| Salesforce solution architect | <ul><li>Define the solution for gathered requirements in coordination with the Salesforce technical architect.</li><li>Provide justification for any customizations and code used in solution design.</li><li>Define the systems integration specifications, Salesforce data model, system landscape, and OAuth flows in coordination with the Salesforce technical architect.</li><li>Confirm coverage, context, and completeness of the full solution.</li><li>Facilitate environment setup and monitor deployment among environments.</li><li>Conduct solution design revisions throughout the project.</li></ul> |

*(continued)*

***Table 9-1.*** (*continued*)

| Salesforce Title | Roles and Responsibilities |
|---|---|
| Salesforce project manager | • Onboard and offboard team resources.<br>• Manage ongoing team roles and responsibilities.<br>• Manage project timeline, client deliverables, and milestones.<br>• Manage project risks, issues, decisions, and assumptions.<br>• Manage daily project operations, project status, and metrics.<br>• Manage stakeholder and project team communication.<br>• Manage communication with external vendors and technology partners.<br>• Oversee timely and accurate implementation of the solution.<br>• Manage project scope, budget, and team allocations.<br>• Coordinate formal sign-offs and client acceptances.<br>• Coordinate go live, system freeze, communication strategy, and cutover plans for all releases. |
| Salesforce business analyst | • Conduct discovery and requirements gathering sessions.<br>• Develop backlog of requirements and/or user stories.<br>• Evaluate and capture business needs as per their viability with Salesforce technology capabilities.<br>• Conduct analysis and generate documentation including process flows to elaborate and explain critical and complex business concepts.<br>• Develop and maintain Salesforce configuration workbook.<br>• Capture UI/UX requirements with the context of Salesforce UI/UX capabilities.<br>• Develop and maintain data dictionary for commonly used terms and nomenclature consistency.<br>• Coordinate all project documentation in coordination with team members.<br>• Coordinate development and delivery of release notes with input from technical team members.<br>• Develop and manage requirements traceability matrix (RTM) across project scope, business requirements, technical design documents, testing documents, and training materials. |

(*continued*)

***Table 9-1.*** (*continued*)

| Salesforce Title | Roles and Responsibilities |
|---|---|
| Salesforce administrator | • Responsible for out-of-the-box Salesforce configuration, performance, and security testing of the solution.<br>• Configure out-of-the-box security, visibility, and sharing settings.<br>• Confirm and validate all technical requirements.<br>• Identify and mitigate technical risks associated with assigned solutions. |
| Salesforce developer | • Responsible for programmatic development, performance, and security testing of the solution.<br>• Follow coding standards and best practices for all programmatic development.<br>• Adhere to code versioning and source code management practices.<br>• Run code coverage tests during code promotions.<br>• Troubleshoot deployment and code integration issues.<br>• Confirm and validate all technical requirements.<br>• Identify and mitigate technical risks associated with assigned solutions. |
| Salesforce integration architect | • Co-design and validate the integration specifications with the Salesforce solution architect.<br>• Define source to target mappings for systems integration.<br>• Coordinate ETL construction and data integration transformations needed when using an ESB (e.g., MuleSoft).<br>• Design the integration patterns, protocols, frequency, and criteria used for each integration.<br>• Define internal and external IDs used for integrations.<br>• Design data update vs. data override conditions for all integrations.<br>• Coordinate and co-design data conversion plans. |

(*continued*)

***Table 9-1.*** (*continued*)

| Salesforce Title | Roles and Responsibilities |
|---|---|
| Salesforce data architect | • Develop data schema and data type definitions as per business requirements.<br>• Define source to target mappings for any data migrations.<br>• Coordinate the development of a Salesforce data dictionary.<br>• Define and validate data attributes such as master-detail, junction objects, lookups, roll-up summaries, and formula.<br>• Define internal and external IDs used for data migrations.<br>• Coordinate the setup and configuration of data security, access, and data sharing rules.<br>• Design and coordinate necessary validation rules for data intake and data integration points to ensure data quality.<br>• Manage data sharing and visibility with external users via customer community portals, Site.com, and Visualforce pages.<br>• Design data update vs. data override conditions for data migrations.<br>• Coordinate and co-design data conversion plans. |
| Salesforce quality assurance specialist | • Develop test strategy, test plan, test scripts, and test reports.<br>• Manage manual vs. automated testing.<br>• Manage the various forms of testing such as unit tests, regression tests, systems integration tests, user acceptance tests, performance tests, data migration tests, and usability and accessibility tests.<br>• Classify and report defects vs. requirement change requests.<br>• Coordinate the processing of defects and change requests with the team and retest.<br>• Co-author, verify, and validate all acceptance criteria and definition of done.<br>• Develop automated test scripts as needed.<br>• Manage testing tools to optimize and manage test activities. |

(*continued*)

***Table 9-1.*** (*continued*)

| Salesforce Title | Roles and Responsibilities |
| --- | --- |
| Salesforce training specialist | • Define and obtain agreements on training deliverables and training prerequisites and training assumptions.<br>• Identify stakeholders for different training sessions.<br>• Define all identified user training needs.<br>• Develop training plan, training outlines, training materials, job aids, and quick reference guides.<br>• Set up and configure learning management tools.<br>• Define training schedule and training delivery plan.<br>• Conduct general Salesforce overview training.<br>• Conduct application-specific trainings.<br>• Conduct application administration training sessions. |
| Salesforce change management specialist | • Define change management and user adoption needs.<br>• Develop a change management plan.<br>• Define and document usability requirements to increase user adoption.<br>• Lead change management activities and communication efforts.<br>• Document changes to business processes, systems, and technology compared to legacy scenarios.<br>• Support the technical experts in incorporating help text and training support capabilities within the solution. |

Now that you have the methodology and the right team assigned to your project, let's look into the design and setup of the next DevOps archetype, that is, environment management strategy.

# Environment and Release Management Strategy

When companies pay for Salesforce licenses, the licenses include a set of Salesforce sandboxes, which are essentially replica environments for the development and testing of code similar to other technology providers such as Microsoft, AWS, and others.

The number of Salesforce sandboxes available with the licenses depends on the license editions.

For more details on how many and what kind of sandboxes are available for each edition of Salesforce licenses, refer to the Salesforce article "Sandbox Licenses and Storage Limits by Type."[2]

Salesforce being a multi-tenant architecture requires all code and customizations to be developed and tested in one of the sandbox environments before deploying to production. As a matter of fact, no code can be written directly in any production environment of Salesforce. Direct changes to the production environment are strictly restricted to point and click configurations via the setup menu. This is mainly because all code written in Salesforce needs to pass a 75% code coverage test before any code can be deployed into the production environment. Code coverage in Salesforce refers to testing any Apex classes, triggers, and custom Lightning components with corresponding test classes that contain sample test records to test the behavior of the respective classes, triggers, and custom Lightning components. This code coverage requirement protects Salesforce from malicious activities and code recursions from code written by any one client and also ensures that no single customer's code monopolizes or disrupts any other customer's Salesforce use, given that several customers share the same multi-tenant production environment.

Salesforce sandboxes differ from each other based on type, storage size, production data transferability upon refresh from production, and refresh interval time. All sandboxes created initially or refreshed over time can only be refreshed from the production environment. When initially created or refreshed, the metadata and, in some cases, the actual production data get transferred over to the newly created or refreshed sandboxes. Table 9-2 provides a quick reference to the different types of sandboxes and the key distinctions between each type.

---

[2]Sandbox Licenses and Storage Limits by Type, https://help.salesforce.com/articleView?id=data_sandbox_environments.htm&type=5.

***Table 9-2.*** *Salesforce Sandbox Types*

| Sandbox Type | Storage Size | What Transfers from Production? | Refresh Interval | Commonly Used For |
|---|---|---|---|---|
| Developer | Data: 200 MB Files: 200 MB | Only metadata | Daily | Development and unit tests |
| Developer pro | Data: 1 GB Files: 1 GB | Only metadata | Daily | Systems integration and regression tests |
| Partial copy | Data: 5 GB Files: 5 GB | Metadata + subset of production data | 5 days | Quality assurance tests |
| Full copy | Same size as production | Metadata + all of production data | 29 days | UAT (User Acceptance Testing), performance tests, and data migration tests |

Even though sandboxes are created from the production environment, they are completely isolated from the production environment, which is not impacted by any changes made by the developer or the admin in any of the sandboxes. In order to move the development and configuration from one sandbox to another and ultimately to the production environment, one needs to utilize a deployment method to deploy from one environment to another.

At the time of this writing, there are eight methods to conduct deployments in Salesforce. Table 9-3 provides an overview of the eight methods of deployment, when to use them, and their limitations (if any).

***Table 9-3.*** *Salesforce Deployment methods*

| Deployment Method | Advantages | Disadvantages |
|---|---|---|
| Change sets | • Point and click UI to select, add, and deploy components from any sandbox to another and also to production.<br>• Does not require using a local file system or downloading any software on local machine.<br>• Audits all previous deployments.<br>• Same components can be deployed to multiple orgs.<br>• Ideal for partial or small deployments. | • No code version control options.<br>• No rollback options.<br>• Selecting and creating component package is cumbersome.<br>• Retrying failed deployments is cumbersome.<br>• Not ideal for large deployments. |
| Migration tool (e.g., ANT) | • Deployments and retrieval of source code can be scheduled as daily batch process.<br>• Post-deployment steps can be automated.<br>• Ideal for multistage release processes due to scripted retrieval and deployment of components. | • Requires initial setup.<br>• No easy way to identify and select dependent components.<br>• Deployment error messages are nonintuitive and complex to resolve. |
| IDE (e.g., VS Code) | • Project-based development.<br>• Deployment to any org.<br>• Synchronizing changes.<br>• Selecting only the components you need. | • Some setup required.<br>• Not always upgraded at the same time as other Salesforce products.<br>• Repeatable deployments require reselecting components, which can be time consuming and introduce errors. |
| Force.com Workbench | • Ad hoc queries.<br>• Deploy or retrieve components with a package.xml file.<br>• Metadata describe functions available.<br>• Lightweight data loads possible. | • Not an officially supported product. |

*(continued)*

***Table 9-3.*** (*continued*)

| Deployment Method | Advantages | Disadvantages |
|---|---|---|
| Salesforce CLI | • Scripted commands and automated tasks.<br>• Passwords can be hidden to authenticate access to sandbox and production. | • Company firewall could cause issues and block execution. |
| Unmanaged packages | • One-time setup of a development environment.<br>• All components along with their dependencies can be bundled within a single package. | • Packages cannot be upgraded with new versions. The entire package needs to be redeployed.<br>• Requires development in a Developer Edition org. |
| Managed packages | • Best suited for AppExchange product development.<br>• Deployment can be as simple as installing an AppExchange product. | • Access to code is limited or hidden.<br>• Unique namespace can be bothersome or a blocker.<br>• Difficult to modify or delete components.<br>• Requires development in a Developer Edition org. |
| Unlocked packages | • Combines the advantages of managed and unmanaged package deployments.<br>• Can be created with or without a unique namespace.<br>• Unlocked packages can be upgraded with newer versions, without replacing entire package. | • Requires enabling DevHub and packaging feature on DevHub, which are irreversible settings.<br>• Dependent on version control system.<br>• Requires development with scratch orgs. |

Now that we understand the environment strategy and the deployment methods, let's talk about the two ways in which source code can be maintained throughout the development and delivery process.

# Org-Based Development Approach

The traditional approach to manage code has been to develop and maintain the golden copy of the entire code in a single Salesforce sandbox. This single sandbox can either be the sandbox where all developers and admins develop their code/configurations or an integration sandbox where the code is merged from multiple sandboxes where developers and admins independently develop/configure their code/configurations. This approach of maintaining the golden copy of all Salesforce developments within a Salesforce sandbox is referred to as an "org-based development" (OBD) approach. You may have already predicted that such an approach has several risks and drawbacks. Here are some key drawbacks and risks:

- Risk of accidentally refreshing the sandbox with the golden copy and losing the entire code/configuration.

- Risk of overwriting or deleting each other's code/configuration.

- No version control available and hence no option to roll back to any earlier version.

- Merging code and resolving conflicts is entirely manual and possible only through trial and error.

Org-based developments are effective when the Salesforce implementation is small and straightforward with only the out-of-the-box Salesforce functionalities being configured. However, the org-based development approach can quickly become complex and time-consuming as multiple revisions are needed. Not to mention that the biggest risk of org-based development is wiping out some or all code/configurations with no recovery or rollback options. Tracking every developer and administrator's changes manually in a shared development sandbox is unrealistic because change logs within Salesforce provide minimal information about the changes made, such as user name and timestamp of the change. Change logs are great for acknowledging changes, but there is no automated option to revert back any of the changes.

If an org-based development approach is not the best option, then what is?

# Source-Driven Development (SDD) Approach

In a source-driven development approach, a Source Code Versioning Management (SCVM) tool is used to manage an online directory of folders (a.k.a. repository) in the structure of the Salesforce metadata. All metadata and corresponding Salesforce components are retrieved out of Salesforce and managed in this online repository such that the external online SCVM tool becomes the source of truth for all code/configurations across all environments of Salesforce within an enterprise. This removes the dependency on any single Salesforce environment to be maintained as the source of all code/configuration, which is proprietary intellectual property of your organization. Every time a change is made to the code or configuration in Salesforce, a copy of the change is also committed (i.e., saved) to the online SCVM tool. All changes committed by various developers and admins are consolidated into a single source of truth within the SCVM tool and then retrieved regularly from the SCVM tool to continue with further development with the latest version of code on every machine of the developers and admins.

There are several source code versioning tools such as Git, Subversion (SVN), Concurrent Versions System (CVS), Team Foundation Server (TFS), Visual SourceSafe (VSS), and Mercurial; but the most popular SCVM tool by far is Git. There are some initial setup steps required to integrate and commit your Salesforce changes constantly to the SCVM tool, but after the initial setup, the code committing and versioning is seamless and routine.

Here are some key benefits of using a Source Code Versioning Management (SCVM) tool:

- **Code versioning** and single source of truth maintained independently in an external repository eliminating dependency on Salesforce sandbox(es) as the source of truth for all code.

- **Early detection of code conflicts and dependencies** reduces rework and prevents overwriting or breaking each other's code.

- **Latest version of code available to all** team members due to frequent commits into the centralized code repository giving instant access to the latest code/configuration to build upon.

- **Peer review** of code and configuration can be conducted independently without interrupting the work activities of developers and admins.

- **Code backup** is centralized, frequent, and incremental instead of a full backup at the end.

- **Rollback options** include the ability to roll back to any previous version of code committed to the repository.

- **Release notes** can be easily generated from version history and commit descriptions added by the developers, admins, and peer reviewers.

All SCVM tools have something called "branching" features, which allow parallel concurrent disparate versions of code across different Salesforce sandboxes at different stages of implementation. It also supports code conflict resolution and dependency resolutions between different developers and admins by staging conflicting codes in separate branches and then merging them together in a single branch to create a single conflict-free version of the final code. Another benefit of branching is to support peer review and architecture review of codes being committed via something called pull requests.

Ideally, each branch corresponds to a sandbox environment used in the project. A more advanced system approach is to further decompose the branches to be tied to each feature of the application being developed.

Although there are various ways to design the ideal branching strategy, Figure 9-4 presents a simplistic but effective example of a branching strategy that can be implemented in most projects as is.

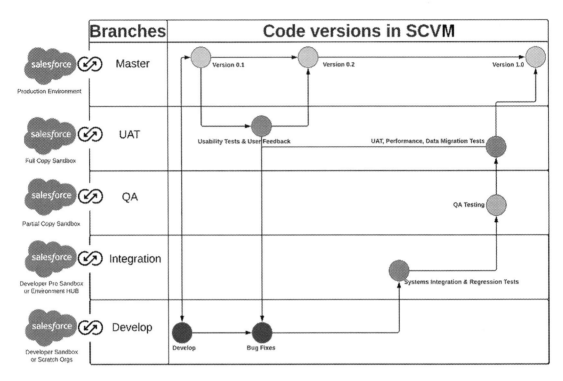

***Figure 9-5.*** *Sample Branching Strategy*

In Figure 9-5, the strategy shows five branches corresponding to each environment of Salesforce needed in a typical Salesforce implementation. Here we have a master branch that corresponds to the true source of code that corresponds with each minor release to nonproduction environments and the major release to production.

The other four branches correspond to Dev, integration, QA, and UAT environments. A day in the life of a developer or admin working within a source, code-driven development is as follows:

1.  The developer starts off their day by pulling changes from the master branch to their local repository to ensure they have the latest version of code/configuration to build upon.

2.  Once the developer completes a unit of work on the same day or over a few days, they pull the changes one more time from the master branch to ensure there has been no new code merged by other developers that could cause conflict with their recently developed unit of work. Any conflict found at this time in the developer's local repository is resolved by the developer by

updating their own code or overwriting the code pulled from the master branch with their recently developed unit of work.

3.   If a continuous integration (CI) tool *(more on CI tools a bit later)* is set up, then the CI tool monitors any new changes in the "Dev" branch of the SCVM and deploys the new changes to the developer sandbox of Salesforce.

4.   Upon successful unit testing in the developer sandbox, the changes in the development branch are merged to the "integration" branch of the SCVM.

5.   Once again the CI tool monitors the new changes in the integration branch and deploys the new changes from SCVM to the developer pro sandbox used for integration testing.

6.   Upon successful integration testing in the partial copy sandbox used for integration testing, changes from the integration branch are merged to the "QA" branch in SCVM.

7.   Once again the CI tool monitors the new changes in the QA branch and deploys the new changes to the partial copy sandbox used for quality assurance testing.

8.   Upon successful quality assurance testing, changes from the QA branch are merged to the "UAT" branch in SCVM.

9.   Once again the CI tool monitors the new changes in the UAT branch and deploys the new changes to the full copy sandbox used for User Acceptance Testing (UAT).

10.  Finally, after all testing is concluded in the UAT environment, the final version of the code in the UAT branch within the SCVM is deployed to production.

The earlier indicated sample branching strategy is an environment-based branching strategy. However, you can also consider a feature-based branching strategy, especially when working with larger teams, where work is distributed among the team based on features to be developed.

Now that we talked about the role and benefits of SCVM tools and branching strategy, let's talk about how to further automate the DevOps process to create a factory-like assembly line that automates frequent integrations of code/configurations and deployments across multiple sandboxes and production at the same time.

# Continuous Integration and Continuous Deployment (CI/CD) Strategy

Continuous integration refers to the practice of frequently merging the work efforts of all developers and administrators into a single unified version of code and then using a continuous integration and continuous deployment (CI/CD) tool such as Jenkins, Azure DevOps, or GitLab CI to create a DevOps pipeline, which is another way of saying setting up a factory-like assembly process to monitor and collect the latest version of code in the various branches of the SCVM and deploy it in the designated Salesforce sandboxes and even production environment with limited to no manual intervention.

The concept behind a CI/CD tool is to integrate the constant flow of solution development and test fixes with the delivery of solutions to the market by leveraging a factory-like assembly line setup. Most CI/CD tools have the ability to consolidate new versions of code with existing versions automatically when no code conflicts are detected. They also have the ability to revert back to any version of the code that needs to be rolled back to. Without a CI/CD tool, it is a highly cumbersome and time-consuming effort to detect code errors and manage error-free deployments to any single org, let alone simultaneous deployment in multiple sandboxes at the same time.

Now let's talk about an exciting and recent feature of Salesforce known as "Salesforce DX," which is Salesforce's long-awaited feature to support source-driven development within a multi-tenant architecture.

# Salesforce DX

Salesforce recently launched a feature called "Salesforce DX," which is based on the principles of the source-driven development approach. Salesforce DX is available as a free platform feature with almost all editions of Salesforce licenses. Salesforce DX brings with it four new features that change Salesforce DevOps in a significant manner; they are

- **Salesforce CLI**: A new command-line interface specifically for retrieving, modifying, and deploying Salesforce metadata

- **Second-Generation Packages**: A new packaging model with version upgrade capabilities and more

- **Environment Hub**: Centralized environment management console to manage all Salesforce environments from one location

- **Scratch Orgs**: Temporary sandboxes provisioned for a limited time with all Salesforce features to develop, test, and integrate new features with a SCVM branch upon completion.

# Salesforce CLI

Salesforce CLI is a command-line interface proprietary to Salesforce, with commands that allow automatic creation, update retrieval, deployment, and management of Salesforce metadata for any org connected to it. Developers can use Salesforce CLI to clone projects from the SCVM repositories and make code commits to the connected SCVM. Salesforce CLI also allows creation of scratch orgs, which are temporary and disposable Salesforce sandboxes that can emulate any edition or version of Salesforce to built and test features. Salesforce CLI can also be used to synchronize source code between scratch orgs, sandboxes, SCVM, and the developer's local repository.

# Scratch Orgs

A scratch org is a temporary, disposable Salesforce environment that can be instantly provisioned using Salesforce CLI. Scratch orgs are created and provisioned for a short period of time between 7 days and 30 days. Scratch orgs are ephemeral in nature, meaning a temporary environment is created on demand for a specific set of development activities and terminated once the intended development is completed. Scratch orgs are similar to sandboxes but are not restricted by any Salesforce edition or license type. A scratch org is fully configurable, allowing developers and admins to emulate any edition and any standard feature of Salesforce. Obviously when the features are released in production, only those functions and features that are allowed by the license types and edition available in the production org work. The scratch org configuration file in which any developer or admin works can be copied and distributed to other team members, such that all developers and admins use the same settings and configurations to build and test their respective features and feature sets. Each scratch org generates a unique project config file which is committed and merged into a Salesforce package within Salesforce DX.

# Salesforce Package(s)

Packages are similar to a repository created within Salesforce DX that automatically creates a project directory to manage all config files generated from the scratch orgs. A package can be created for the entire org or a single application or a single feature of Salesforce. The metadata within a package can be independently tested and deployed to any environment within Salesforce. Eventually the package along with the Salesforce metadata contained within it is frequently committed to and retrieved from the SCVM tool.

The package-based development approach is most useful when organizing and modularizing Salesforce developments into a conflict-free, interoperable structure of metadata that can be deployed over multiple releases to production. Packaging is not a new concept in Salesforce. However, the latest version of packaging available with Salesforce DX is known as the second-generation packages, also known as "2GP." The key distinction of a second-generation package from its predecessor is that the second-generation package can be evolved with new versions of the package being deployed instead of redeploying the entire package during each release. Each version of a second-generation package is an immutable and independent artifact that can be added on top of previous versions of the package.

A package version contains the specific metadata and features associated with that package version, and installing a package version is similar to deploying metadata. Another benefit of package-based deployment is the ability to detect which metadata in your Salesforce org came from which package, allowing for isolated and directed troubleshooting.

# Environment Hub

The environment hub can be seen as the environment management console that allows you to provision, connect, view, and log into any scratch or Salesforce org from a central location. If your company has multiple environments for development, testing, and trials, the environment hub lets you streamline your approach to org management. The environment hub resembles the structure of an actual Salesforce sandbox, but it is more than a sandbox. It tracks all active scratch orgs being used by developers and assembles all commits made by developers from their respective scratch orgs. The environment hub centralizes and constantly identifies any conflicts from commits made by any developer or admin to any single scratch org.

In addition to the preceding new features, Salesforce DX uses the migration tool from its Force.com platform to retrieve and push metadata to any Salesforce org, but the key feature of DX is that it can pull all metadata from all scratch orgs into one single version.

Salesforce DX does not replace the need for a SCVM tool or a CI/CD tool; however, it adds to the benefits of using SCVM. The idea behind maintaining this centralized repository outside of a Salesforce sandbox is to maintain frequent versions of all code/configuration from all sandboxes. It also does not replace the need for a CI/CD tool such as Jenkins, Azure DevOps, or GitLab CI that enables automated integration and deployment of code in the various environments. In addition to a SCVM and a CI/CD tool, its great practice to use an application lifecycle management (ALM) tool such as Jira or Trello or Azure DevOps, which is used to manage every aspect of an implementation from project planning, requirements gathering, and testing to deployment tracking. It is ideal to manage the entire backlog of business requirements and user stories within an ALM tool instead of loose documents and multiple versions of Excel worksheets. Another addition to the DevOps toolset is a static code analysis tool such as SonarQube, which can inspect code continuously in static mode as it is written. Usually, errors are found in code after it runs through a compiler. However, static code analysis tools can detect code anomalies, security vulnerabilities, and most importantly whether any piece of code has sufficient test coverage to pass Salesforce's 75% test coverage requirements.

Figure 9-6 illustrates a sample implementation of Salesforce DX in conjunction with the ALM, SCVM, and CI/CD tools to represent an ideal DevOps approach.

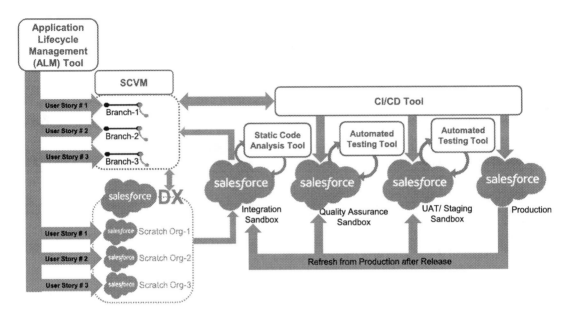

***Figure 9-6.*** *Sample Salesforce DX Implementation*

# Testing Strategy

The primary objective of an effective testing strategy is to test instantly, continuously, and frequently from start of development until product launch.

But before we talk about how to formulate the best testing strategy, let's take a look at the different types of testing that need to be considered.

Table 9-4 provides the nine types of testing that need to be ideally conducted for every mid- to large-sized Salesforce implementation.

***Table 9-4.*** *Types of Testing*

| Test Type | Test Description | When and Where Is This Done? |
|---|---|---|
| **Unit test** | In this form of testing, each unit of code in a single component is tested. This testing is carried out by the developer upon completion of their development of the component. | During development in the developer environment or scratch org. |

(continued)

***Table 9-4.*** (*continued*)

| Test Type | Test Description | When and Where Is This Done? |
|---|---|---|
| **Static code analysis test** | Systematic examination of source code to identify overlooked programming flaws such as unused variables, empty catch blocks, and unnecessary object creation; checks for test code coverage requirements and security vulnerabilities. | At the time of committing or merging code into the SCVM repository in the developer environment or integration environment. |
| **Integration test** | A high-level software testing process in which testers verify that all related systems maintain data integrity and can operate in coordination with other systems in the same environment. The testing process ensures that all subcomponents are integrated successfully to provide expected results. | Integration environment. |
| **Quality assurance test** | This testing is done by a specialized team of testers who certify that the system components function as per the technical design. This type of testing is the most elaborate type of testing that requires development of formal test cases that cover the definition of done for the solution. | Upon deployment of code to the QA environment. |
| **User acceptance test** | In this form of testing, actual end users test the software to make sure it can handle required tasks in real-world scenarios, according to their business requirements. | Upon deployment of code to the UAT environment. |
| **Performance test** | Includes stress and load testing. Coordinated with Salesforce. Done using LoadRunner, Silk Performer, RedView. | Upon deployment of code to the UAT environment or a separate stage environment preferably in a full copy sandbox. |

(*continued*)

***Table 9-4.*** (*continued*)

| Test Type | Test Description | When and Where Is This Done? |
|---|---|---|
| **Smoke test** | Preliminary testing to reveal simple failures severe enough to reject a prospective software release. | Part of post-deployment steps and upon each deployment to any environment. |
| **Regression test** | A type of software testing that ensures that previously developed and tested software still performs the same way after it is changed or interfaced with other software. | Part of post-deployment steps and upon deployment to the integration, QA, and UAT environments. |
| **Data migration test** | Testing that data is correctly migrated and that data integrity is maintained between systems. | Upon deployment of code to the UAT environment or a separate stage environment preferably in a full copy sandbox. |

Now that we know the different types of testing, there are two ways to accomplish all the testing. All the testing can either be done manually or via automated testing using test automation tools such as Selenium or Qualitia. Both testing approaches have their advantages and disadvantages.

Although manual testing is labor intensive, for short-length, straightforward, and informal projects, it is definitely more efficient to conduct manual testing. However, in large and complex projects, the efficiencies gained from automated testing can reduce testing efforts by as much as 70%[3] compared to testing manually.

Automated testing requires investment in test automation tools and significant resources to develop automated test scripts. Figure 9-7 illustrates the decision criteria that one must consider when choosing an automated testing approach over manual testing.

---

[3]70% efficiency is indicated based on our own professional experiences implementing automated testing and is not an industry established benchmark.

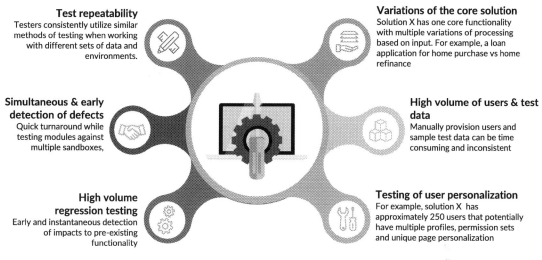

**Test repeatability**
Testers consistently utilize similar methods of testing when working with different sets of data and environments.

**Variations of the core solution**
Solution X has one core functionality with multiple variations of processing based on input. For example, a loan application for home purchase vs home refinance

**Simultaneous & early detection of defects**
Quick turnaround while testing modules against multiple sandboxes,

**High volume of users & test data**
Manually provision users and sample test data can be time consuming and inconsistent

**High volume regression testing**
Early and instantaneous detection of impacts to pre-existing functionality

**Testing of user personalization**
For example, solution X  has approximately 250 users that potentially have multiple profiles, permission sets and unique page personalization

***Figure 9-7.*** *Decision Criteria for Choosing Automated Testing over Manual Testing*

Although automated testing requires a substantial investment in an automation testing tool such as Selenium or Qualitia, along with some dedicated resource time to design and write automated test scripts, there are several benefits that can be reaped within the first few weeks of implementing automated testing. Some of these benefits are outlined in Figure 9-8.

**Increased Test Coverage**
Full comprehensive end to end regression of modules, which improves over every sprint and automated test.

**Quick Defect Discovery and Resolution**
Quick turnaround while testing modules against at least N Sandboxes

**Additional Time**
Allows testers on additional tasks, which can include adding scope/test coverage, performing negative/edge testing, and improving custom config testing.

**Populate Volume Data**
Allows us to more closely mimic production and support future/continuous testing.

**Time Saved on DevOps Tasks**
Testers save time on these repetitive and required tasks, which include User provisioning and Configurations/Data Loads.

**Front-End & Backend Validations**
Automation Testing will perform UI Validation along with data configuration for common validation tests.

**CI/CD Integration**
Regression suites will integrate with existing Automation framework.

***Figure 9-8.*** *Benefits of Automated Testing*

Now that you know the benefits of implementing automated testing, how do you implement an automated testing approach?

Figure 9-9 outlines a step-by-step process to setting up an ideal test automation approach for any implementation.

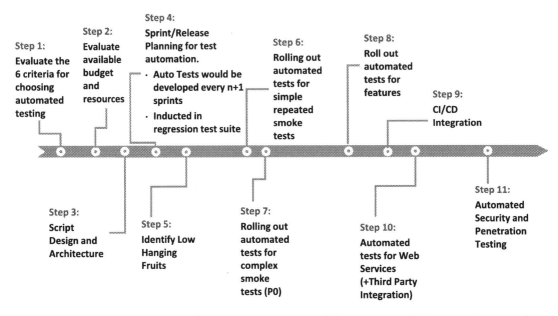

***Figure 9-9.*** *11 Steps to Implementing a Successful Automated Testing Approach*

Regardless of whether your testing strategy includes manual testing or automated testing, it is crucial to incorporate all nine types of testing indicated in Table 9-4 to ensure a healthy and self-sustaining solution to be delivered as the final outcome from testing.

The last but crucial archetype of an efficient DevOps process is the setup and execution of a governance and monitoring structure.

# Governance and Monitoring

A good governance and monitoring structure must include at least the following three types of committees:

1. Steering committee

2. Center of Excellence (COE)

3. Data governance committee

# Steering Committee

The members of this committee own the overall vision and strategy of the Salesforce implementation. It is usually made up of project sponsors and business and IT stakeholders. The steering committee sets the project priorities and oversees the implementation budget. The steering committee is also responsible for developing the tactical road map for all phases of the Salesforce implementation. A better way to think about the steering committee and its agenda is to compare it with the initial project kick-off meeting. Kick-off meetings are conducted only once in the lifetime of a project. However, the steering committee meetings follow a similar agenda as kick-off meetings on a regular basis, such as meeting weekly, monthly, or quarterly. The steering committee course-corrects issues such as scope creep, insufficiency of deliverables, or unsatisfactory project progress. Steering committees also review and prioritize requests brought in by the Center of Excellence (COE) team. The steering committee evaluates the potential impact and costs of including COE suggestions to the implementation budget and road map.

It also acts as the final escalation point for disagreements that the project teams are unable to resolve on their own.

# Center of Excellence (COE)

The key purpose of establishing a Center of Excellence (COE) is to achieve the following:

- Identify and execute business priorities for the Salesforce implementation.

- Leverage the expertise across involved stakeholders, processes, and technology.

- Maintain scalability, sustainability, and healthiness of the Salesforce application.

At its most mature state, it is a highly formalized and self-directing committee that is responsible for supporting business users and shepherding the most complex of projects to successful completion. The COE promotes the use of best practices derived from multiple implementations as a means of repeating the successes from past implementations in every implementation going forward. The COE should consist of stakeholders that look both inside and outside the organization to capture new knowledge and best practices.

# Data Governance Committee

Data governance is a process that monitors data usability, data quality, and data compliance in adherence to data privacy and data security standards set for each industry.

The key responsibility of a data governance committee is to maintain unified business definitions across the organization and develop data quality and data security standards across all enterprise-owned technologies.

At the time of writing this chapter, a new terminology subsequent to DevOps has evolved called "DevSecOps." Let's take a moment here to shed some light on the key differences that we've have noticed in the DevSecOps practice compared to the DevOps practice that we discussed in this chapter.

## DevOps vs. DevSecOps: What's the Difference?

Through this chapter, as we talked about DevOps, a huge amount of focus was on methodology, source-driven development, version control, and ease of code integration and deployment. However, application security and accessibility requirements come as an afterthought or much later during testing or are entirely missed in the initial version of the launched solution. Addressing any security flaws after development and testing often requires a significant amount of rework and refactoring of the application, which could be a time-consuming and unbudgeted expense. The term DevSecOps is the industry's response to solving this issue by embedding application security and accessibility front and center within the standard DevOps process.

The key difference between a standard DevOps and a DevSecOps practice is the process of addressing application security and accessibility requirements within the requirements gathering, development, integration, testing, and deployment stages. In a DevSecOps practice, security practices are included since the initial planning and design sessions. Since security is a necessary evil that is camouflaged in happy path scenarios, the integrity to implement the highest security standards within each code or configuration eventually depends on the developers and admins who build the components while managing the ongoing pressure to complete development on time and within budget. DevSecOps is yet to mature in the coming years with better strategies, best practices, and tools to make security first and foremost in the DevOps process.

# Chapter Summary

In this chapter, we covered

- The six archetypes that constitute an ideal DevOps practice

- A brief overview of the traditional development approach and the benefits of DevOps

- The three common delivery methodologies

- The roles and responsibilities of a Salesforce delivery team practicing DevOps

- An overview of Salesforce environments and the various methods of deployment from one sandbox to another and to production

- Differences between org-based development and source-driven development

- The benefits of using a Source Code Versioning Management (SCVM) tool and branching strategies

- An overview of continuous integration and continuous deployment strategy using Salesforce DX

- An overview of the various types of testing and when and where such testing needs to be conducted

- An overview of automated testing as an alternative to manual testing, the decision criteria to choose automated testing over manual testing, and the benefits of automated testing

- An overview of the 11 steps to implementing a successful automated testing approach

- An overview of governance and monitoring consisting of, at minimum, a steering committee, a Center of Excellence (COE), and a data governance committee

- Finally, the difference between DevOps and DevSecOps

# APPENDIX A

# Salesforce Authorization Flows

This appendix will provide a flow diagram for each Salesforce authorization flow to assist an architect in choosing the correct authorization flow when designing system access to and from Salesforce. This appendix will focus on the nine primary authorization flows used in Salesforce, including

- Web Server Flow

- User-Agent Flow

- JWT Bearer Flow

- Device Flow

- Asset Token Flow

- Username and Password Flow

- Refresh Token Flow

- SAML Assertion Flow

- SAML Bearer Assertion Flow

---

**Note**   Any other authorization flows indicated in Chapter 7 not listed here are a variation of one of the nine authorization flows mentioned in this appendix. Hence, to avoid redundancy of content, only the preceding nine flows have been covered in this appendix.

---

© Dipanker Jyoti and James A. Hutcherson 2021
D. Jyoti and J. A. Hutcherson, *Salesforce Architect's Handbook*, https://doi.org/10.1007/978-1-4842-6631-1

# Web Server Flow

A **Web Server Flow** is mainly used to integrate an external web-based application with the Salesforce API, leveraging the industry standard OAuth 2.0 authorization code grant type authorization protocol.[1]

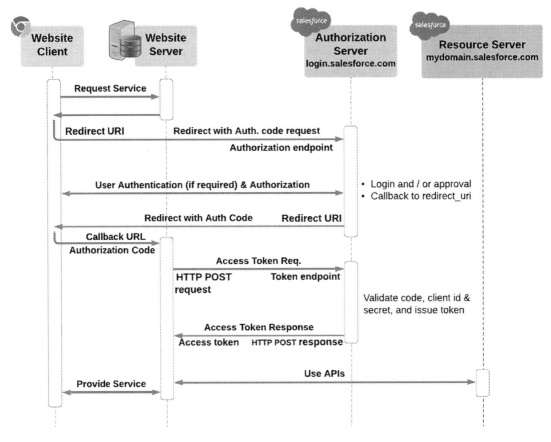

**_Figure A-1._**  _Web Server Flow Illustration_

Figure A-1 presents an example scenario demonstrating Web Server Flow:

1. An external website wants to obtain information from an object within your Salesforce instance.

2. The website makes a request to its own server for authorization.

---

[1]https://tools.ietf.org/html/rfc6749#section-4.1.

3.  The website server redirects the authorization code request to the Salesforce authorization endpoint of your instance (i.e., endpoint defined by you within your Salesforce-connected app).

4.  The user is redirected to the Salesforce login page. After a successful login, the user is asked to approve the website's access to the object data within your Salesforce instance.

5.  After the user approves the website to access the data, Salesforce sends a callback to the website with an authorization code.

6.  The website passes the authorization code to the Salesforce token endpoint, requesting an access token.

7.  Salesforce validates the authorization code and sends back an access token that includes associated permissions in the form of scopes.

8.  Then the website sends a request back to Salesforce to access the information needed by the website. The request includes the access token with associated scopes.

9.  Salesforce validates the access token and associated scopes.

10. The website can now access the Salesforce data.

---

**Note**    The user never sees the access token; it will be stored by the website within a session cookie. Salesforce also sends other information with the access token, such as the token lifetime and eventually a refresh token.

---

# User-Agent Flow

A **User-Agent Flow** is mainly used when the user authorizes a desktop or mobile app to access data using an external system or embedded browser. Client apps running in a browser using a scripting language such as JavaScript can also use this flow. This flow leverages the industry standard OAuth 2.0 implicit grant type authorization protocol.[2]

---

[2]https://tools.ietf.org/html/rfc6749#section-4.2.

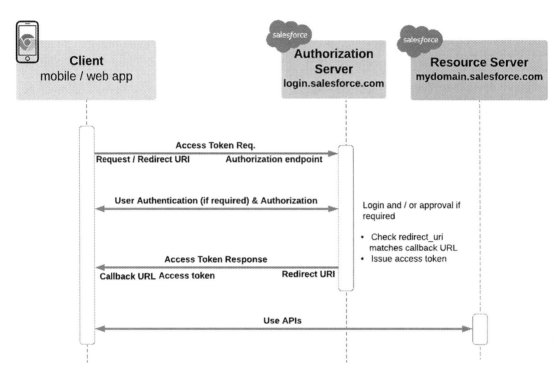

***Figure A-2.*** *User-Agent Flow*

Figure A-2 presents an example scenario demonstrating User-Agent Flow:

1. The end user opens the mobile app.

2. The Salesforce-connected app redirects the user to Salesforce's login page to authenticate and authorize the mobile app's access.

3. The user logs in and approves access requested by the mobile app.

4. The connected app receives the callback request from Salesforce and gets redirected to the URL in the redirection URL along with the access and refresh tokens.

5. The connected app uses the access token to access data on the user's behalf and presents it within the mobile app.

**Note**    This authorization flow is least secure because the access token is encoded into the redirection URL and is exposed to the user and other apps on the device. Also, the authentication is based on same-origin policy, which means that the redirect_URI must match one of the callback URL values specified in the connected app.

# JWT Bearer Flow

A **JWT Bearer Flow** is mainly used to authorize long-term access for remote systems without requiring them to log in again each time they need to access Salesforce. JWT stands for JSON Web Token. This flow uses a certificate generated by both systems to sign the JSON Web Token request each time one of the authorized systems needs access to the other system. This flow does not require user interaction; however, it does require a trust relationship to be established between the integrating systems. This flow is best for server-to-server integrations without requiring user authorizations each time data is exchanged.

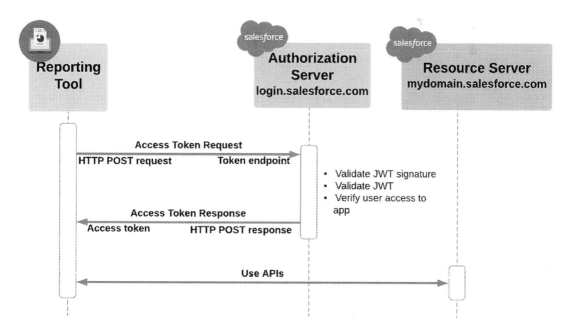

***Figure A-3.***  *JWT Bearer Flow*

Figure A-3 presents an example scenario demonstrating the JWT Bearer Flow:

1. An external Salesforce reporting tool needs to pull data from Salesforce to generate a sales report.

2. In this case, the Salesforce-connected app sends the JSON Web Token to the defined token endpoint. The JSON Web Token enables identity and security information to be shared across the two systems' security domains.

3. Salesforce validates the JSON Web Token based on the digital signature previously set up to authorize the external reporting tool.

4. Salesforce ensures that that the presented JSON Web Token is still valid and that the connected app is till approved for access.

5. Salesforce issues an access token to the reporting tool.

6. The reporting tool can now access the required data from Salesforce.

# Device Flow

A **Device Flow** is mainly used to integrate Internet of Things (IoT) devices with limited input or display capabilities such as smart TVs or smart devices such as Amazon's Alexa. Device Flow can also be used to integrate with command-line apps such as Git. When using this flow, users need to use a web browser or a mobile device that has more input capabilities to connect the device and to configure additional capabilities.

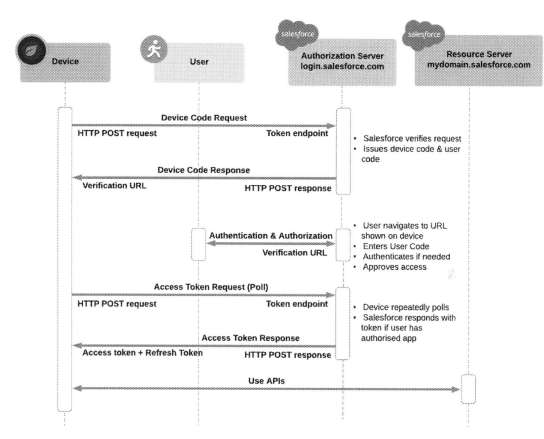

***Figure A-4.*** *Device Flow*

Figure A-4 presents an example scenario demonstrating the Device Flow:

1. The user wants to connect Salesforce to their IOT-based home thermostat *(such as Google's Nest)* to control their home temperature.

2. The user opens the Bluetooth app in their home thermostat to connect with their mobile device that has the home thermostat app installed for additional configuration.

3. After connecting the mobile device to the home thermostat via Bluetooth connection, the user opens the home thermostat app to set up the device.

4.  The home thermostat app is set up as a connected app within Salesforce, in which case the thermostat app posts a request to the Salesforce endpoint for authentication.

5.  Salesforce verifies the request and returns a human-readable user code, verification URL, and device code.

6.  The thermostat app on the user mobile device displays the human-readable code provided by Salesforce and requests the user to enter the code by navigating to the verification URL to add the new thermostat device to the user's account.

7.  The user goes to the verification URL on their mobile device and enters the code to activate the device.

8.  Once verified, the user authorizes the thermostat app to access data in Salesforce and vice versa.

9.  The thermostat app on the user's mobile device begins polling the Salesforce token endpoint for an access token.

10. Salesforce sends an access and refresh token to the thermostat app on the user's mobile device.

11. The user can now control the thermostat device via Salesforce.

# Asset Token Flow

An **Asset Token Flow** is used to integrate IoT devices such as smart watches and mobile devices that are not limited by their input capabilities for setup and use. In other words, it is not dependent entirely on the device capability for device registration and data exchange with Salesforce, as in the case of devices integrated using the Device Flow described earlier. The Asset Token Flow leverages the JWT Bearer Flow to identify the device and a back-end server used by the device to process the stream of data and events exchanged with Salesforce. The JWT tokens allow registration of the device within Salesforce and to link the device data with data stored in Salesforce objects.

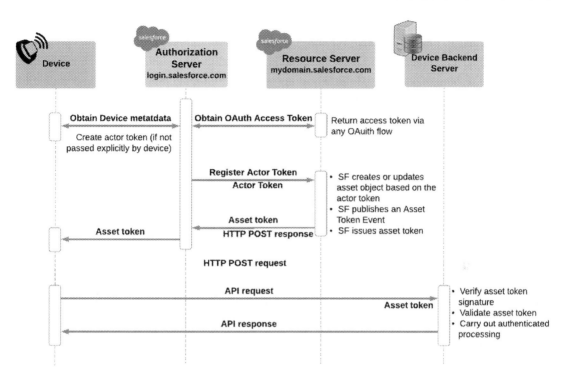

***Figure A-5.*** *Asset Token Flow*

Figure A-5 presents an example scenario demonstrating the Asset Token Flow:

1. User wants to register their wearable smart watch with Salesforce to exchange health data collected by their smart watch.

2. User logs into a Salesforce app to register their smart watch device, where they provide all data needed from the smart watch to register the device.

3. Salesforce stores the device information in the standard asset object.

4. The connected app configured within Salesforce generates an actor token that identifies the user and an asset token that identifies the data based on the data provided in the asset object.

5. The asset token is sent to the back-end server of the device and stored in the device and completes the device registration process.

6. After the device is registered, the device transmits data to its back-end server.

7. The back-end server of the device uses the earlier provisioned asset token to exchange user health data with Salesforce, without requiring re-logins into Salesforce *(similar to JWT Bearer Flow)*.

# Username and Password Flow

A **Username and Password Flow** can be used to authorize a remote system using the user's username and password that the user uses to log into Salesforce. However, this is the least recommended option for designing integrations, since it exposes the user's username and password in the URL. Although, the username password can be stored within named credentials to mitigate exposure of user credentials, it should be only used for integration with highly trusted remote systems and other grant types such as Webserver Flow or JWT token flow are not feasible.

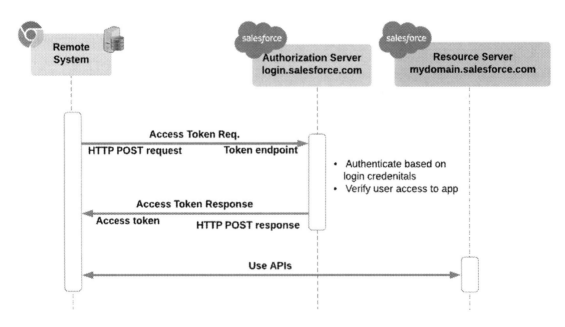

*Figure A-6. Username and Password Flow*

Figure A-6 presents an example scenario demonstrating the Username and Password Flow:

1. A connected app is configured to integrate a remote system with Salesforce.

2. The user's username and password is stored in the connected app (or stored in a named credential and referenced within the connected app).

3. The connected app requests an access token by sending the user's login credentials to the Salesforce token endpoint.

4. After verifying the request, Salesforce grants an access token to the connected app.

5. The remote system gets access to any data that is accessible by the user themselves.

# Refresh Token Flow

A **Refresh Token Flow** is mainly used to obtain a new access token to start a new session when the current session expires as per the session timeout limit set within the system. The prerequisite for a Refresh Token Flow is to have a valid preexisting session that has expired. The refresh token extends the access for the remote application or user without requiring any reauthentication or reauthorization steps, if nothing has changed within the remote system or user's access privileges.

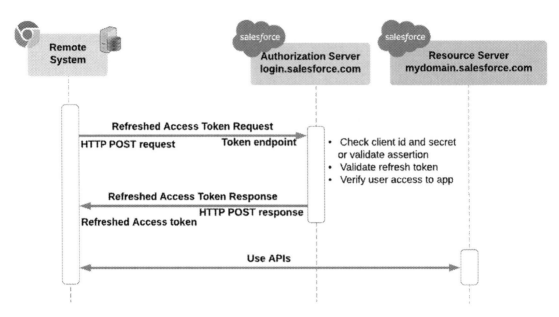

***Figure A-7.*** *Refresh Token Flow*

Figure A-7 presents an example scenario demonstrating the Refresh Token Flow:

1. An external system is in active session with Salesforce, and the session is about to expire.

2. As soon as the session expires, the connected app related to the remote system uses the existing refresh token to request a new access token.

3. After verifying the request, Salesforce grants a new access token to the remote system.

4. The remote system seamlessly enters into a new session with a reset session timeout. All of this happens within milliseconds and typically does not cause any interruptions when transferring from one session to another.

# SAML Assertion Flow

A **SAML Assertion Flow** is an alternative way to connect remote systems with Salesforce within organizations that already use SAML-based SSO to access Salesforce. A SAML assertion is an XML security token issued by an identity provider and consumed by a service provider. The service provider relies on its content to identify the assertion's subject for security-related purposes.

With this flow, the remote system can federate itself within the API using a SAML assertion, the same way users federate within Salesforce via single sign-on. The biggest advantage of this flow is that it does not require configuring a Salesforce-connected app since the SAML assertion manages the authentication and authorization details within this flow.

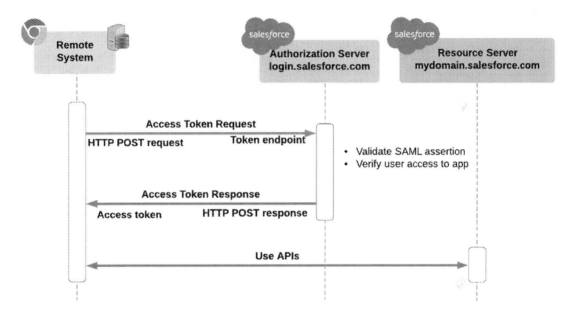

***Figure A-8.*** *SAML Assertion Flow*

Figure A-8 presents an example scenario demonstrating the SAML Assertion Flow:

1.  A SAML configuration is set up in Salesforce connecting the remote system.

2.  The remote system exchanges a SAML assertion for an access token.

3.  After verifying the SAML assertion, Salesforce grants an access token in the response, granting the remote system access to Salesforce.

> **Note**    This flow cannot be used by the remote system to connect with more than one Salesforce org. Login flows cannot be used for authentication with this flow, and this flow does not work with Salesforce communities. Also refresh tokens cannot be issued with this flow.

# SAML Bearer Assertion Flow

A **SAML Bearer Assertion Flow** is mainly used to authorize a remote system that has been previously authorized. The SAML Bearer Assertion Flow is similar to the Refresh Token Flow with the exception that the SAML Bearer Assertion flow uses a signed SAML 2.0 assertion to request an OAuth access token instead and the digital signature applied to the SAML assertion authenticates the authorized app.

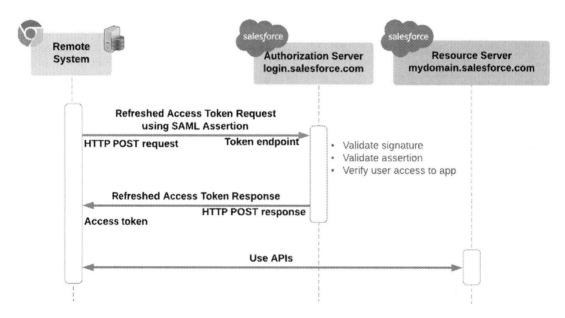

***Figure A-9.***  *SAML Bearer Assertion Flow*

Figure A-9 presents an example scenario demonstrating the SAML Bearer Assertion Flow:

1.  A connected app is configured using a digital certificate.

2.  This certificate corresponds to the private key of the remote system.

3.  When the connected app is saved, a consumer key is generated and assigned to the remote system.

4.  When the remote system requests access to Salesforce, the connected app posts the SAML bearer assertion to the Salesforce token endpoint.

5.  Salesforce validates the signature using the certificate registered for the connected app. In addition, it validates the audience, issuer, subject, and validity of the assertion.

6.  Assuming that the assertion is valid and that the user or admin had authorized the app previously, Salesforce issues an access token to the remote system and grants access.

---

**Note**    Refresh tokens cannot be issued with this flow either.

---

# APPENDIX B

# Salesforce Integration Patterns

This appendix will provide a one-page flow diagram for each Salesforce integration pattern to assist an architect to better understand the pattern. This appendix will focus on the six most popular integration patterns used in Salesforce, including

- Request and Reply

- Fire and Forget

- Batch Data Synchronization

- Remote Call-In

- UI Update

- Data Virtualization

## Request and Reply

A **Request and Reply** integration pattern supports synchronous communication where message is sent to an external system and the sender is expecting a return of information.

© Dipanker Jyoti and James A. Hutcherson 2021
D. Jyoti and J. A. Hutcherson, *Salesforce Architect's Handbook*, https://doi.org/10.1007/978-1-4842-6631-1

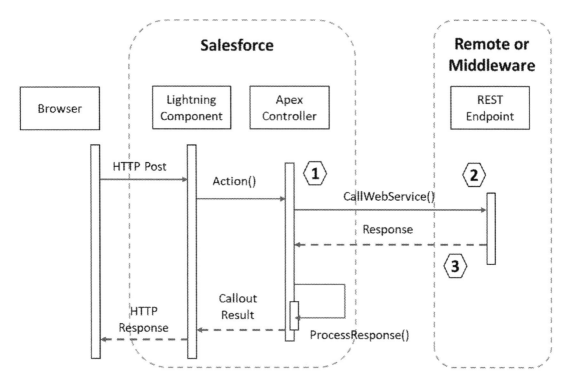

***Figure B-1.*** *Request and Reply Integration – Synchronous Remote Process Invocation*

Figure B-1 presents an example flow using a Request and Reply integration pattern. The pattern is initiated when

1.  The Apex controller makes a remote web service call to the remote system or middleware after the browser user initiated an action.

2.  The service call remains open while it waits for a response from the remote system.

3.  The remote system returns a response to the Apex controller which processes the response.

# Fire and Forget

A **Fire and Forget** integration pattern supports asynchronous communication where message is sent to an external system and the sender is **not** expecting a return of information.

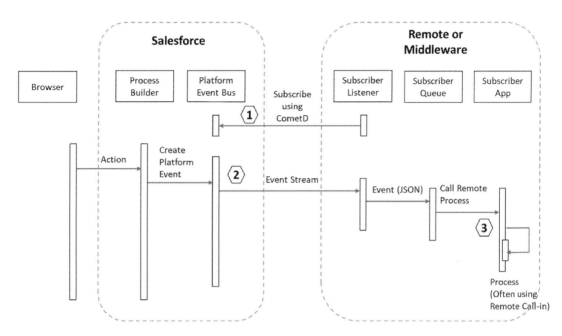

***Figure B-2.*** *Fire and Forget Integration – Asynchronous Remote Process Invocation Using Platform Events*

Figure B-2 presents an example flow using a Fire and Forget integration pattern. The pattern is initiated when

1. The remote system (app) subscribes to a CometD platform event as a listener.

2. The Salesforce process creates an event on the event stream after an action is recorded.

3. The remote system listens to the event stream and recognizes an event. It calls a remote process. The system must be prepared to handle the same event processing more than once.

# Batch Data Sync

The Batch Data Sync integration pattern is a common pattern used to support data migration in and out of a receiving system.

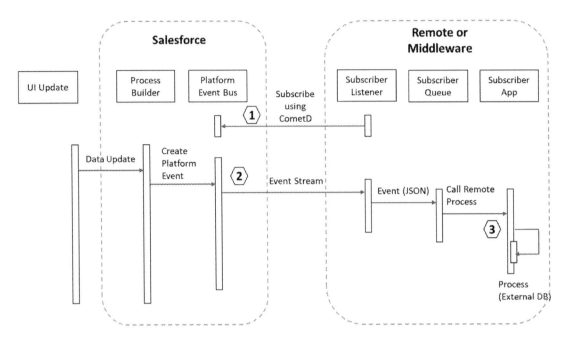

***Figure B-3.*** *Batch Data Sync Integration – Asynchronous Remote Process Invocation of Change Data Capture*

Figure B-3 presents an example flow using a Batch Data Sync integration pattern (similar to the Fire and Forget pattern). The pattern is initiated when

1.  The remote system (app) subscribes to a CometD platform event as a listener.

2.  The Salesforce process creates an event on the event stream after a record creation or update is recorded.

3.  The remote system listens to the event stream and recognizes an event. It calls a remote process to update change sync in the external database. The system must be prepared to handle the same event processing more than once.

# Remote Call-In

The **Remote Call-In** integration pattern is used to support synchronous communication where a message is sent from an external system to the receiving system.

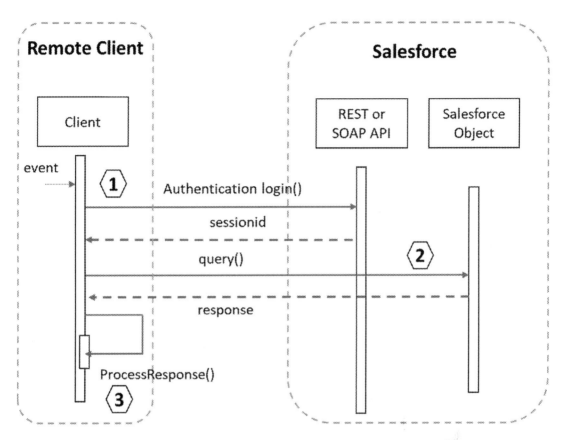

***Figure B-4.*** *Remote Call-In Integration – Synchronous Remote Call Using SOAP or REST*

Figure B-4 presents an example flow using a Remote Call-In integration pattern. The pattern is initiated when

1. An event at the remote client initiates login call to Salesforce and, if authenticated and authorized, returns a sessionid.

2. The remote client makes a remote call using either SOAP or REST API call to Salesforce to query, update, create, or delete data.

3. Salesforce returns a response to the client which processes the response.

# UI Update

The **UI Update** integration pattern is used to update the receiving system UI based on changes in the sending system.

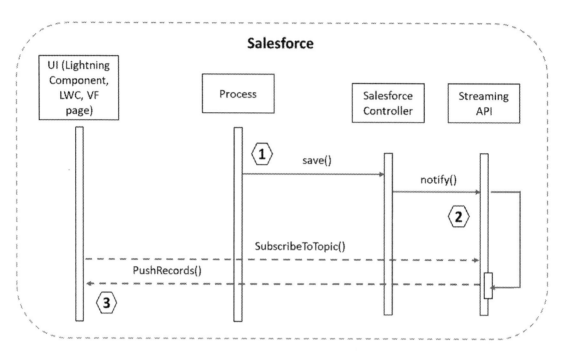

***Figure B-5.***  *UI Update Integration – Using Change Data Trigger*

Figure B-5 presents an example flow using a UI Update integration pattern. The pattern is initiated when

1. A UI is expecting to automatically see if a process updates a given field. The save of the process makes the record change.

2. The controller notifies Streaming API of the change. A PushTopic is defined with the event trigger and the data included in an update.

3. A JavaScript-based component can use the PushRecords to update the UI.

# Data Virtualization

The **Data Virtualization** integration pattern is used to support synchronous communication where a message is sent from an external system to the receiving system and presented as a **virtual** object.

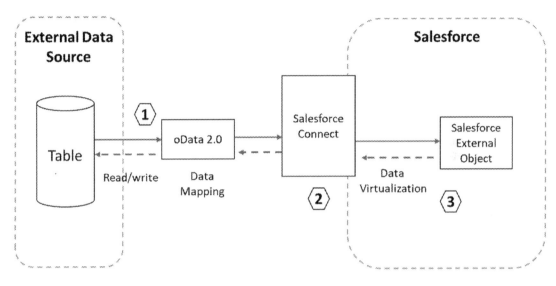

***Figure B-6.*** *Data Virtualization Integration – Using OData and Salesforce Connect*

Figure B-6 presents an example flow using a Data Virtualization integration pattern. The pattern is initiated when

1. Read/write access is established using OData to manage and map the external data source.

2. Salesforce Connect provides authentication and authorization and management of the OData data mapping.

3. Salesforce external object is defined and presents a virtual data object.

# Salesforce Sample Artifacts

This appendix will present a set of artifacts that we created for practice business discussions and mock CTA reviews. The goal of this appendix is to give you different ideas on how to create and present your architectural design. We are including the following artifacts:

- System landscape
- Data model
- Role hierarchy
- Project management/governance
- Integrations/SSO/OAuth
- Actors/licenses

## System Landscapes

The system landscape examples highlight different approaches that we created to present how an existing enterprise environment will be changed with a proposed system solution. The diagrams all assume that Salesforce is existing or will be added to support the new system design. Figures C-1 through C-4 are examples of system landscape diagrams.

355

© Dipanker Jyoti and James A. Hutcherson 2021
D. Jyoti and J. A. Hutcherson, *Salesforce Architect's Handbook*, https://doi.org/10.1007/978-1-4842-6631-1

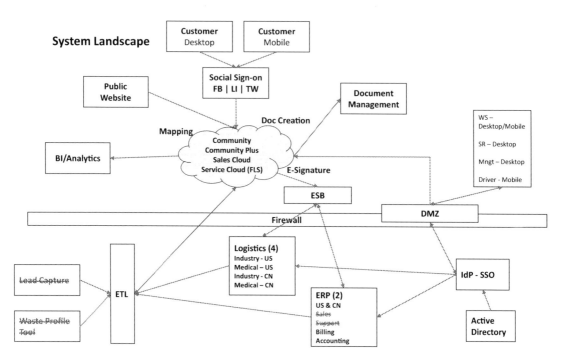

**Figure C-1.** *System Landscape for Greenhouse Recycling Corp*

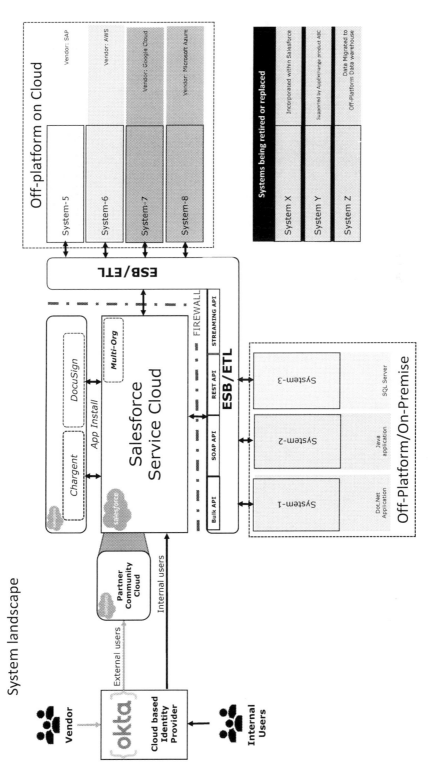

*Figure C-2.* *System Landscape for Example System*

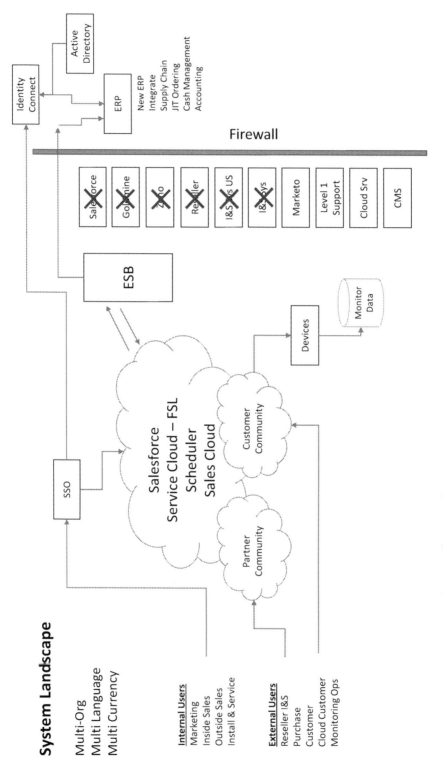

***Figure C-3.*** *System Landscape for Mock CTA Review*

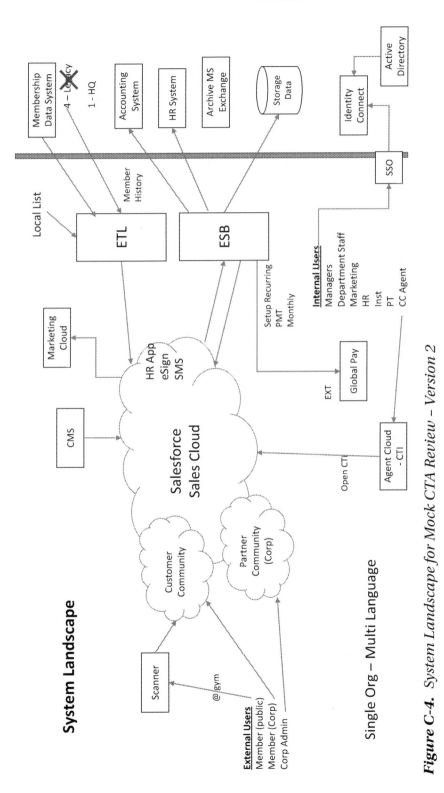

*Figure C-4.* *System Landscape for Mock CTA Review – Version 2*

# Data Models

The data model examples shown will present different approaches that we have used to present with a proposed system solution. The data models use an ERD to depict the objects, object relationships, and important elements used in the design. Figure C-5 through C-6 are examples and considerations used in data model diagrams.

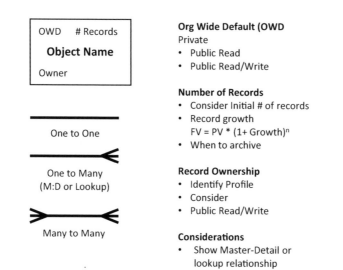

*Figure C-5.  ERD Elements, Relationships, and Consideration*

# Data Model

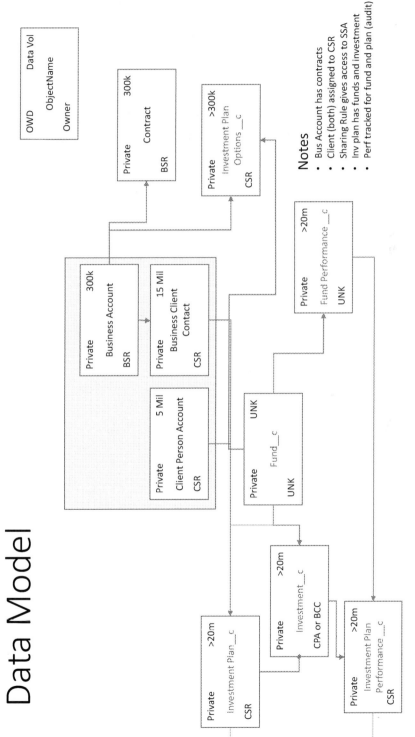

| OWD | Data Vol |
|-----|----------|
| | ObjectName |
| Owner | |

**Business Account**
Private    300k
BSR

**Business Client Contact**
Private    15 Mil
CSR

**Client Person Account**
Private    5 Mil
CSR

**Contract**
Private    300k
BSR

**Investment Plan Options __c**
Private    >300k
CSR

**Fund __c**
Private    UNK
UNK

**Fund Performance __c**
Private    >20m
UNK

**Investment Plan __c**
Private    >20m
CSR

**Investment __c**
Private    >20m
CPA or BCC

**Investment Plan Performance __c**
Private    >20m
CSR

### Notes
- Bus Account has contracts
- Client (both) assigned to CSR
- Sharing Rule gives access to SSA
- Inv plan has funds and investment
- Perf tracked for fund and plan (audit)

**Figure C-6.** *ERD Elements, Relationships, and Consideration*

# FUSIAOLA Options

Figure C-7 is a variation of the FUSIAOLA artifact presented in Chapter 2. This version focuses on the objects, systems, actors/licenses, and integrations given.

# System, Object, Actors, Integration

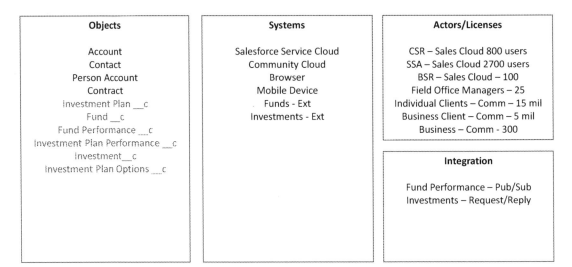

| Objects | Systems | Actors/Licenses |
|---|---|---|
| Account | Salesforce Service Cloud | CSR – Sales Cloud 800 users |
| Contact | Community Cloud | SSA – Sales Cloud 2700 users |
| Person Account | Browser | BSR – Sales Cloud – 100 |
| Contract | Mobile Device | Field Office Managers – 25 |
| Investment Plan __c | Funds - Ext | Individual Clients – Comm – 15 mil |
| Fund __c | Investments - Ext | Business Client – Comm – 5 mil |
| Fund Performance __c | | Business – Comm - 300 |
| Investment Plan Performance __c | | |
| Investment __c | | **Integration** |
| Investment Plan Options __c | | Fund Performance – Pub/Sub |
| | | Investments – Request/Reply |

***Figure C-7.*** *Systems, Objects, Actors, and Integration Artifact*

# Lifecycle Management Artifacts

Figures C-8 and C-9 show different approaches to present lifecycle management.

## Environment management

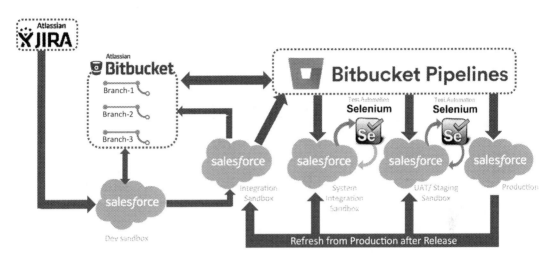

***Figure C-8.*** *Environment Management – Sandbox Management*

# Release Management

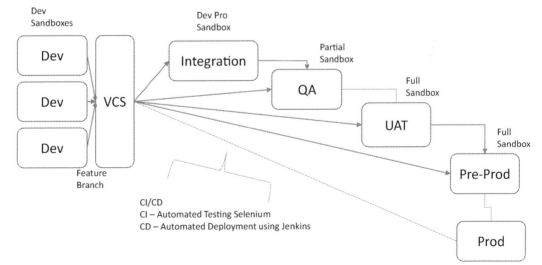

***Figure C-9.*** *Release Management – Sandbox Management*

# Artifacts Used During a Mock CTA Review

Figures C-10 through C-17 provide an example of a set of artifacts used for mock CTI board review.

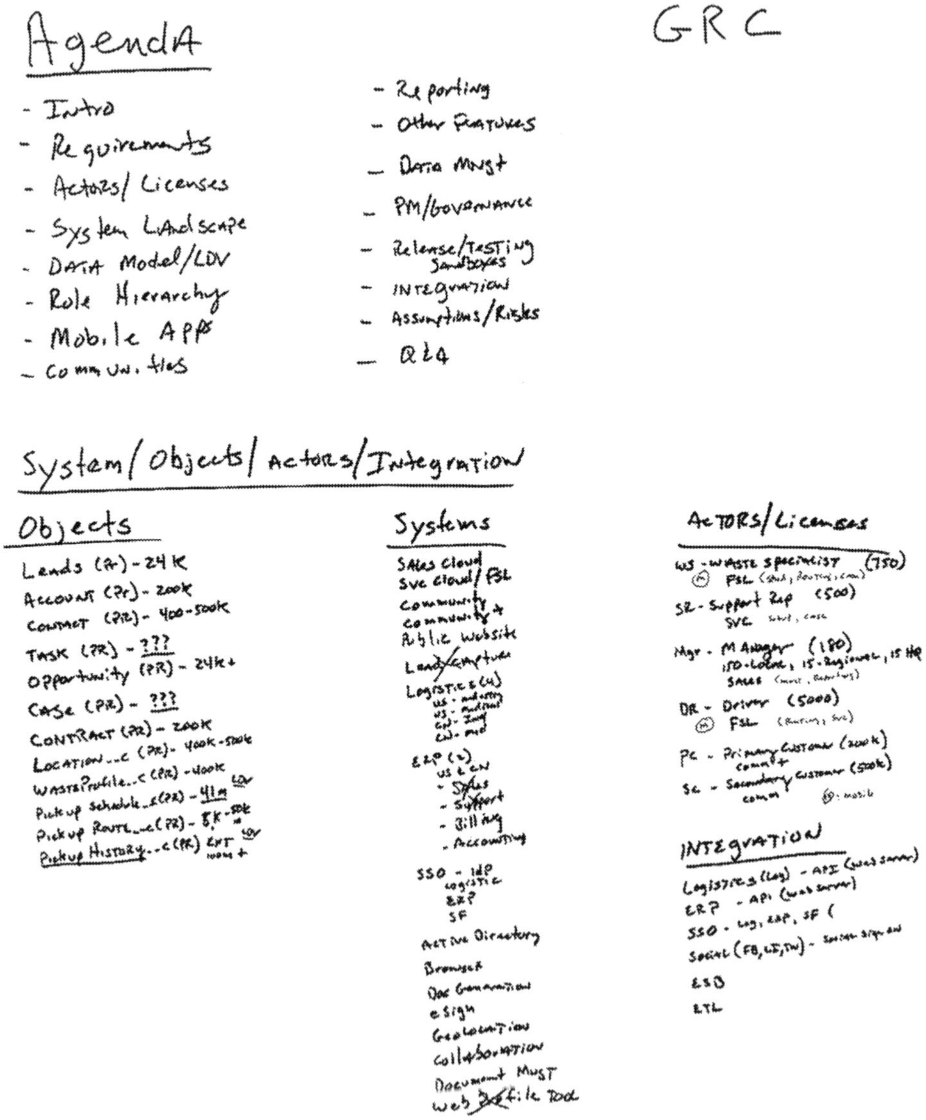

*Figure C-10.*  *Agenda with a System, Objects, Actors, and Integration Artifact*

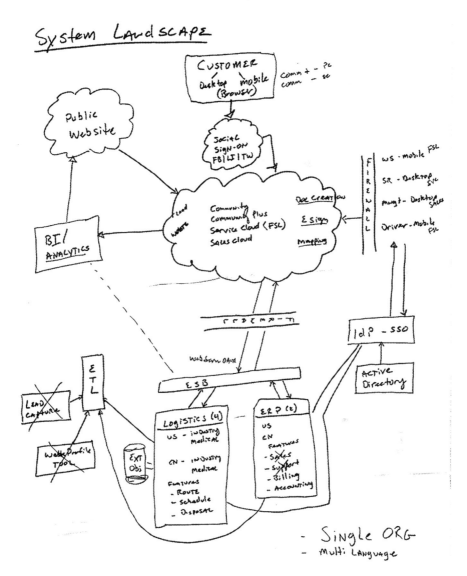

***Figure C-11.*** *System Landscape Artifact*

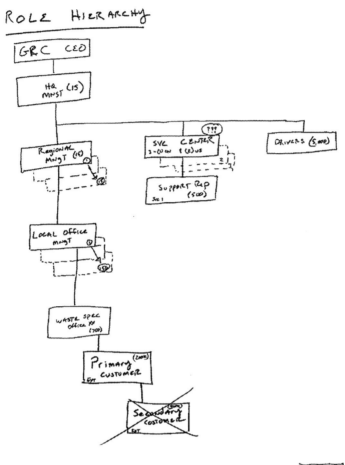

***Figure C-12.*** *Role Hierarchy Artifact*

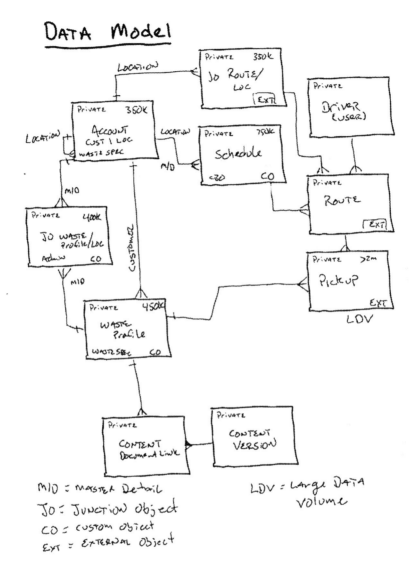

**Figure C-13.** *Data Model Artifact*

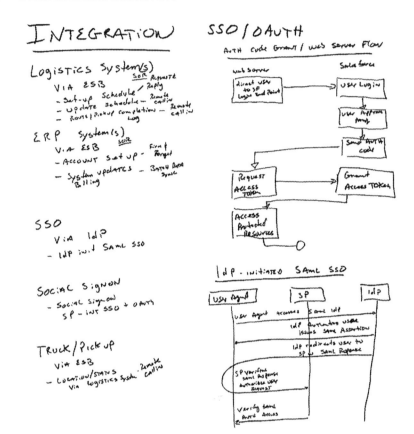

**Figure C-14.** *Integration and SSO/OAuth Artifact*

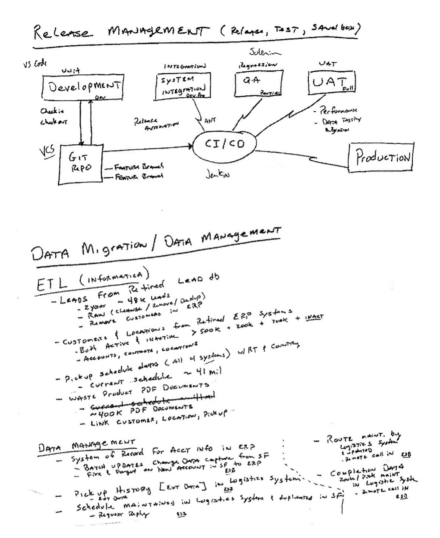

***Figure C-15.*** *Release Management and Data Management Artifact*

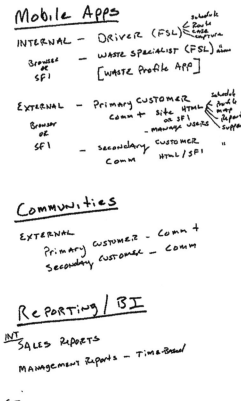

**Figure C-16.** *Mobile App, Communities, and Reporting/BI Artifact*

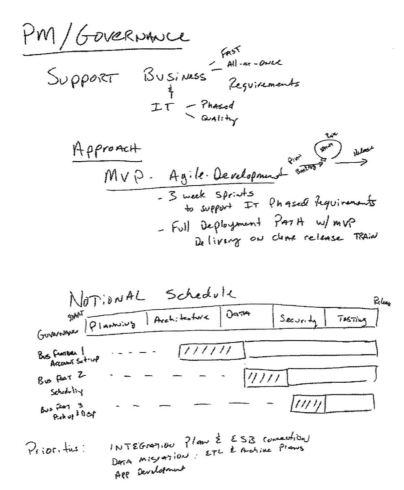

**Figure C-17.** *Project Management and Governance Artifact*

# Index

## A

Access, 233, 234
Access control, 148
Access grants, 165
Account skews, 134
Ackoff knowledge continuum, 114
Agile methodology, 300, 301
Apex-managed sharing, 161
Apex programming language, 16
Apex runtime engine processing
        apex code, 16
Apex sharing, 27
API protocol types, 194–197
AppExchange products, 57, 104–106
Application design
    declarative development options, 91–96
    options, 91
    order of execution, 102–104
    programmatic options, 96–100
Application design architecture, 25, 26
Application-level security, 167, 168
Application lifecycle management (ALM)
        tool, 321
Architectural artifacts, 31
Architecture, Salesforce
    application design architecture, 25, 26
    data architecture, 26
    development lifecycle
        management, 28
    IAM domain, 27

    limitations, 29
    mobile domain, 28
    salesforce integration domain, 27
    security architecture, 26, 27
Artifacts
    data model, 360, 361, 367
    FUSIAOLA analysis (*see* FUSIAOLA
        analysis)
    integration and SSO/OAuth, 368
    lifecycle management, 362
    Mobile App, communities, and
        reporting/BI, 370
    project management and
        governance, 371
    release management and data
        management, 369
    role hierarchy, 366
    system landscape (*see* System
        landscape artifact)
Asset token flow, 338–340
Assumptions, 51
Asynchronous communication, 203
Auditing, 150
Audit trails, 170
Authentication, 49, 50, 148, 234–237
Authorization, 49, 148
    flows, 240–243
    OAuth 2.0, 239–243
    OpenID Connect Framework, 239
    scopes, 243

© Dipanker Jyoti and James A. Hutcherson 2021
D. Jyoti and J. A. Hutcherson, *Salesforce Architect's Handbook*, https://doi.org/10.1007/978-1-4842-6631-1

Printed in the United States
By Bookmasters